O2B18

Classmates Recall the 40s and 50s

By D. E. NELSEN

With the Help of My Friends

PublishAmerica
Baltimore

First printing

PublishAmerica has allowed this work to remain exactly as the author intended, verbatim, without editorial input.

ISBN: 978-1-60749-515-4
PUBLISHED BY PUBLISHAMERICA, LLLP
www.publishamerica.com
Baltimore

Printed in the United States of America

The Senior Class of
Memorial High School
Announces its
Commencement Exercises
Friday Evening June Tenth
Nineteen hundred sixty
Eight o'clock
Memorial High Gymnasium

ALMA MATER
(What it means to me)

Hail to the Purple: Purple represents the depths of our love, respect and commitment to Beloit Memorial High School.

Hail to the White: Pure white, representing our youth, idealism, innocence and naiveté.

Hail to our Alma Mater: Our beloved home away from home.

Beloit High: Our refuge of learning and our garden from which grew long lasting, fruitful friendships.

Long May our memories keep you bright: May the echo of our voices and the spirits of our youth reverberate through your hallowed hallways forever.

Loyalty we pledge to thee: You will always be uppermost in our hearts and thoughts as we traverse the pathways that you opened for us to travel.

Faithful to you we will ever be: As long as we are alive, nothing but reverence and sincerely joyous thoughts of you will be expressed.

All Hail, all Hail, we sing our praise to you Beloit High: We, the Class of 1960 salute you. As Bob Hope would say, "Thanks for the memories!"

Written by Donald B. Cuthbert
Director of BMHS Bands

Table of Contents

FOREWORD

The United States Census Bureau records indicate that between the years of 1940 and 1955, over sixty-seven million children were bon in the United States. Sixty-seven million plus people, who lived through the same era, had many of the same experiences are still alive today to recall those special growing up and hometown memories just like my classmates and I do.

Extended families, sometimes three or four generations living under the same roof were common. If Grandma and Grandpa didn't live in the same house that we did, surely they lived within a few city blocks. Being part of an extended family gave all of us the feeling of security, being part of something larger than ourselves and an overwhelming sense of unity. Daily or at least weekly visits to relatives were as common an occurrence as was brushing your teeth or the customary Saturday night bath, with our boats or little rubber duckies and the bar of Ivory soap that floated.

So, whether you lived on the east coast, the west coast or somewhere in between; I encourage you to read of our memories and recall your very own special hometown memories. Who knows, perhaps, you too, will be driven to chronicle your memories to pass on to your progeny as my classmates and I hope to do with this literary effort.

Every time I hear "Memories, like the corners of my mind," from the Broadway Musical "Cats," or when I hear "Traditions" from Fiddler On The Roof, I am reminded of what my great grandmother used to say in her soft yet rather raspy Pennsylvania Dutch sort of way. "Donny, sit down here next to me and listen to Old Grandma for a spell. I've got something important to tell ya. You may not know it yet, but it does the soul good to pause and reflect upon one's life every once in a while. I seem to be doing a lot of that lately. You must stop and think about where you come from, what you have done and to be sure you are on the straight and narrow, don't ya know? Be certain that you are doing yourself good and not doing harm to others. Take time to reflect upon the good times and even the not so good times, you know, the trying times that test your mettle and builds your character." I didn't understand at the time what in blazes she was talking about. I asked Dad what she meant and he told me, "What she meant was that everybody should take time to take inventory of what he or she has experienced and to contemplate the significance of your very own existence. You know, are you worth your salt or are you just a bump on a log?"

I told Dad that Old Grandma went on to say, "You know, consider the impact you have on yourself and those around you. You don't affect just you, don't ya know?"

Old grandma, as we all called her, was just short of one hundred years old when she died. Her stories and her philosophy of life lives on in most if not all of her descendents to this very day. She was right, you know. You can't hope to carry on and understand family traditions if you don't remember and embrace the past yourself.

I cannot think of a better place to begin our introspective soul searching than with a retrospective stroll down Memory Lane. So, if you grew up in the 40s or the 50s, from "The Days That Will Live In Infamy," to the "Dawning Of The Age Of Aquarius," I invite all of you to join my classmates and me on the path of a million or more memories. Some of the memories you will read about are memories that are common to each and every one of us who had the pleasure of growing up during the 40s and 50. Some of the memories that are shared in this book are truly unique to one or to very few people, but are nonetheless valid and worthy of sharing with you and our offspring.

If you were born after the decade of the 50s or even at the tail end of the 50s and were too young to remember those times, I am ever so sorry. You, unfortunately, missed out on some of the best living that ever existed.

As my classmates and I are about to attend the fiftieth anniversary of our graduation from high school, I find myself thinking, maybe even daydreaming, back to the good ole days of my youth more and more the older I get. Strange, isn't it, I sometimes have difficulty remembering what my wife served for dinner last night, where I left my reading glasses (usually propped high above my forehead), where I put the car keys or where I parked the car in the Mall parking lot, but my memories from elementary school through college are as clear as a crystal ball. Go figure.

During my soul and memory searching processes, which included talking with many classmates and some of their similarly aged friends, I experienced a true epiphany. A friend and fellow co-worker of Don Marske's, a fellow named Kurt Leininger, presented me with that epiphany. He told me that his parents are still alive, approaching the celebration of their one-hundredth birthdays and that he talks with them about what their lives were like back in the olden days. It dawned on me that I know more about the roots of my family tree, both here in America as well as the trees that grew in England and Denmark, than I do about my parents and grandparent's lives as young people.

By way of English class and of course American History, selected reading of American authors and poets such as Edgar Allen Poe, Henry Wadsworth Longfellow, James Fennimore Cooper, Henry David Thoreau, Walt Whitman and Robert Frost as well as a shelf in my home office that is laden with well worn, oft read, historical biographies, that I realized that I know more about those people as well as an ancestor of mine, Ralph Waldo Emerson, than I do about most of the newer branches, sprouts and leaves and yes, even a few nuts, too, on my very own family tree.

It was at that point, the point of admission of ignorance of my very own family, that this literary endeavor became more than just a lighthearted trip down memory lane to share with my children and grandchildren, hoping they may glean a bit of an insight as to what makes Old Grampy tic. The focus of the book is to record so far unrecorded memories as seen by children growing up in the 40s and 50s.

So, I decided to open the blank pages of this book to a select few classmates and their similarly aged friends to pass on their own special memories to their progeny. As the rolling stone gathered speed, I have invited all of the remaining 347 classmates from our graduating class of approximately 423, to join me in long distance phone calls, E-mail messages, hand written letters, text-messaging and most of all chronicling their very own memories between the covers of this book.

As a result, this endeavor has taken on a wholly different purpose and scope. The way I see it, if we do not share our memories and our experiences with our offspring, the most beautiful part of our lives, the non-documented part, will just wither and die. Paraphrasing what General Douglas McArthur said at his good-bye speech at West Point, "Old soldiers never die, they just fade away." Metaphorically speaking, our history and our memories will be turned to dust. Knowledge of our wondrous years will inevitably be blown away in the tornado of time, to be lost forever in the vastness of eternity if we don't take the time to share it now!

So, from just a lighthearted trek down memory lane, for our seventeen grandchildren, this book has become a legacy that my classmates and our friends want to leave behind for future generations, a legacy, if you will, for our children and their children. It will be written in the traditions of oral history with the benefits of word processing, the scanning of old time photographs and, of course, the marvels of e-mail, text messaging and the cell phone economy of unlimited long distance calling.

Growing up in the 40s and the 50s was truly living during the good ole days. The pages that follow contain memories as they pop into our heads, more often than not, in a non-sequential, random order. Unfortunately, but realistically, that is the way older minds tend to work. In Chapter seventeen, "My Classmates Tell All," you will have the opportunity to read of their special memories. Collectively, we hope to paint for you a picture of what it was like being reared, for example, in a small Mid-western town, a town that even though its claim to fame was being a manufacturing town, a town whose genesis was the power generated from the mighty Rock River, it was surrounded by and influenced greatly by the farming community and the families that we loved and respected so much.

As you will read, the farming community played a very important part in our physical, financial as well as social upbringing.

My classmates and I were born in late 1941 or early to mid 1942, so we don't have cognitive memories of our own of those days leading up to and following the Japanese attack on Pearl Harbor and the Aleutian Islands or any of the battles that took place until we were at least four years old, just as the war was finally won. Growing up during the war years following the war that was to end all wars, consciously or subconsciously, those times formed us into the people we became and are today. Add to that the stresses of the cold war with the constant threats and fears of nuclear war and bomb shelters, I hope that you will readily understand why our generation is and was exceptionally patriotic.

Fortunately, for the most part, we were of the pre-hippie and pre flower children era. I am not aware of any of our classmates being mortally wounded in Vietnam. I know of no classmates who ran to Canada to avoid the draft or any who hide behind the shield of conscientious objection. Rather, most of us just rolled up our sleeves, had our hair cut to a nubbin, went to where we were ordered to go and dug in to fight the fight for the duration.

Haven't you found aging to be an interesting process? It seems to me to that it is not always enjoyable, but it truly is always interesting. Some may condemn aging as a cursed event, the winding down of the clock of life or the rusting of body and soul, but many of us look upon our golden years, maybe not always so golden, as to have the opportunity and the luxury of time to give of ourselves to and for the benefit of others.

It truly is a crying shame how the schematic of life is drawn. That schematic dictates that most of us will have and raise children when we, for the most part, cannot financially afford to rear them. Then when we have the financial wherewithal to support a family, we are just too old to physically endure much more than brief visits from our grandchildren. It is only when we pause to ponder, that many of us truly realize what it is that we have been placed here on this earth to accomplish. As you read on, you will understand what I mean.

In spite of the reflections that we see staring back at us from the fogged up bathroom mirror each morning as we towel off, brush our teeth and comb what little hair we have left, I don't know about you, but I do not see a sixty-six year old man. In my mind's eye, I see a young and vibrant, redhead lad of eighteen. I do not see a rotund belly, wrinkles, a nearly completely bald head with the exception of a ring of white hair that stretches from ear to ear on the back of my head, a bushy white beard and moustache or the abundance of liver spots. No, I do not believe I am suffering from the early stages of Alzheimer's or dementia. Maybe I am just psychologically trying to hold on to the good ole days. I guess it is amazing the tricks that our minds play on us? Or perhaps, it is God's way of telling us that it is time to make an appointment with our ophthalmologist.

My psychological preparation for attending the fiftieth anniversary reunion has not only found me searching out former classmates, but has given me the privilege of rekindling friendships from my youth. I have been told by many of my classmates that they too have and are now reaching out to old classmates and friends as a result of our telephone and e-mail conversations. It may have taken nearly fifty years for many of us to once again reach out and touch our friends, but by God we re doing it now and will never stop if I have anything to do about it. All of this talking has set my mind to remembering the good ole days when I was svelte and in excellent physical shape. The remembering of those skinny years, those years of youthful vigor and exuberance has given me the determination to make a silk purse out of this sows ear which is my obtuse body. Come hell or high water, by the time of the reunion, I will have lost one hundred fifty pounds or more. That weight loss will put me just three pounds over my graduation weight. I weighed in at 177 pounds soaking wet the day I entered the Army. My goal, by September of 2010 is to tip the scales at 180 pounds. I want all the ladies and gents that I look forward to hugging at the reunion to be able to get their arms around me. There is one down side to my intended weight loss. I will have to purchase a foam filled fake belly to fill out my Santa Claus suit. If my cheeks aren't quite as plump as they should be to portray the Jolly Old Elf, I'll just stick a little cotton between each cheek and gum.

I know that I am repeating myself ("Knock off the verboseness, Nelsonavitch. How many times do I have to tell you?"), as Mr. Lafky would chide, but I feel so strongly that I feel it bears repeating: Over the past several months, many long telephone conversations and E-mail messages with classmates and friends have convinced me that we, now the older generation, need to share our memories and experiences with our children, grand children and great grandchildren. Share the memories with them to let them know a little bit more about us, but also in the tradition of oral history, it is our responsibility to pass our story on to the next generations, lest it be lost forever.

As you read the following memories of our growing up years during WWII and living through the Truman and Eisenhower administrations, I hope that you, too, will reconnect with your younger self and share with your offspring those never to be repeated experiences of a much calmer, slower paced life before jet airplanes, rockets, Sputnik, text messaging, instant messaging and cell phones came along.

While our memories may be slightly different than your memories, (I don't believe there are many frozen ponds or creeks in southern California to ice skate on) while we may have even started life in a different region of the country, our classmates eventually came together in the BMHS Class of 1960. However, you do not need to have been reared in our hometown to get a chuckle out of reading this book. Whether you were raised in Chicago, Los Angeles, Fargo, St. Louis, Salt Lake City, New York, Topeka, Tampa, Anchorage, Boston or Freeport or even our rival cities of Madison and Janesville, I'd be willing to wager that we share more in common than we have differences. Chronicling our memories has been a more effective tonic for me than a healthy swig of Geritol, Hadacol or a vitamin B-12 shot, not to mention the sulfur and molasses tonic that my mother administered. You see, you do remember the good ole days.

DEDICATION

My friends, fellow classmate contributors and I dedicate this book to the entire class of 1960, as well as to our children, our grandchildren and all readers of the younger generations, you know, the generation "X" people and now the newest, the Millennia's. We would like to especially dedicate this book to our classmates who are no longer with us. (The list that follows at the end of this dedication is as current as the information available to the reunion committee at the time of publishing. I am truly sorry for any omission, should any occur) Jumping into adulthood at the beginning of the Vietnam War as we did, I am pleasantly surprised that we know of none of our classmates who were killed in the service to their country in southeast Asia. We fondly remember each of our classmates and want them to know how much we appreciate their friendship and the role that they all played in the mosaic that makes up our lives.

It truly is a blessing to have so many friends accompany me as we stroll down memory lane together. Yes, in some cases, it might even be considered to be Lovers Lane, inasmuch as a dozen or more classmate romances blossomed into marriage as of 1980, the twentieth anniversary of our graduation. Personally, I cherished each and every one of their friendships as a child and as an adolescent. Ironically, now that I am nearing the age of antiquity, I honestly believe that I appreciate their friendship even more today. I am saddened by the fact that the location of so many classmates is unknown. Downsizing residences and favoring cell phones rather than landlines has meant that many classmates just cannot be located. We sure had a good time growing up during those more innocent, less hectic Good Ole Days, didn't we?

Please, get yourself a cup of coffee, a soda or "Pop" as you may have called it, or maybe a nice glass of wine or a beer, find a nice comfortable chair, sit back and put your feet up and join us as we walk down the path of memories from the 1940s through the 1950s.

I promise you it will be a smooth trip. The only bumps in the road, as you will see, will be the bumps, lumps and knocks that I unfortunately was unwillingly forced to endure. At the time they were happening, I saw absolutely no humor in any of the incidents. Today, however, I look back and have a real good belly laugh. Read on and see if that isn't your reaction.

As you read, I am sure that you will quickly recognize that the most memorable moments from our youth are in fact many times our most embarrassing memories, too. So, friends, sit back and have a laugh or two with us or at our expense. If so inclined, shed a tear or two as you read of some of the more poignant memories that may be shared.

IN LOVING MEMORY
OF OUR DECEASED CLASSMATES
MAY YOU REST IN PEACE

Raymond Anderson—Richard Armstrong
Duane Ast—Edwin R. Barnes
Shirley A. Bates—Judith A. Belken
William H. Beltin—Betty J. Blakely
Theodore H. Brooks—Nancy Ann Bue
James E. Burden—Sharon K. Busjahn
John Cain—Charles D. Card
Michael T. Champeny—Everett Chase
Charles H. Christenson—Eleanor L. Davis
Linda M. DeWees—Mary Elliot
Sharon L. Evenson—Sonja I. Everson
Rachael A. Fairman—David N. Faust
Charles W. Florey—Richard A. Foslin
Allen Gillham—Robert Owen Gilmour
Dotty R. Goff—Karen M. Grenier
Lee R. Harrell—Glen E. Hauser
Herbert J. Helser—Larry Hickman
Sharon L. Hovland—Ivan J. Hudson, Jr.
October Johnson—Thomas K. Kohl
Sharon Kay Kuehl—James H. Kuhnle
Ronald D. Lee—Yvonne R. Lindermann
Gail F. Martin—Marsha L. Maves
Edward McBriar—Delores G. Mehring
Mary Ann Nequette—Rosetta Nichols
Ronald Osborn—Warren A. Ovist
Jerry R. Pate—Marty J. Peebles
John H. Pinson—Carl L. Reichard
Duane Riese—Julianne K. Ross
LeAnn M. Rusconni—Judith A. Sandvig
Ronald Schmidt—Marsha L. Scott
Jerry L. Sheldon—Trudy A. Scott
Karen E. Spooner—Jannice J. Stout

Lynn M. Sulanke—Mary L. Tarrant
Deanna Teed—Elizabeth Thomas
Lavonna J. Topham—Donald E. Walrath
Caren L. Walters—Carol J. Walters
Hope C. Weberg—Margo A. Wienke
Ray Woltors—Robert Worden
Diane Worsley—Terry K. Zander
Fred W. Zinn

CHAPTER ONE
Let's Take It from the Top

It has become abundantly clear to me that strolling down memory lane is not unlike driving up or down a winding, twisting mountain road. At times it appears that one meets oneself coming around the next switchback curve. It is almost impossible, at least for me, to go from point "A" in one year to point "B" in a different time frame without incorrectly remembering the actual sequence of memories and events. Recognizing my inability to remember everything in absolute chronological order, I hope that you will bear with me as I wander the path, back and forth through the days of our youth and hopefully explain how and why they were such wondrous times, much calmer times and most certainly more innocent times. The intention is that the memories be as accurate as possible, as accurate as a sixty-six year-old memory will permit me to record.

Surely, many of you have either been asked or have questioned yourselves as to what your earliest memory is. I believe, for the most part, most of us do not remember much of anything on our own until the age of three or four, possibly even five years of age. What we remember of those days that preceded our own cognitive memories are the stories that we remember Mommy and Daddy telling about our first three or four years of life. How much of those related memories are void of embellishment is a question whose answer that will remain locked in the vault of time.

Sometimes, a tragic or life changing event takes place that is written indelibly on our souls. For example, my parents told me that when I was only eleven months old, my parents drove Dad's black 1939 Chevy Coupe to Oregon, Wisconsin to visit my father's mother at a nursing home where she was living out her final days. I was told that I was sitting on my mother's lap in dad's car, which was parked at the curb, and saw an old lady standing at the parlor room window, waving. My mother says that I was jumping up and down on her lap as she tried to hold me up for the old lady to see. I do not personally remember those events, but Mother told me years later that without warning, an intoxicated driver of another car came barreling around the corner and crashed into the rear end of father's Chevy Coupe. I understand that I was ejected from Mother's arms and thrown to the floor of the car under the heater box. I'm told that upon our return home, I took my first steps. I guess I was no worse for wear. What is amazing is that the old lady, my parental grandmother, died just a month after that visit.

Five or six years later, my father showed me an old fashioned, leather bound photograph album that he found in the attic behind some dusty boxes and other assembled attic trash. "Say Donny, do you know who this is? Does she look familiar to you?" he asked, pointing to the picture of a very old lady dressed in a very long, very ugly dress. Her hair was piled high on her head like an old librarian and she wore a scowl on her face that made her look as though she was about mean enough to skin a bear with her bare hands. Mind you, I had never seen that old photograph album, let alone the picture, and the last time I am told that I laid eyes on my paternal grandmother was when I was eleven months old.

"I remember her," I said. She's the old lady I saw in the window."

The next vivid memory I have took place when I was just a little over two years old. I remember mother walking through the front door of our home with a blanket cradled in her arms. All of a sudden, the blanket stared to move and make ear piercing crying sounds. I do not remember anything about my baby sister until two years later, but I surely do remember that crying blanket.

At four and a half years old I remember my parents gave my sister and me a newborn baby brother. Unfortunately, he died when he was only ten days old from some deformity in his digestive system. I remember how sad Mom and Dad were and I remember the white box that rested on the Library table behind the davenport. From that point on, I seem to be able to remember more and more of my every day life, the friends that I had, trips to the dentist, Santa Claus, colored chicks, bunnies and Christmas.

For example, during the summer when I was four years old, I clearly remember that my Aunt Helen took care of my sister and me while our mother was hospitalized. (I guess that must have been the same time my little brother, David, was born) At that time, Diane was two years old and really taking the terrible twos to heart. Sis could be real nice one minute and then as if by a light switch being thrown, Sis could turn into a little devil in the blink of an eye.

One night when Aunt Helen put us to bed and tucked us in, she gave Diane her customary bedtime bottle. Little Damien emerged and threw the bottle at our aunt. That was the last baby bottle that Diane ever had. Aunt Helen's reasoning was if Diane was old enough to throw her bottle at her with such accuracy, then she was old enough to drink from a cup or go thirsty for all she cared.

Several weeks after mother's discharge from the hospital, on a hot and very humid August afternoon, I remember Mother placing an old galvanized washtub in the bright sunshine in our back yard and filling the tub with water from the garden hose, then topping it off with a kettle or two of boiling hot water to take the chill off the cold water. That little galvanized washtub was my sister's and my swimming pool. Sunscreens obviously were not available way back then. Mother slathered us with Johnson's baby oil. The net effect was similar to pouring olive oil in a hot skillet. If I remember correctly, both Sis and I got much more sunburn than we did wet, but it was memorable anyway, and that's what counts, right? After Sis and I were given our evening bath, mother rubbed Unguinteen on our shoulders. Supposedly it would magically reduce the pain of the sunburn. NOT! I wonder what snake oil salesman talked mother into buying that worthless ointment.

The changing colors of the leaves of the hardwood trees from green to brilliant hues of red, orange, gold and yellow were a harbinger of things to come. Of course, when winter came around, the cold, blustery days and nights in Beloit, Wisconsin, opened the door to the most spectacular experiences and memories. At least they were and are my most special memories.

I cherish magnificent memories of playing inside of our firmly packed igloos that Dad helped us make and the handmade barriers of large hand rolled boulders of packed snow that we lined up in front of our igloo. They were intended to keep our igloo safe and sound when subjected to barrages of snow balls from our neighbor's children. Of course they, too, had their very own fort, but none of them had an igloo. Back and forth across the driveways, volleys of snowballs would fly. It now warms my heart to remember those days, but at the time, if we had not cleared the remnants of our snowball fights from the driveways by the time our fathers came home from work, it wasn't going to be our hearts that our fathers would warm.

Hours upon endless hours were passed in pretend play in our frozen, eighteen-inch thick walled igloos. Sometimes the igloo was a fortress, sometimes a pirate ship; sometimes it was King Arthur's castle. But the most fun of all was pretending that our snow and ice structure was Santa's ice castle.

We had an old braided rug, a refuge from Grandma's basement, on the floor and pictures that my sister and I had drawn with Crayola crayons hanging from a nail or sticks that we pounded into the frozen walls. Once Diane and I took our little chairs and table out to the igloo. We had fun drawing and coloring until Ma found out what we had done. She went off like a Roman candle and it was nowhere close to being the fourth of July.

Light shining through the two windows that Dad had cut in the curved walls of our igloo gave plenty of illumination for us to be able to play card games, read or pack and stack snowballs in anticipation of the next snowball fight. I accidentally left the crayons out in the igloo one night. The next day we tried coloring, but for some reason the Crayola Crayons just kept breaking.

We didn't really object to the nose biting and cheek numbing cold. Even though our mittens were usually soaking wet, all four or five pairs that Mother had stuffed into the pockets of our coats, and even though Mother had securely tied a scarf or two around our heads to protect our faces from the cold, our cheeks were inevitably frost bitten and our toes were tingling.

The only complaining that could be heard was when Mother would call for us to come inside to warm our obviously chilled bodies and have a nice hot cup of hot chocolate with melted marshmallows. None of us wanted to go inside. We didn't want the neighbor kids to have time to make a whole bunch of snowballs when we were inside. But, once inside, we'd gulp down the hot chocolate, eat a cookie or two and then plead for dry mittens to replace those which were lined up in front of the hot air registers to dry, and then run back outside to continue our snowball battle. Thank God that Grandma Case liked to make lots and lots of hand knitted children's mittens. Does that sound familiar?

I cannot forget sledding down the packed snowy slopes or Horace White Park or the even steeper and longer hills on the east end of the Municipal Golf Course near the Beloit Memorial Hospital. Many times after Dad picked us up at the park, we would stop at the Little Bungalow and have a cup of hot chocolate and share a piece of chocolate cake. As I got a little older, tackling the hill beneath the one hundred-twenty foot tall ski jump at the Big Hills was the venue of choice. Of course the nearly vertical landing hill about scared the be-Jesus out of me, but I loved it nonetheless.

The signature feature of the Big Hills was the enormous ski jump the county had erected for the use of the county residents. If I remember correctly, the ski jump was one hundred twenty feet tall and drew ski jumpers from all over the country. The landing slope was exceptionally long, straight and as steep as was the ski jump. Can you imagine any governmental organization or any parks commission today, in our litigious society, doing something as foolish and legally sensitive as providing the youth, or even adults, with an opportunity like that to have fun?

The landing hill beneath the ski jump was the steepest but cleanest straightaway run in the park with a big curve at the end of the run that rose in elevation to help slow our forward motion. It was by far the longest, too. Boy oh boy, the courage that it took to climb aboard our American Flyers or toboggans and launch ourselves over the precipice and down what seemed to be a nearly vertical slope. At first I wondered if I would be pulled off the sled by gravity or if I would fall off the sled, tumbling and sliding along side the sled as we raced for the bottom of the hill. We must have been traveling at least a gazillion miles per hour. I don't know if it was fear or if it was centrifugal force that slammed my stomach into my throat and bounced it off the roof of my mouth, but there it rested.

There were two significantly negative aspects to that experience, however. First was the fact that even though we had traveled hundreds of yards, it took only a few seconds to go from the top of the hill to the end of the run. Unfortunately, in order to have the same thrill again, without the aid of ropes of any kind, we had to trudge back up the hill, dragging the sled or toboggan, in order to go down again.

Usually, if you rode a sled down the hill you had to pull the sled back to the top yourself. With a toboggan usually two or three kids accompanied you so you had help dragging the heavier toboggan up the hill. In either case, four or five runs and we were plumb tuckered out!

As long as we're already at the Big Hills Park, let's jump out of our heavy winter coats, leggings and galoshes and into our summer togs.

Several times during each spring and summer, three or four generations of both sides of my family would gather at the Big Hills park for a Sunday morning breakfast cooked outdoors over an open fire. I don't remember how many people joined in the outdoor feast, but I remember my cousins David and Denny and I had to peel enough potatoes to feed a small army. Once peeled, Mother and a couple of her sisters would thinly slice the potatoes in preparation for the big feed.

In your imagination, can't you just see and smell the home fries as they lay sizzling in a pool of butter on the grill, turning a deep golden brown on their edges? Sometimes, if they remembered to bring them along, gigantic Bermuda onions were sliced into thin rings and fried along with the potatoes. Sometimes they even added thinly sliced red, yellow and green bell peppers to the potatoes. What a treat!

One of our relatives lived on a farm in Stoughton, Wisconsin and raised chickens for their egg production. I don't remember what kind of chickens Uncle Arnold raised, but each and every egg had a brown shell and usually half of the eggs contained a double yolk. Needless to say, we had plenty of really fresh eggs and pounds upon pounds of smoked bacon that would be consumed by the gathering. Coffee was brewed in an old-fashioned enamelware coffee pot suspended above a wood fire from a wrought iron shepherds hook like staff. Mother always threw thee or four broken eggshells into the pot. I don't know why, but she did. Maybe seeing Festus put eggshells in the coffee pot on Gun Smoke gave Mother the idea.

Dad and some of my Uncles fried dozens of eggs, some over easy, some fried hard and lots and lots of scrambled eggs with broken up pieces of sharp cheddar cheese mixed in. What seemed like hundreds of sliced potatoes and at least fifteen or twenty pounds of bacon sizzled on one side of the heavy three-foot by four-foot cast iron grill. The aromas were enough to drive you crazy with anticipation. Oh my, the smells, the mouth-watering aromas that came wafting off of that grill. I am gaining weight as I remember.

Have you ever tasted toasted home made bread that was cooked over an open fire? If not, allow me to tell you how we did it. First of all, all of my cousins and I were sent into the woods with Grandpa Nelsen's old bucksaw to search out and cut down small saplings that had a pronounced "Y" in their trunks. When we followed our noses back to the breakfast site, one of the men would sharpen each end of the "Y" with his pocketknife and then secure a thick, hand cut slice of lightly buttered home made bread between the spread arms of the stick. It was kind of like a big slingshot without the inner tube straps.

We children did our part by holding the sticks and bread close enough to an open fire to toast the bread, but not too close. Sometimes, if we were not as attentive as we should have been, a piece of bread would char beyond any semblance of digestibility. Or even worse, some were even ignited and went up in flames. I don't remember which was worse, the adults laughing at the burner or the custom that the burner had to take a big bite of the botched toast.

As the burned toast will attest to, not all memories of those family cookouts are sweet memories. For example, one of the memories from the Big Hills that lingered for several days after our morning cookout was the inevitable case of Poison Ivy that one of us was bound to get. A good scrubbing with warm water and some God awful foul smelling soap accompanied by the subsequent dousing of Calamine Lotion did nothing to relieve the itching and pain. In spite of those little set backs, those picnic breakfasts make my mouth water sixty years later just thinking about them.

Children of Generation X may have been brought up with the Frisbee, but we beat them to the punch. Each summer my friends and I would ride our bicycles to one of the dairy farms on the outskirts of town. We made certain that we did not attract the attention of the farmer as we leaned our bicycles against the barbed wire fence and crawled through the fence to play our little game. Picking out the driest cow chips that we could find, we played catch or tag with one of the free bovine Frisbees. We had a great time until someone inevitably picked up a not so dry cow chip and hurled it at one of the guys. On the ride home, we tried our best to position ourselves down-wind, or was it up-wind from the smelly companion.

Some times, under the cover of darkness, we would sneak into the pasture, walk up to a cow, and with all our might, we would tip the poor thing off her feet. Thank God we never got caught or even worse, smushed as the cow lost her balance and fell to the ground bellowing all the way down.

Summers heralded the earning season for many of us. Once we had reached the ripe old age of nine or ten, we hired ourselves out to a local farmer to de-tassel corn in the fields. For you younger people and for you city-slickers, detaching the tassels from the corn stalk redirected the growing energy from the stalk to the production of large, fully kernelled ears of corn while eliminating any chance for cross-pollination. While for the time, ten cents an hour was good money, we paid a dear price for the pocket full of change that we had accumulated at the end of the week. Corn tassels are very abrasive. Unless we were fortunate enough to have a pair of dad's old leather gloves to protect our hands, at the end of the week our hands were a bloody mess. The things we wouldn't do to earn a little pocket change. About the only thing that help heal the cuts and abrasions on our hands was a frequent slathering and vigorous hand rubbing with Corn Huskers Lotion, an old time mineral oil based remedy.

An older farming memory for me started back to when I was four or five years old. Moore Street, the street that our home was on, was one of the thoroughfares used by the pea farmers to take their pea harvest to the Green Giant processing plant. A parade of International Harvester, Farmall and John Deere tractors pulling large staked hay wagons heaped high with pea vines would slowly chug their way past our house. Neighborhood children from as far away as three or four block to the east and west of Moore Street sat on the curb waiting for the opportunity to snatch a pea vine or two from the wagons as they passed. Have you ever tasted the sweet succulence of fresh peas right out of the pod? Let me tell you, there ain't nuttin better! I wonder why cooked peas never tasted as good?

Way back in the olden days of my youth, many families still had the old-fashioned iceboxes. At least two or three times a week the ice man in his leather apron and his long leather sleeve would deliver large blocks of ice to our neighbors homes. Of course, a gaggle of children in the neighborhood would be patiently waiting at the curb in hopes that the nice iceman would chip off a chunk of that clear frozen delight for us to suck on. If he did crack off a chunk for us, he always wrapped it in a piece of brown paper to protect our delicate little fingers, If the ice man disappointed us, we could always count on the Meadow Gold milk man to give us a piece of ice as he made his way door to door delivering bottled milk to our houses. Yes, I said bottled. Real, honest to goodness glass bottles. The pressed paper or aluminum cover that sealed the bottle, many times had a secret symbol printed on its underside, which entitled the holder to a free bottle of milk, a quart of whole cream or even a pound of sweet Wisconsin butter.

You know, of course, that Wisconsin at that time was considered to be the Dairy State. At times my father was known to stretch the truth almost to the breaking point, certainly to the brink of credulity, so we never really knew if Dad was serious or if he was just pulling our legs. Dad once told us that there was an official law in Wisconsin that required restaurants to always serve a slice or chunk of cheddar cheese when apple pie was served. He would emphasize his point by saying, "Apple pie without the cheese is like a kiss without a squeeze."

That may have just been his sense of humor, but I do know for a fact that the Wisconsin Legislature enacted a law that forbade the sale of Oleo Margarine in the state. The neighboring state of Illinois, only eight blocks from where I lived, did approve of the sale of Oleo Margarine, but it was not colored. To make it look more like butter, the processors inserted a color capsule into the plastic bag of what looked to be lard. The purchaser would have to break the color capsule and knead the mess into a palatable spread. Fortunately, Dad would have no part of "that stuff" on his dinner table. He wasn't going to break the law for something so disgusting as colored lard.

Remember, on a previous page, I mentioned that a relative of ours owned a farm where he raised chickens. Well, the story of that farmer relative, Uncle Arnold, does not stop with the supplying of bacon and eggs for the Sunday Morning cookout. Each Labor Day weekend, our extended family would gather at Uncle Arnold's farm for the annual Chicken Slaughtering and Canning Festival; red, white and blue flags and all.

The men caught the chickens, hens and roosters alike, as they pecked at the ground for small pebbles to help grind what they had just eaten. One by one, the men would hand off the chicken to one of us young boys. Our job was to hold the chickens by their legs, place the chicken's head between the two large nails someone had pounded part way into the chopping block and pull back gently on their legs, exposing the chickens' necks to what was to come. I remember standing next to the chopping block holding the cackling and wing flapping chicken by its legs, my eyes closed so that I didn't have to witness the gory event. Dad or one of the other men would lop off the chicken's head with one mighty blow of the executioner's axe. As you might guess, when we heard that last screeching cackle, many times one of us boys would let go of the chicken. You know what happened next, don't you? Yep, somehow that headless chicken would chase us around the barnyard. It was kind of reminiscent of Incabad Crane and the headless horseman.

Once we had recaptured the headless chicken we had to carry it by its legs, head down, or at least where its head used to be, so the blood could drain from its lifeless body. Obviously our trousers were covered with stinky chicken blood by the time we were done. We had been instructed to take the fresh kill to the barn where the women folk, ladies for you members of the younger generation, had several large cast iron cauldrons filled with water that were suspended over a large fire of hard wood. (Jumping ahead nearly fifty years; one of the Amish sayings that tickles me is, "A plump woman and a big barn never done no man any harm.") When the water was boiling at a galloping roll, one by one they took the chickens from us and holding them once again by their leg, dipped the chickens in and out of the scalding hot water to loosen the skin's hold on their feathers. Then the sopping wet, stinky chicken was handed back to the delivery boy and he received instructions as to how to properly pluck the feathers, pinfeathers and all. I did not care for those hot, slimy and stinky chickens, yuck. The feathers would stick to our hands and clothing, we smelled as bad as the chickens. As I said, we had blood all over out clothing. God how I hated even the thought of chickens. At that time, I wondered why anybody would want to eat a chicken.

The second day, the day after all the cackling, killing and mayhem, the lady folk worked feverously in the kitchen to pressure cook and can the chicken. Some of the Mason jars contained just chicken and a little chicken or vegetable stock, while others contained chicken noodle soup, Chicken Chop Suey, or Chicken and gravy with potatoes, onions and carrots, etc. All of this was going on in the inside kitchen as well as in the summer kitchen located on the back porch. While the women did the preserving, the men folk helped Uncle Arnold with chores and little fix up jobs around the farm.

We kids played horseshoes, softball and bad mitten and drank glasses upon glasses of Grandma's homemade lemon aide. Of course, there was always a heaping plate of grandma's chocolate chip cookies or homemade sugar cookies.

At the close of the day, we always had a big cook out of hamburgers and hot dogs with potato salad, sweet corn and fresh strawberry short cake with freshly beaten whipped cream. Tall glasses of ice-cold milk were a must. You can bet your bottom dollar that not one of us was looking forward to chicken for supper.

The best part of the whole process was working as an entire family and of course the delicious meals that we had during the long cold Wisconsin winters. Sometimes, if we were really lucky, Mother would heat some of the soup and pour it into Thermos bottles for my sister and me to have for lunch at school. Man oh Manaschevits, was that soup ever good! Homemade noodles, carrots and onions with large slivers of chicken suspended in a hot schmaltzy broth tasted wonderful. The kids who had brought PB&J sandwiches for lunch were jealous. I don't know if there is any validity to calling homemade chicken soup "Jewish Penicillin," but I can tell you it was a rare occurrence for either Sis or me to catch a cold.

A trip down memory lane, especially for the benefit of our grandchildren and our great grandchildren would not be complete without a glimpse into our home, Father's cars, Sunday afternoon worship of Vince Lombardi and of course cheering for the Milwaukee Braves.

My parents purchased a two-bedroom home from the carpenter who built the house in 1940. It was a modest bungalow with a fairly large screened-in front porch. All of the woodwork in the house was solid oak ass were the floors and all of the doors in the house. Dad paid whopping $3,400 cash for the house and never carried a mortgage on the house.

The kitchen was so small that there was only enough floor space for the stove, sink and refrigerator. The two bedrooms were of reasonable size and were sufficient until I was five years old and my sister was three. At that time my parents decided that I needed to have my own room. Remember the screened in front porch I told you about? It was a porch. It did not have a basement under it; just cement blocks to raise the porch floor level to that of the rest of the house. At that time cement blocks with ventelation holes were used to prevent moisture from rotting the floorboards from the bottom up.

During the winter the winter winds howled through those openings, sometimes amplifying the sounds made by the rushing wind. Those openings in the foundation blocks produced a low-pitched eerie howl that at first scared the be-jeepers out of me. The porch was enclosed and knotty-pine boards were nailed to the insulated walls. Reddish-brown asbestos tiles were affixed to the floor.

At the end of the summer I had my very own room. All was well until the first blast of arctic air came from the northwest. I awakened to frost on the inside of my windows. When I stepped out from under the goose down comforter on my bed and my bare feet hit the tiled floor, it was like my feet had been plunged into a bucket of ice cubes. That next night and every night during the winter, I wore a pair of thick wool socks that grandma had knitted for me.

As you will learn, my father wasn't very good with carpentry tools, but he was a whiz with a bucket of paint and paintbrush. Dad had such a painting fetish that the floor of the garage and the floor of our basement were always painted with a battleship gray paint. In the basement Dad painted a light green marbles rink with a two-inch white ring surrounding it.

In one corner of the basement stood a cylindrical cast iron, gas-fired water heater. There was nothing automatic about it. About half an hour prior to taking a bath, Dad would go downstairs and light the water heater with an Ohio Blue tip stick match. We'd wait, and then wait some more. Finally, Mother would give my sister a bath and then it was my turn to bathe in the less than hot, soapy water that Diane had just emerged from. I often wondered if she had left a little additional liquid in the bath water for her big brother.

Dad always had a Chevrolet. "I'm a Chevy man and damned proud of it," he would boast to my Uncle Bob who favored Fords. Dad's cars were always black until 1955 when he purchased a mint green and white two door Chevy Belaire. We really felt special to have a two-tone color car like the rich people had. During the spring and summer, almost every Sunday after church and dinner, we would pile into the car and visit one relative or another. If we happened to go to Janesville, Sis and I knew that we would get an ice cream cone on the return to home

By today's standards, we were poor folk. Dad insisted on purchasing quality, but would not go into debt for it. "Simple enough to remember,

Donny, if you don't have enough money to buy it, don't buy it." I really wish I had learned that lesson better than I did.

Dad was a real nut when it came to yard work. Each spring he get a load of dirt that was dredged from a farmer's pond and would then spread it on top of the lawn along with a little Kentucky Blue Grass. Weeks after the dirt had settled and the new grass spouted, it was my task to crawl all over the lawn with a bucket and pick up the thousands of little white snail shells that had been hidden in the pond dirt. Today I wonder why he just didn't have me smash them up to add nutrients to the soil.

Dad didn't stop there when it came to giving his lawn tender loving care. As soon as a Dandelion dare sprout in his lawn, Dad pulled his Dandelion digging jackknife from the utility drawer (junk drawer) and get down on his hands and knees to dig that sucker out. As if that weren't eccentric enough when Crab Grass showed its unacceptable appearance in the blades of Kentucky Blue Grass, down on his hands and knees again would go Dad to pull each offending weed out by the roots. Then of course, if God had not favored us with what Dad considered to be an appropriate amount of rain, he would sit in a lawn chair, read the Beloit Daily News and water the lawn with a hand held hose while puffing away on a John Ruskin cigar.

You know what? I don't think our yard looked any better than any other yard in the neighborhood, in spite of all of the pampering that Dad lavished on it.

Now for just a brief blurb about my extended family that in one way or another influenced the way I grew up. You have already read of my paternal grandmother. My paternal grandfather was killed in a farming accident when my father was a young man. Unfortunately, I never asked Dad about Grandpa and know very little about him except his Bucksaw used to cut down their annual Christmas tree. I proudly am the keeper of Grandpa's bucksaw for the time being. At my demise it will be handed down to my eldest son to keep until he is ready to pass it down to his eldest son.

You will read about my maternal grandfather later on. His mother, Emma Shoemaker lived with Grandma and Grandpa Case up to just a few months prior to her one-hundredth birthday. Right up to the end she was able to sit on the floor, legs straight out in front of her and pull on her long, opaque stockings, shoes and then tie the laces. She definitely was a grand old lady. The stories that she told us of her youth that went back to prior to the

American Civil War always held our rapt attention. What a storyteller she was. The interesting thing about her was that she never went to a doctor in her ninety-nine plus years of life.

My maternal grandmother, on the other hand, was a reincarnation of Miss Carrie Nation, the infamous axe-wielding prohibitionist. Grandma was so into the Christian Temperance Union that she forbade Grandpa from even thinking about consuming anything alcoholic. Little did Grandma know that the Wolfe Brothers Crook cigars that Grandpa chewed from one end and smoked from he other, were dipped in rum? Grandpa gotch ya, Grandma, and you didn't even know it. Yea, Grandpa, you put it over the old hot head, didn't you?

My Aunt Do (short for Dorothy) made the best, the tastiest baked beans and homemade ketchup that I have ever tasted.

My Aunt Pauline (Polly) contracted Tuberculosis in the late 1930s and was confined to and cared for in a sanatorium in Janesville. I can still remember standing on the lawn beneath her third-story room and waving to her as she stood waving from the open window. That memory goes back to when I was five years old. After aunt Polly had greeted my sister and me she threw to small change purses that she had made to us from her perch on high. That was over sixty years ago and I still carry my change in that little brown change purse with the white stitching.

My mother's youngest sister, Aunt Winnie (Winifred) taught me two very valuable lessons. The first lesson was not to put your fingers in the way of a closing car door. The second had to do with bathroom etiquette. One day while at Grandma's a bunch of my cousins and I were playing outside on the lawn. Sooner or later the call of nature summoned me to the bathroom. The downstairs bathroom was right off the kitchen where aunt Winnie was washing dishes. I ran in the back door, slid into the bathroom and started emptying my near to burst bladder. No sooner had I started that Aunt Winnie hollered from the kitchen, "Shut the door, Donny, I can hear you O—O!"

My Aunt Helen, my father's younger sister really was more of a loving mother to me than was my birth mother. Up to her dying day, in 2003 she still called me Donny. Every time I saw her and had the honor of being with her in her later years, I would take her out to a soda shop for her favorite treat, a Hot Fudge Sundae with extra hot fudge and two cherries popping out of a bed of freshly whipped cream. When she was finished I would defy anyone to show me a single trace of what had been in the deep-fluted dish. Aunt Helen had extracted the last bit of fudge and ice cream from the dish with her index finger. "Waste not, want not," she would say.

Later on in the book you will see references to ski jumping and the nuts that dared to fly down the steep slope and crash into the ground below. Two such nuts were my cousins Bud and Denny Caldwell.

It would be impossible to end this chapter without telling you a bit about my favorite female cousin. Shirley is ten years my senior, so it is only natural that I would look up to her. Shirley was the John McCain of the 40s and most certainly the most maverick of the grandchildren. Now don't misunderstand me. Cousin Shirley was as straightforward and honest as any person that I have ever known. She always said what everyone, at least anyone with any common sense at all, believed but either had more sense than to say or was too afraid to say. You go, girl!

All in all, we not only had an interesting family, we had a warm and loving family, at least most of the time. I sure miss Aunt Do's baked beans and Grandma's homemade spicy pumpkin pie and the smell of Grandpa Case's Wolfe Brothers Crook cigars and most of all great grandma's (Old Grandma, as we called her) stories about her good ole days and learning from her no nonsense philosophy of life.

CHAPTER TWO
World War II and Beyond—the Hot and the Cold

I have a few, very few, vague memories of WWII inasmuch as I was born in November of 1942. What I do remember is Mother pulling me in my red Radio Flyer wagon up and down the streets with a bunch of old pots and pans in the wagon. I must admit that my memory of those days comes from photographs taken with a little Kodak Brownie camera that my Aunt Winnie always carried. I learned much later that Mother was collecting scrap metal to aid the war effort. Making pots and pans into bombs seemed to be the patriotic thing to do at the time, I guess.

The other vague memory I have from the very end of the war was that Dad kept sacks of flour and sugar in the attic of our home. He had to access the attic through a rather small rectangular opening in the ceiling of his closet. He had access to the flour and sugar from the bakery where he specialized in the creation of French and Danish pastries. I don't think he had permission, but he did have access.

I specifically remember hearing my father say one evening at the supper table that he needed four new tires for the car, but rationing made that neigh unto impossible. "I know, I'll let it get around that I have three hundred pounds of sugar and five hundred pounds of flour that I will trade a portion thereof for four new tires."

Ultimately he made the trade, two sacks of flour and one sack of sugar for the four tires. I hope he wore thick gloves when he retrieved the sugar and flour from his secret attic stash because, knowing what I now suspect, those sacks of sugar and flour were more than likely to have been very hot inasmuch as they were obviously an ill-gotten bounty from the storeroom of the bakery. Dad wouldn't break the law by buying Oleomargarine, but he did misappropriate contraband flour and sugar from the bakery. I guess you could say that my father was a selective law abider.

I don't remember V-E Day, but I do remember V-J Day because of the radio broadcasts that my parents listened to. I am certain that what I remember wasn't the news, but rather the hugging and kissing and joyous banter that exuded from my gleeful parents. I didn't understand what the big deal was or why Mom and Dad were so happy. Later when I questioned Mother in my naïve, childish way, Mother told me they were happy because friends, relatives and neighbors would soon be coming home from the war!

The end of the war was a happy time for all, except for the men like my father who worked in what was determined by the government to be vitally needed positions or people who worked for manufacturers who made products needed for the war effort. Fairbanks Morse, for example, where Dad and so many other fathers in Beloit worked, made large diesel engines. Therefore, they were precluded them from serving in the armed services. They were fulfilling an extremely important service to the country, the military and the safe guarding of most of the world.

Mom, sis and I were glad that Dad didn't have to fight in the war. We were all happy to have him home every evening, even if he got home from work long after Sis and I had gone to bed. When he was home in the evening, we looked forward to Dad tucking us in our beds and telling us one of his homespun bedtime stories before we said our prayers. I remember sometimes being awakened late at night by my father bending over my bed and kissing me on the forehead as he straightened my covers. I guess he had just gotten home.

I know that he was thankful that he was able to be at home to see my sister and me grow up, but, in spite of all of those blessings, I later realized that deep down Dad felt that he hadn't done his part. I guess Pop was a little ashamed that others had to do the fighting and even dieing in his place. I do not ever remember my dad talking with relatives who had returned from the war about their experiences, even when they told how the diesel engines in the tanks and ships had done yeoman's work under very difficult situations. At least I do not recall my father ever initiating the conversation.

Those of us who were born in the early forties have very few cognitive memories of our own from the days of World War II. I am not even certain that I was aware of the momentous act Harry Truman ordered when he instructed that an atomic bomb be dropped on Japan. We do have a much more vivid memory of the Korean War and especially the Cold War that followed.

Children today are most certainly living much more complicated lives than did we back in the olden days as my grandchildren call the 40s and 50s. That does not mean that kids of my time didn't experience fear and stress. Yes, those good ole days were filled with more stress than any child should have ever have been subjected to, let alone have to endure on a daily basis in school and even more stressful times lying in bed just thinking.

To explain my rationale for that statement, let me lead you down that branch of memory lane that veered off the road of happy times. Let me take you back to the air raid drills that we endured in school. Classmates, do you remember the teachers instructing us to turn out the lights, lower the window shades, sit on the floor beneath our desks and to close our eyes, and cover our faces with our hands? Do you remember stuffing cotton balls in your ears to protect your hearing? Now I ask you, if by chance a bomb should hit your school, what the hell good was good hearing if your ears were separated from the rest of your exploded body?

Do you remember the joking about sitting under your school desk, spreading your legs as far apart as you could, putting you head between your legs and kissing you butt goodbye? Or, did your air raid drills take you to the safer confines of an iron rebar reinforced concrete bomb shelter in the basement of the school? In either case, on a scale of one to ten, the needles on the dials of our stress meters were pushing past ten on the way to who knows where.

Add to those stresses, the blackout drills with room darkening shades pulled down and all of the lights inside the house dimmed or shut off. There wasn't one blessed bit of comfort to be found in such an exercise, just more fear.

As if enduring those dreaded air raid drills wasn't stressful enough. Even though my best friends in the whole world, my classmates, were in the same boat that I was in and even though they surrounded me, many times holding hands and praying the Lords Prayer together, somehow I felt so very alone with my fears.

Many were the nights that I lay in my darkened bedroom, alone and trembling in my bed. Thoughts went through my mind of Ruskie airplanes dropping bombs on my house. What if a bomb exploded and caught our house on fire? What if a piece of shrapnel from the exploded bomb came flying through Sis's bedroom window and hit her? What would Sis and I do if Mom and Dad were killed? I prayed every night for God to keep us safe from those mean SOB's on the other side of the world.

Please, don't think for a moment, not even a single second that our stress wasn't frightening enough to postpone the onset of much needed sleep. God forbid that I should hear the droning sound of the engines of a propeller driven airplane as it flew high above our house on its way from Chicago to New York City or beyond. Was it one of our airplanes or had one of those Commies snuck over our border and was headed straight for our house?

I lay there in my bed waiting to hear the shrill whistling sounds that I understood falling bombs make just before they explode. Finally, sleep engulfed me and I remember sometimes actually having happy dreams. I dreamed about ridding a pony and having a Red Ryder BB Gun in its leather scabbard hanging from my saddle. Pure fantasy inasmuch as I have never ridden a horse of any kind nor have I ever owned a BB Gun. On more than one occasion, however, I had a recurring dream of bombs exploding in the middle of Moore Street and waking up when I hit the floor. I know now that I had just fallen out of bed as have so many children, but back then I just knew it was the Ruskies attacking.

That, my younger friends, was stress spelled with an **"S"**! To top it off, in the very late 50s, there was a lot of talk and television programming and advertisements for bomb shelters and the stocking of essentials such as water, batteries, and of course prepared foods in the communal bomb shelters with their yellow and black symbol.

When all is said and done, I wouldn't trade my stress for the stresses of growing up today, not by a long shot. While kids of my generation did in fact endure stress, I believe the innocence and quality of life that we lived far outweighed the occasional threat from the Soviet Union.

Now that I stop to think about the carefree nature of life back in the good ole days, I do not remember ever locking our front door. I'm not even sure that we had a key for the lock of even if the lock worked. In the summer time I remember going to bed at night with the front door wide open to catch the breezes. I do not remember anyone ever stealing anything from a parked car. I never heard about child molestation, car jacking, drive-by shootings or drug abuse. I do remember neighbors sharing the bounty from their Victory Gardens, the exchange of heaping plates of homemade cookies, neighborhood picnics and roofing bees when one of the neighbors needed a new roof. No way, never in ten thousand years, would I trade my informative years for an opportunity to grow up in today's society.

In fact, if I had my druthers, I would consider having been born two or three generations prior to my actual birth. To emphasize that longing, my next book (already started) chronicles the adventure of a friend and my undertaking the construction of a genuine two room log cabin complete with stone fireplace and chimney. No power tools for we two Mountain man wannabes. Building the cabin would be accomplished with only an axe, adz, Grandpa's buck saw, a hand held one and one half inch diameter auger, a hand held bit and brace that also had a straight screwdriver bit, hand hewn pegs and a two hatchets.

So, you see, I am serious about wishing I could have lived a hundred years before I was born. I must admit, however, that I probably would have starved to death if my life depended upon providing venison for our table with a flintlock rifle and black powder. Believe me, I have tried. In seven years of attempted deer hunting in the mountains of Pennsylvania, I have never fired a shot. Once I was close enough to actually hit the deer, but when I pulled the hammer back to cock the flintlock rifle, the slight "Click" made by the hammer being pulled back jolted the deer into overdrive. Before I knew what happened, the deer had disappeared into a stand of pine trees.

Catching fish and even an occasional snapping turtle and blasting a duck, a pheasant or grouse from the air with my black powder double barrel shotgun proved to be a lot more productive. Too bad it would take about fifty or sixty ducks and a wagon load of pheasants, rabbits and quail to come close to the quantity of meat harvested from an average sized deer.

Chapter Three
Was it Medical Care or Child Abuse?

The first day of spring heralded two significant events in my early childhood other than the Crocus and tulips sticking their heads through the last vestiges of the winter's snow or the sighting of the first Robin. One was the annual spring-cleaning of the house. I didn't mind that too much inasmuch as all I had to do was use the wood-handled metal rug beater and beat the dirt from the rugs that my mother had draped over the taut clothesline in the backyard. Sure, I inhaled a lot of dust and I sneezed so hard and so many times that I almost peed my pants, but all in all, it was a lot of fun. That task gave me the opportunity to release my aggression in a parentally accepted manner. The whole time I was flailing at the rug, I was thinking about what I would like to do to the class bully, but was too afraid to attempt in real life. Boy did I ever give that bully, I mean the rug, the thumping of its life. Psychologically, I beat the snot out of that bully.

The second, the more disgusting, and I mean a really gut wrenching, chills down your spine, tears to your eyes kind of distasteful event was a preventative medicinal concoction that Mother administered to my sister and me. Of course Diane and I protested and tried to run and hide from her pursuit with a teaspoon and bottle of her potion. Eventually she cornered us and said, "Shut up and swallow. It's good for you. You don't want to get sick, do you?" So, Sis and I were forced take the spring tonic that was formulated from sulfur and molasses. Do you have any idea how bad that stuff tasted. You do remember that sulfur smells like rotting eggs, right? I can tell you, with my right hand raised to God, it don't taste no better than it smells!

To top it off, in the fall, usually the first day of the new school year, I began yet another of one of Mother's ritualistic prophylactic medical blessings, the ingestion of a cod liver oil capsule each morning with breakfast. It didn't have any taste going down, but two or three hours later, like clockwork, the belching began. I was teased unmercifully when some of my classmates got a whiff of my breath. I was known as stinky fish breath for several months until I discovered, one day, that I could fake swallowing that miserable capsule and then spit it out in the toilet bowl and flush it to a more suitable destination. The capsule was off to a destination where stinky fish reside. I suppose it ultimately ended up as fish food in the Rock River. Maybe that is how the Carp got so big. And to think, Mother thought she was so smart in getting me to take her prophylactic disease fighting medication. Psychologically, in my young mind, I showed her, but in truth I always counted on her believing that her obedient little boy had in fact swallowed the capsules.

God forbid that you ever got plugged up in our house. If Mother's calculations indicated that either my sister or I had failed to make the proper number of deposits in the porcelain bank, she would immediately break out a tablespoon and the bottle of Fletchers' Castoria or an even larger, more disgusting, bottle of castor oil.

Did you ever have to swallow castor oil? Did you ever try to mix castor oil with any other liquid? It does not mix well, does it? In fact, the castor oil just floats on top of whatever you are attempting to mix it with. For example, if you mixed it with Seven-Up, by the time you put the spoon down and went to gulp it down, the castor oil had already separated from the Seven-Up. As you tipped the glass to drink, the castor oil would slide to the bottom of the glass like an oil slick and the first thing that you drank was the Seven-Up. Then at the very end came that bolus of crude oil. Of course, it was the oil slick that lingered on your taste buds long after the memory of the Seven-Up had dissipated. I suspect those remedies would be considered by many today to be child abuse. What an expletive deleted thing to do to a kid! Oh to come back as my mother's father. I'd make her take the same dose of medicine; only I would double or triple the dose.

I recall, not so fondly, the Smallpox vaccination and the humungous scab on my left arm that itched worse than the pair of wool pants Mother made for me from grandpa's old suit. That plastic dome with the air holes that was taped over the scab wasn't all that comfortable either. Like most gangly boys, I'd continually bang into doorjambs, hitting that darn left arm every time. I am surprised that Mother didn't have Diane and me vaccinated against Malaria, the Bubonic Plague and Leprosy and what ever other malady that she read about in Reader's Digest, National Geographic or Life Magazine.

With Mother in the house, a kid couldn't even play hooky by feigning illness. No matter how convincing I was, or perhaps because I was so convincing, at the first mention of not feeling well, Mother was on the party line telephone, telling whichever neighbor was talking at the time that she had a serious medical emergency and that she needed to call the doctor right away.

Those were the days when doctors actually made house calls. More than once my faking came to a screeching halt when I saw Dr. Kishpaugh park his 1936 Hudson in our driveway and then walk into my bedroom, place his hand on my forehead, utter a concerned Hmmmmm and open his little black bag from which he withdrew a sterilized glass syringe and needle that looked to be big enough to be used by a veterinarian on a horse or cow, maybe even an elephant. Miraculously, before Dr. Kishpaugh could stick that big needle into my tender little tush, I confessed to feeling much better and promised that I would go to school right after lunch. I wonder how much money Dad had to pay for the bogus house calls. I wonder if Dr. Kishpaugh really would have jabbed me in the hinny with that gigantic needle?

I have been told that I always seem to leave the worst for last. You know, "I have some good news and I have some bad news. Which do you want to hear first?" Well, being a creature of habit and a little on the anal retentive side, I have followed true to form. Once again, I have saved the worst for last.

My bedroom had a window that looked out to the street at the front of our house and another window that looked out to the side yard. In the summer time I always got a goodly amount of cross ventilation, especially through the font window as it faced west and caught most of the westerly breezes. I usually lay at the foot of my bed to take full advantage of the refreshing zephyrs. I remember being awakened many times by rain blowing through the screen hitting me in the face as a thunderstorm came blowing out of the west. I loved the lightning and the rumbling thunder and that fresh smell of Ozone that always accompanied a good rain. Sis, on the other hand, either cried out for Ma or Dad or put her pillow over her head and cowered in her bed.

Very early one morning, just before sunrise, I heard the wailing of a siren getting louder and louder and saw the red flashing lights of an ambulance reflecting off the neighbors' freshly painted house as it came to a screeching halt in front of the house directly across the street from our home. The attendants unloaded a cart from the ambulance and rushed into the house. It seemed like they were inside the house for an eternity as many neighbors who also had been awakened by the wailing siren, still dressed in their pajamas and nightgowns, congregated on the sidewalk outside the house. Some were drinking a cup of coffee while others puffed nervously on their Camel, Lucky Strike, Chesterfield or Raleigh cigarettes. About a half hour later, the attendants emerged from the house pushing the cart they had carried into the house. On top of the cart lay a heavily laden rubberized bag. I could hear many of the bystanders gasp and quietly ask questions of the attendants. At the time, I had no idea what the significance of that early morning wake up call was, but I was destined to learn its significance in a few months.

Several months later I learned that the old lady that lived in the house across the street had turned on the all of the gas burners as well as opened the oven door of her gas range and just sat down on the kitchen floor waiting to die. That was really sad, but at the same time, made me very thankful that we had an electric stove. How could someone do that to himself or herself? Why? I wondered, is she in Heaven now?

The following summer I developed an abscess on one of my baby teeth and had to go to a dentist to have it extracted. As soon as I was seated in the dentist's chair of intolerable torture, the roly-poly dentist came at me with a mask saying, "Donny, I'm just going to give you a little bit of gas to make you go to sleep."

Hearing that, what I believed to be the pronouncement of my very own death sentence, I bolted from the chair, nearly knocked that fat, mean old dentist on his keister and ran down the hall and down the stairs to the street. Once my PF flyers hit the pavement, I was off at full speed in search of a safe place to hide. I found my safe haven, or at least I thought I had, in the back booth of the Walgreen Pharmacy's soda fountain and ice cream bar. I had just enough time to order and begin to drink a cherry Coke that cost me my last ten cents when Mother came storming in. She was huffing and puffing as she wagged her finger at me. Her face was as red as the cherry in the cherry Coke. I, the escapee, had been recaptured. Drats!

When you read what happened next, I want you to promise me that you won't laugh. What happened to me was no laughing matter. Mother grabbed me by my left ear and led me down the street and back upstairs to the dentist's office, tugging my poor left ear all the way. In later years I always wondered if the cause of my big ears could be traced back to mother's constant ear tugging. Thank God Mother was ambidextrous and didn't favor one ear over the other. Can you imagine going through life with one big ear and one normal sized ear?

No sooner had I been thrust back into the chair than that lard bucket dentist climbed on board, with one leg draped over each arm of the chair, his gluteus maximums pressing my flailing legs to the chair. Try as I might, I couldn't move him. For a fleeting moment or two, I thought seriously of kicking him in the you know where and what and making him see stars in the daylight, but luckily for me, his cheeks of adipose tissue and my better judgment prevailed.

So, I was forced into a gas-induced slumber while Mother stood behind the chair with her hands firmly grasping my shoulders, pinning them to the back of the chair like the wrestler, Gorgeous George, would pin his opponent to the mat, as Dr. Sipple tugged and yanked at my infected tooth.

That was a terrible experience. It was an experience that haunts me to this day. Every time I have to schedule an appointment with the dentist, I cringe. If I am lucky enough to go to heaven and if there is the remotest possibility that Dr. Sipple is there, so help me, when God has his back turned, I might just knock Dr. Sipple's teeth down his throat!

But, that wasn't the end of that experience. Things just seem to be going from worst to worser and to worserest, don't they? The ultimate insult to my sensibilities came the next morning, after having suffered through every thing that I was subjected to the previous day. When I slid my hand under my pillow, expecting to find a quarter that I expected would be left by the Tooth Fairy in exchange for my tooth. The tooth was gone, but all I found was a neatly folded note that read, "Sorry, Donny, the tooth fairy does not leave money for a boy who behaved so badly at the dentist's office as you did yesterday."

You can't blame me for not liking dentists, now can you? I must tell you, I wasn't very happy with the Tooth Fairy either.

CHAPTER FOUR
Cowboys, Indians and Bandits Galore and Other Assorted Tales

Certainly, through the decades of the forties and well into the fifties, television did not exist for most of us. Well, maybe it existed, existed in the large picture window of the appliance store downtown or in the home of a rich friend or relative. As far as our house goes, it most certainly was AWOL. Listening to the radio and letting our imaginations run free, we conjured up all sorts of mental images. Sometimes my sister and I would use Crayola crayons and butcher's paper to draw pictures of what we were listening to on the radio.

An example of just how much radio played a part in our everyday life took place every Saturday morning at precisely eight A.M., I could be found knocking on the front door of my friends who lived two or three doors away from us. We had a standing date to play cowboys, Indians and bandits in their attic.

The Olson family had an old-fashioned wooden console Zenith radio stored in their attic. Ron and John and I had strategically positioned boxes, trunks, hung blankets and such so that as we listened to the Lone Ranger, The Cisco Kid, Hopalong Cassidy, Sky King, Gene Autry, Roy Rogers and Dale Evans and others, we acted out what we were hearing on the radio. We were decked out with our six shooters strapped to our hips in their leather holsters, wearing red bandannas tied around our necks, Cowboy hats atop our heads and Cowboy boots, if we were lucky enough to have a pair. I, unfortunately, was the buckaroo with the PF flyers.

At precisely noon, the three buckaroos, Ron, John and I would holster our six guns, turn off the radio and go to my bunk house where mother always had a bowl of Tomato, vegetable beef or Chicken Noodle soup and a hot grilled cheese sandwich waiting for each of the hungry cowboys. If we were really lucky, and if Mother was in a generous frame of mind, we might even be surprised with a grilled cheese and bacon sandwich. Heehaw! T'was a lot better than hardtack and beans, a lot less gas, too. Get along little doggie.

Galloping down the sagebrush and tumbleweed-strewn path of memories, reminds me of a joke that I heard when I was a kid. See, I warned you these would be random thoughts. Ain't this about as random as you can get? Anyway, it seems that there was a young boy in the fourth or fifth grade. For the purposes of the story, let's call him Harry.

The teacher had given the class an assignment to write a short story with a moral. When young Harry got his paper back from the teacher the next day, he had a big red **F** on his paper. Not understanding his teacher's obvious error, Harry raised his hand and said, "Teacher, why did I get an F? I didn't misspell not even one word and my mom checked my story to make sure I used proper punctuation, and my story was very short, wasn't it? So why did I get an F?"

"Well, Harry, you didn't follow instructions. Your story did not contain a moral. You must follow directions, young man, if you want to get a good grade in my class."

"Oh, but it did, it did contain a moral!" he insisted.

"O.K., young man, if you are that confident of even the slightest inkling of a moral being present in your story, you may come to the front of the room and read your story out loud to the rest of the class. I promise you, if just one of the boys or girls can tell me what the moral to your story is, I will change that F to a B. No, on second thought, I will go so far as to give you an A minus. Fair enough?"

"You promise? You'll give me an A minus?"

"Yes, young man, it is a promise," she said, knowing that none of the students would be able to find the non-existent moral.

So, Harry stood next to the teacher's desk and read the following short story to his classmates:

"One day the Lone Ranger and Tonto were riding their horses, Silver and Paint, through the woods when a bunch of bandits ambushed them. The Lone Ranger and Tonto took their lariats from their saddle horns, swung the lariats in big looping swirls and captured all of the bandits and tied them up. Then the Lone Ranger and Tonto made the bandits walk all the way to town there they were put in jail. The End"

"O.K. class," the teacher said, "is there anyone who can tell me the moral of Harry's story, that is, if there is a moral to be cited?"

From the back of the classroom a little girl, Marcia, said, "I can, teacher. You're gonna have to give Harry the A minus as you promised."

"Oh really, young lady, and pray tell what might the moral be?"

"Well, teacher, it seems to me that it taught those bandits not to mess around with the Lone Ranger and Tonto."

Do an about face as we go back to the importance of the radio in most homes during the 40s and 50s. The radio in our home played a prominent role in our family's daily life. My father and I always listened to Gillette's Friday Night Fight of the Week while Mother and my sister did some sort of girlie thing.

Dad would sit on the edge of his chair, eating his nightly bowl of Kellogg Corn Flakes as I lay on the floor at his feet listening to the announcer's blow-by-blow account of one boxer trying to beat the snot out of the other. I swear, sometimes I think I would see Dad wince as the announcer told of a particularly solid blow that had been landed. I know for a fact that more than once I saw Dad slam his fist into the pillow that he always had on his lap as we listened to the fight for just such purposes. It was almost as if he thought he was delivering the mighty blow that the announcer had just described.

See what a vivid imagination can do for you? You don't have to be young to use your imagination. You need not be a physical specimen of athletic stature to let your imagination entice you into believing that you are a heavyweight boxer. Your imagination can take you anywhere that you would like to go or be any thing that you want to be, no matter what your age may be. Imagination worked for my father and Dad was really old.

On the lighter side, we religiously listened to The Jack Benny Show, The Hit Parade, The Great Gildersleeve, Amos and Andy, The Ted Mac Amateur Hour, Fibber McGee and Molly and of course Ma Perkins was an absolute must listen to, in our home. Of course we never missed an episode of Bob Hope and Groucho Marx's 'You Bet Your Life. In chapter thirteen I ask if you remember how and why Groucho Marx's TV program was taken off the air. If you don't remember, I think you will find the answer to be quite interesting.

Our family life, our weekly routine, was typical to most of our middle class neighbors. I know that I, and most of my friends, always listened to The Green Hornet and The Shadow. You remember, "What evil lurks in the hearts and minds of man? Only The Shadow knows."

A most comical incident, an incident that has nothing to do with radio, but nonetheless a comical incident, has found us taking yet another random detour on memory lane. When you get to be my age, sometimes thoughts and memories can be fleeting. So, inasmuch as the following thought just popped into my head, I believe is important that I share it with you at this time, lest it fade from my memory. The memory is too funny to chance delaying its presentation, even if it has nothing to do with the subject at hand, radio. What you are about to read really happened while my fifth grade classmates and I were enduring the tutelage of a substitute teacher.

The day before Miss Mataye's absence, she had given us an assignment to create a food diary, a diary of the various food groups that we consumed that evening, the quantity, the calculated calories, as well as what we had eaten for breakfast the next morning with the same qualitative and quantitative descriptions. You remember that three part nutritional pyramid chart that hung on the classroom wall, don't you? She wanted us to take this assignment seriously because, as she said, "After all, students, you are in fact what you eat." I often wondered why I didn't look like a potato or a piece of meat. If I ate a worm, would I look like a worm?

Mid-way through the day, the substitute teacher called on one of my classmates to read his diary. When Harry Satness got to the breakfast portion of his food diary, he reported, "For breakfast I 'et' seven pancakes, two strips of bacon, one sausage patty and a whole bunch of butter and maple syrup and two glasses of Ovelteen."

The teacher stopped him at that point and asked, "You mean "ate" don't you?"

To which Harry replied, "Unh-unh, I wanted another pancake caus I was still hungry and I could have "et" the eighth flap jack without no problem at all, but mom said seven was more than enough for a kid my size and besides, it was time for me to skedaddle and to high tail it off to school before I was late."

I am looking forward to seeing Harry at the reunion and reminding him of that knee slapping memory. I wonder if he will remember it as clearly as I do? I wonder if he can still "et" eight pancakes? If he can, he must be as big as a house! Personally, two pancakes is my limit.

Then there was the boy in the class who was so stubborn that he gave the teacher the shivering fits. One day he was acting up in class, as he was prone to do, only a little more intensely than normal. Our teacher tried to reason with him, but as I said, he was a stubborn kid. He wasn't having any part of her logical pleadings; he just wouldn't have any part of it. So, she slapped him on his right hand with her wooden ruler with its copper metal edge imbedded along the length of one side.

Poor kid, the glancing blow of her twelve inches of discipline sliced a wart off his right index finger and he was bleeding like a stuck pig. When I say bleeding, I mean bleeding big time. Blood flowed out of his finger, down the sloping top of his desk and pooled on the floor between his feet. His index finger was bleeding so badly that after the school nurse did her best to stop the bleeding and bandage his finger, he had to be driven home by the principal so that his mother could take him to the hospital to have stitches to seal the wound.

I am sure that more than one of us in the class wished for a few seconds that we, too, had a wart on our hand and that we would receive the mighty blow of her scalpel like ruler so we could go home. No such luck, no warts, no slap and no going home from school until the dismissal bell rang.

I guess children, like fruits and vegetables, ripen at different rates, mellow out if you will. Mike, who had been the bane of the class in elementary school, appearing to be ever ready for a fight, turned out to be a really nice kid by the time we got to junior high.

I remember that when Mike was a member of city council that my father went to him on many occasions, soliciting help in rectifying something that father felt needed addressing in the city. Dad frequently wrote to me telling me of the helpful concern that Mike Melaas showed toward dad's concerns and what a great job he was doing for the city.

CHAPTER FIVE
Not Working Up to His Potential

Have you ever wished that you had never done something or have you wished that you had done a task even better than you had? Have you ever had anything follow around you like a bad smell, or like the black cloud that followed the character in the Lil' Abner comic strip and you couldn't do a blooming thing about it? Boy, do I ever have nightmares about days just like that. Those days seem to have all congregated in the year I was in third grade. Have I got stories to tell you!

For example, the third grade was nothing but one big disaster after another, the proverbial Chinese fire drill. I sure am thankful that I didn't have to repeat third grade inasmuch as I don't think I could have survived another year like the one that I had. For that matter, I'm not so sure that my teachers or the principal could have endured another year like my third grade experience.

The first untoward thing that happened took place on a rainy fall day, a day that was too foul for us to go outside for recess. The teacher told us we could play in the classroom while she stepped out for a moment. She didn't say where she was going, but we all suspected that she probably was going to the boiler room, like all of the other teachers did during our recess, to smoke a cigarette and to drink a cup of coffee.

What do the mice do when the cat is away? They play tag, of course. Just as Miss Brownell reentered the room, she caught me running away from the student who was "It." Running in the classroom was bad enough, but this spectacular run of mine took me across the tops of the desks from one side of the room to the other. Oh-oh was I was going to be in deep trouble. Sure enough, I was in bigger, deeper and more long-lived trouble than I could have possibly imagined.

Every report card that she sent home from that point on made some reference to Donny not working up to his potential. The vindictive woman felt it necessary to remind my parents with each and every successive report card that I had been caught running across the desktops with absolutely no regard for classroom rules or decorum. Never once, not one single time, did she ever give me credit for my athletic prowess.

I guess, in all honesty, Miss Brownell wasn't all that bad. Three or four days before our class picture was to be taken, I was diagnosed with a bad case of Impetigo. Small oozing blisters popped out all over my body. Impetigo is extremely contagious, so I had to stay home from school until all of the blisters had dried up and crusted over. The day before the class picture was to be taken, Miss Browenell telephoned my mother to see if she couldn't possible put scotch tape over my lesions so that I could have my picture taken with the rest of the class. It goes without saying; Miss Brownell was a much better teacher than she would have been as a nurse.

Some time that next spring, you know, one of those days when there was still snow on the ground but the sun was high in the sky. It was just warm enough to melt the snow, melt it into the raw material necessary to pack the perfect snowball.

On just such a day, I wore my favorite Christmas sweater, a dark green pullover with white snowflakes and a white deer knitted into the fabric of the sweater. Unable to resist the perfectly good packing condition of the snow, I bent down and grabbed a handful of snow and packed the snowball to end all snowballs. So impressed with the first snowball, I made another of similar quality. Both of them were excellent specimens about the size of an official softball. What do you do with a work of art like that? You throw it, of course.

My first target was a car that was passing the school on McKinley. As the car neared the end of the fence surrounding the playground, I hurled one of my gems and hit the car in the middle of the trunk. Of course I turned my back and hid my last snowball. I knew I was really lucky the driver had not stopped and come back to the playground.

I methodically looked around the schoolyard to make sure that there were no teachers that would see me launch the perfect snowball. I wasn't going to test my luck on another automobile, so I took aim at the brick wall of the school and gave the snowball my best; my most powerful throw, fully expecting to see it explode on the surface of the brick wall. Remember, I told you this was a bad year? Well, unfortunately the snowball smashed into the windowsill of the principal's office window. Thank God it didn't break the window. The choice of that particular wall was one of my most hair-brained ideas. Of course, I had neglected to look for any of the tattletale upper classmen acting as the safety patrol (to my way of thinking, they were no better than the "Brown Shirt Youth of Here Hitler's army or the SS). One of those delightful sixth grade creeps caught me and took me to the principal's office by the scruff of my neck.

I never wore that sweater again; hoping that by not wearing it the safety patrol would not recognize me in the future. Today I am certain if I had showed up at school in my pajamas or in one of mother's dresses, that SOB safety patrol would still have recognized me. I was doomed until he went to junior high.

All was well until fifth grade. I did just fine academically and socially, but I was about to endure the most devastating twist of fate possible. Every spring, each student, boys and girls alike, received a small brown paper bag that was folded over and stapled at the top. The bag contained thirteen light green marbles and a shooter. We all entered the school district's marbles contest.

I had the great fortune of having an official sized marbles ring painted on our basement floor. Every night after supper, I would practice. I got to be really good. I learned how to rhythmically rub the shooter on a rough section of concrete to scuff the surface of the shooter. The rough surface allowed me to put English on the cat's eye shooter. I could even make it back up after striking its intended target to position the shooter for the next shot. I don't know why I was never able to master that technique with a cue in billiards.

Rarely did I miss or even more rarely did the shooter cross the boundaries of the ring and go out of bounds. At the end of the three-week single elimination competition, the championship match came down to the school's boy's champion pitted against the school's girl's champion.

Yours truly had earned the honor of being named the boys champion of Gaston Elementary School. Roxanne Russell wound up beating all of the girls in the school. So, it was Roxanne Russell and I pitted against each other in the battle of the sexes. It was a precursor of the battle of the sexes between Billy Jean King and Bobby Riggs many years later.

Do you have any idea how humiliating it was to hear "Congratulations, Roxanne Russell, you are the school's new marbles champion?" Do you have any idea how many years the stigma of that defeat followed me around like a shadow? One of my happiest days in school was the day that I learned that Roxanne Russell was going to move out of town.

During the summer between fifth and sixth grades, my parents received a letter from the school district. "Dear Mr. and Mrs. Nelsen: Due to over crowding at Gaston Elementary School, it is necessary that your son, Donald, be transferred to Cunningham Elementary School to complete his elementary school education." Even Ann Marie Kernland who lived less than two blocks away from the school was transferred to Cunningham.

Who did they think they were kidding? There was no over crowding. Gaston just wanted to get rid of the snowball throwing, marbles loser. Oh, well, back to my old friend, Principal Daisy Chapin. As it turned out, our sixth grade year was the last year that Daisy taught or was the principal. At the end of the year her nemesis would go on to seventh grade and my nemesis would retire.

"Rats, I guess Miss Brownell and Miss Mataye were right. Once again, I didn't work up to my potential." This character trait seems to becoming habit forming!

Sixth grade offered me the opportunity of being taught by my first male teacher. What a relief. What an interesting experience. Mr. Arnold Lee excelled in the sciences and world history/geography. For example, in Science class, Pete Peterson, Emmet Smelzer and I made a chicken wire and paper mache volcano with tubing inside that connected to a beaker with a stopper and a long flexible rubber tube to carry steam to the crater of the volcano. Then Mr. Lee put some chemicals in the opening of the crater, lit it with a match, and the volcano erupted. Do you remember the little black, almost Nibs Licorice in appearance pieces of fireworks that we light and as they burned the made a long black snake. Well, the chemicals that Mr. Lee ignited formed lava much like that.

In sixth grade we studied medieval history. We painted a mural that stretched around the three walls of the classroom that did not have windows. The classroom door was even covered on both sides with our artistic rendition of a drawbridge. Most of the mural was painted to look like a castle with the rest of it being the serf's and peasant dwellings and surrounding countryside.

Mr. Lee taught us how to construct suits of armor out of cardboard boxes and tubes which we painted silver. We constructed horses from cardboard and construction paper and suspended them by suspenders made of one of the student's father's old brown suit. We made jousting lances and swords from long cardboard tubes as well as brightly painted cardboard shields. What a joy it was to walk through that drawbridge that was our classroom's door each morning anticipating another lesson in social studies. We even had a medieval dinner and had to eat everything with our hands because knives, forks and spoons were not customarily used back then. We all wore our father's old shirts like a knight's tunic and just wiped our hands and mouth on the shirt tails. Mr. Lee cautioned us not to try this at home! He must have known that our mothers would have had a fit.

Just to prove a point, not once did Mr. Lee write "does not work up to his potential" in my report card. Not once did my sixth grade report card make mention of running across desktops. I even got along with my old nemesis, Miss Daisy Chapin. Not once was I sent to or summoned to her office the entire year. Had I turned the corner or will I continue to hone my insubordinate behavioral skills to employ them on other unsuspecting, probably non-deserving, educational figures of authority? Time will tell.

You know, now that I am seeing my youth through the eyes of a more mature man, I now realize that I was one of those students in elementary school that every teacher dreaded having. I challenged authority to get a laugh. I made silly faces and stuck out my tongue at the teacher when her back was turned. I'd do almost anything to get a laugh. I wonder why I didn't become a comedian? Could I have become a David Brenner or a George Carlan?

CHAPTER SIX
Mom's Predictable Down Home Cooking

A well ordered routine in our home was not restricted to listening to selected radio programs, sitting in the same pew every Sunday at church, twice a day teeth brushings or nightly prayers before we went to bed. We didn't need a calendar in our home to know what day of the week it was.

Mother, in her time honored tradition, knew twelve months in advance what we would have to eat each evening for supper, as we called it. She had long ago learned when the Piggly Wiggly Supermarket would put certain foodstuffs on sale. She'd buy in quantity, thereby assuring her that when she said we were going to have Campbell's Pork and beans two weeks from Thursday, that she would have half a case or more on hand in the root cellar.

If it was Monday, we had left over what ever from Sunday's noon meal, dinner, whether it be roast beef, chicken or ham, that is if we hadn't been treated to a fried chicken dinner at the Cozy Corner restaurant in Orfordville after church on Sunday.

At The Cozy Corner the waitress always asked if we wanted white meat or dark meat. Dad would always order a complete chicken so that we could have what ever we wanted. The waitress would always bring the heart, the liver and the gizzard on a small plate just in case someone wanted to sample those internal organs. At the time, I couldn't imagine anyone wanting to eat a chicken's innards, but now Chicken livers with sautéed onions and bacon with a side of horseradish is one of my favorite meals.

Tuesday's offering was usually fried, pork shops with mashed potatoes with lumpy gravy and some sort of frozen or canned vegetable. Once in a while, especially in the summer, we had fresh vegetables from the neighborhood Victory gardens. Dad always supplied the neighborhood with tomatoes from his seven or eight foot tall beefsteak tomato plants growing behind the garage.

Wednesdays presented us with canned salmon in one form or another. Sometimes it was Salmon croquettes. Other times it was creamed salmon over rice with green peas mixed in. If we were really lucky, sometimes relatives would send us real wild rice from Minnesota and Mother would ladle the creamed salmon over the wild rice. Do you remember the salmon was preserved at such a high temperature in the canning process that the little bones and pieces of vertebrae were so soft that you could eat them?

Wednesday having come and gone, my sister and I would once again be tested with one of father's favorite suppers, Thursday's offering was always, it never failed to be fried liver, onions and bacon. The freshly ground horseradish that always accompanied that meal brought tears to our eyes. The onions and bacon were really good, but the liver was a different story. Can you imagine, willingly eating cow's guts?

Both my sister and I learned quickly that if we didn't eat what was put in front of us, especially liver and/or spinach, we would have to sit at the table until we had cleaned our plates, and I don't mean scraping them off in the garbage can. Try as we might, Mother and Dad did not accept our offers to send our Thursday night suppers to the starving children in Europe.

Do you have any idea how hard a dining room chair gets to be after two or three hours of sitting motionless? Do you realize how disgusting cold liver is? (It would be many years before I acquired a taste for pâte de Foie Gras or sauté chien livres.) Wasn't Popeye the only person who could tolerate the miserable taste of spinach? Why eat it? It never put an ounce of muscle on my scrawny body.

Friday was usually one of the better nights of the week. It was a pickle and catsup hamburger or cheeseburgers and a large order of French fries from Al's Snack Shop and a cold root beer from Showers' A&W Root beer stand. Sometimes Dad would bring home two large containers of Al's mud for us to share as we ate our burgers and fries.

Saturday's evening meal was usually Franc-O- American Spaghetti from the can (now that I think about it, it wasn't until I was seated in the mess hall at Fort Leonard Wood, Missouri during basic training that I tasted real Italian spaghetti with meat balls for the first time) or some concoction of leftovers that Mother threw together. Sometimes the concoction tasted pretty good. Other times, I honestly believe that I would rather have to force beef liver down my gullet than eat what ever her Saturday night blue plate special consisted of. Seriously, when by some strange accident of fate mother actually threw some leftovers into a palatable presentation, I am one hundred per cent certain that she could not replicate the meal if her life depended upon it.

I remember once Mother was determined to make Chop Suey in the brand new pressure cooker that dad bought her for Christmas. That evening is as clear in my memory as if it were yesterday. The entire family was gathered around the radio in the living room, listening to President Harry Truman giving a report on the status of the police action in Korea. (I never did understand the difference between a police action and war. To my way of thinking, soldiers got killed in war and they got killed in police actions, too. Those who died were just as dead, just as missed, whether they were killed during a war or a police action weren't they? Why the euphemism?) President Truman was saying something about General McArthur and the Thirty-Eighth parallel when we heard the loudest noise that I had ever heard. It was almost as if a bomb or a mortar shell had landed in our kitchen.

Mother and Dad screamed at my sister and me to "stay put" as Dad ran out the front door to see what in blazes had exploded and if there was any damage to the house, or, God forbid, that the house was on fire. Mother ran to the kitchen. Looking back, I believe that Mother knew instantly what had happened.

The next thing Sis and I heard was Mother cussing up a storm. Was she ever cussing! If we had been living in a comic book, blue smoke would have been billowing from the kitchen laced with scores of words that would be represented by a jumble of symbols and Arabic letters. She was saying words that Sis and I had never heard before. That was quite unusual, very ironic and totally out of character for Mother. You must understand, each time I uttered a word that I had heard on the school playground, even if I didn't know what it meant and in spite of the fact that I was just reporting what I had heard, I still had to take a big bite out of a bar of Life Buoy soap and hold it in my mouth until soap bubbles were erupting from my nose and mouth and tears were streaming down my cheeks.

I secretly hoped that Dad heard what she had said and that when he came back into the house that he would make Mother take a bite out of the bar of Life Buoy, too. Honestly, I don't believe for a minute that Mother would have taken a bite from the bar of soap, even if Dad had been foolish enough to tell her she had to. After all, isn't what is good for the goose good for the gander? Of course he didn't tell her and she certainly was of no mind to volunteer.

Upon entering the kitchen, mother saw that her new pressure cooker had blown its lid and had blasted Chop Suey, our supper, all over the walls, ceiling, cupboards and floor of the kitchen. The next day when dad pulled the refrigerator away from the wall to inspect, there was even Chop Suey in back of the refrigerator, too. Mother's new white eyelet curtains were stained by soy sauce, juices from the meat and pulverized vegetables. There was Chop Suey everywhere, and not a bite to eat!

When Dad came back into the house, I could see that he was trying his darndest not to laugh out loud as he heard Mother sputtering in the kitchen like a wet hen. Little did he know the work that was in store for him because of that cursed pressure cooker. Mother, was so PO'd that all she could do was grab hands full of the ill-fated Chop Suey and throw it at the walls. Needless to say, we cleaned up as best as we could and went to Al's Snack Shop for supper. Two nights at Al's for burgers and mud in one week, what a week!

Sunday, after church, and after having a PB&J sandwich for dinner, (Mother said she wasn't about to try to cook dinner in such a mess) Dad was on the ladder washing the walls and ceiling while Mother was on her hands and knees scrubbing the floor, insisting that everything in the kitchen needed to be painted and Dad would just have to give her enough money to buy more material for new kitchen curtains. She thought a yellow gingham would go nicely with the yellow paint she insisted father purchase.

That was the last time I, or anyone else, ever saw the pressure cooker. It was relegated to the trash heap. Too bad the metal drives of WWII were no longer in existence. Mum was the word, never again was that blasted contraption to be mentioned in the presence of my mother.

Holiday dinners were usually a treat because we spent most of them at grandmas house. The day after Thanksgiving, on the other hand, was always a day to dread. Mother had a ritual of collecting the carcass of the turkey and favoring us with the most God awful, sorry excuse for turkey soup that you can imagine. It was not unlike drinking dirty dishwater. I am sure that it didn't have a hell of a lot of nutritional value either. What a way to destroy the Thanksgiving Day memory.

While we are on the subject of food, there are a couple of gastronomic traditions that have been handed down in my family from generation to generation. My paternal grandparents, who emigrated from Denmark to the United Sates just as the Civil War in America was drawing to a close, always ate Oyster Stew on Christmas Eve prior to going to church. Mother's ancestors traditionally ate green peas on New Years Day and burned a Barberry candle to bring good luck for the New Year.

Even though Mother married into the annual tradition of Oyster stew on Christmas Eve, that did not mean that she enjoyed, or would even taste the stew. While Dad wouldn't prepare the Oyster stew, he did supervise every step of its preparation. With at least a pint or two of freshly shucked Oysters at the ready, Dad supervised as Mother poured a quart of whole milk, a quart of whole cream and half a pound of butter into a large sauce pan and flavored it with a pinch of kosher salt and approximately a teaspoon of black pepper that had been ground via mortar and pestle. The liquid was heated slowly, being constantly stirred so that the milk and cream would not scorch. At precisely the right moment, Dad would add the oysters and their liquor to the pot. As soon as the oysters stared to curl at the edges, the pot was taken off the fire and the stew as poured into a giant soup tureen that father had inherited from his parents.

Large, hard oyster crackers served two purposes. The first use was to break them in half and place a little freshly ground horseradish on the exposed center of the broken cracker. Father always said that was the traditional appetizer to remind us of the not so good times. Sometimes we'd have a taste of pickled herring to go with the cracker. I guess in the absence of ten or twelve different kinds of herring, this was as close as Dad could come to a Danish hors douvers. The next, and the most important function of the oyster crackers was to steep them in the rich buttery broth until they were almost as soft as the oysters. Crackers dripping of warm cream and butter. Umm—Umm Good! That soup beat Campbell's six ways to Sunday.

As I stated, mother would not partake of her martially acquired ancestral tradition. So, she spent the entire day steaming cubes of beef, pork and veal until it fell apart in her fingers. To the shredded meat she would add a jar of her homemade ketchup and let the flavors marry over very low heat. The BBQ that resulted was then heaped onto a sliced hard roll that dad had baked that morning. With bread and butter pickles on the side, Mother and my sister were ready to sit down to what turned out to be their traditional Christmas Eve supper while Dad and I scoffed down the oysters, crackers and buttery broth.

Mother had a recipe for probably the most delicious cake ever baked. It was a fluffy yellow cake that required thirteen eggs and lots of butter and cream mixed in. The frosting was made of butter, more butter, powdered sugar and crushed Nabisco Vanilla Wafers, with dollop or two of very strong black coffee added for that special taste. The only time she made it was to take it to a bereaved's home after a funeral. Thank God we didn't get to eat it very often. On the other hand, I wish she had associated that cake with something more joyous than a funeral, something that occurred much more frequently, like maybe Saturday night supper, or perhaps to follow the insult to our taste buds that occurred each Thursday night. (Liver night) At least that way we would have at least one pleasant memory of Thursday night's supper.

I vividly remember one summer's day. Precisely at twelve noon, my father came home, which he never did, and was about ready to skin my mother alive. It turns out that Mom and Dad had a serious difference of opinion about something the night before. Mother must have lost the argument and decided to make Dad pay. Before Dad ate breakfast, Mother made and packed his lunch as she always did. The difference was that she made dad's lunch sandwiches out of thinly shaved pieces from a bar of Ivory soap rather than the Limburger cheese that he had expected. I guess I'd have to give mother credit for ingenuity and spunk. While she most certainly earned an A in stupidity, I'd have to give her failing grades for common sense. Nothing but nothing comes between a man and his Limburger cheese sandwich, nothing!

Father said that he should have suspected something was array when the cab of his truck didn't smell like Limburger cheese with his lunch box sitting in the sun on the front seat of his truck. Dad stood in the kitchen doorway and watched mother prepare the stinky cheese sandwich correctly and then he left as quickly as he arrived.

One lament must be shared with you. My father, being of Danish heritage and the son of dairy farmers, insisted that Mother's cooking contain a goodly portion of butter and whole cream. Even at breakfast, our toast was dripping with butter and our cereal, whether it be Wheaties, Corn Flakes, Cream of Wheat, hot oatmeal, Farina or Mapo, sometimes even Sugar Pops, it was always smothered with fresh whole cream and at least two teaspoons of sugar, sometimes even brown sugar.

While the meals were usually tasty, (How could butter and cream be anything but tasty?) I am certain that being raised on a diet such as I have described, set me up for the cardiac problems and obesity that I have suffered in my latter years. I suppose that diet had a lot to do with the blocked main descending artery of my heart two or three years ago that required a Roto-Rooter job and a subsequent Stint. Needless to say, my cardiologist has restricted my butterfat and sugar ingestion. In fact, she has just about restricted everything that tastes good, smells good, looks good, is fattening or is immoral.

I understand her concern, but there are no calories or grams of butterfat in remembering, are there? She cannot take from me the memories of the rich food, especially Grandma's deserts such as "Elkow, or maybe it was Elcow, or maybe even Elko." Unfortunately, I do not know of the existence of her old recipe nor do any of my relatives. I guess the recipe died along with the last of the old Danes.

If you remember the title of this chapter, I said that Mother's cooking was predictable. I didn't say it was innovative, now did I? Sometimes, like Thursdays, it was down right awful. The saddest thing of all was that I wasn't smart enough to wrangle supper on Thursday nights from one of my friends. I didn't indicate that she had eclectic tastes or a collection of recipes that contained anything but meat and potatoes. Plain meat, boiled, roasted or fired. The potatoes sustained the same fate except sometimes they were smashed. Occasionally I was subjected to pickled pig's feet or sardines, neither of which I remember fondly. A little further down memory lane you will understand why I include Uncle Mert's sauerkraut is in the list of non-edible treasures.

While my Italian friends would sit down to a big plate of pasta and meatballs smothered in a rich spaghetti sauce, mother would just open two or three cans of Franc-O American Spaghetti. As I said, I never tasted real spaghetti and sauce or Lasagna until I was in Basic Training at Fort Leonard Wood, Missouri.

Other delectable foods I never tasted until I no longer sat at Mother's table were, eggplant, anything Mexican, escargot, as well as a myriad of international delicacies. I had no idea of what the heck a lobster was and I wondered why people would actually eat clams (fish bait, from my experience) and raw oysters? Mom was good with cream and lots and lots of butter, but she was void of any other culinary skills, including thinking outside the box of her normal, boring routine. How could anyone in their right mind love the taste of Spam and would not be willing to try something as good as Pizza. It wasn't until high school that I learned how delicious Pizza is.

There was a good tasting, fun filled aspect to my parents cooking. My father was a skilled baker, having worked in bakeries during the Depression years and well into the mid 50s. He could bake the best smelling, best tasting bread and dinner rolls in the county, but his real forte was Danish and French pastries.

Dads had impressive strength in his hands. His biceps and his triceps bulged form all of the hand kneading of bread dough. So proud of his arms strength was Dad that I couldn't leave the house until he had given me a lesson or two in the finer points of arm wrestling. To Dad, that meant to beat my—! Try as hard as I might, I could never beat him until the day after Thanksgiving when he was eight-nine years old. That was a sad day for me. I knew I could finally take him. I could feel the weakness in his grip and there wasn't that customary pulsating rhythm in his arm. As much as I wanted to win just one arm wrestling match with my father, I just couldn't do that to him. I grimaced and made it appear that I was trying my darndest to beat him, but after a minute or so, I feigned a muscle cramp and gave up. He slammed my right hand to the dining room table and proudly proclaimed, "The old man's still got it, Sonny."

Getting back to the yarn of Dad's baking skills. His specialty was French and Danish pastries. It was always exciting to be awakened early on a Sunday morning to the aroma of butter horns, or his famous cheese and jelly filled Danish pastries. Have you ever eaten a Danish pastry seconds after it came out of the oven?

Mother had a bit of a sweet tooth. She was particularly good at making seasonal treats such as date and hickory nut filled cookie swirls, peanut butter cookies filled with roasted peanuts and of course my favorite, crispy ginger snaps.

From time to time we would coat our hands with butter and helped pull Mother's homemade taffy that had been boiling on the stove for hours. Sometimes she flavored the taffy with peppermint, anise and/or cinnamon. She was famous for her white divinity fudge with pecans as well as the caramel coated apples on a stick that she always gave to all of the trick-or-treaters who came to our door on Halloween. No worry back then about someone putting stickpins or razor blades in the candied apples.

Homemade peanut brittle, chocolate covered pecans, chocolate covered raisins and chocolate covered pretzels all came from mother's kitchen as did molasses flavored popcorn balls which were periodic treats that encouraged my sister and me to behave. My job was to unwrap all of the caramels without eating even one caramel. Do you have any idea how difficult that was to do?

In the spring we always drove the backcountry roads looking for wild asparagus. In the summer Mother and her sisters would make homemade ketchup, can corn relish, watermelon pickles, bread and butter pickles and dill pickles. In the fall we would once again drive the country roads in search of Hickory nuts and black walnuts to dry in the basement for the following year's baking. I remember one time Mother was on her hands and knees in a ditch along a backcountry road beneath a rather productive Hickory tree. She was finding hundreds of hickory nuts. I can still see her reach for a stick to move the fallen leaves with when the stick came to life, turned and bit her on the wrist. Mother's stick was a small garter snake. Needless to say, Dad and I did the rest of the hickory nut gathering from that time on.

When my sister and I were young, at Easter time, my parents gave my sister and me each a little bunny rabbit and three or four colored chicks. Dad built a good-sized hutch and we kept the bunnies in the hutch behind the garage. He also built an elevated cage for the chickens. We fed them fresh grass, lettuce, carrots and of course rabbit pellets and gave them fresh water twice a day.

Each Saturday morning it was my job to clean out the cage, put fresh straw on the bottom of the cage and clean their water bottles. The chickens were fed cracked corn, oats and whatever insects we found in Dad's garden. The chicks were cute until their adult feathers came in. Diane and I lost interest in them at that point. They quickly became dad's responsibility. More than once, when the rooster crowed at the crack of dawn, I could hear mother say, "Leonard, I'm going to kill that damn rooster."

The strangest thing always happened a week or two after the first serious frost in November. The rabbits just disappeared and aunt Helen and Uncle Ross came for supper. I now know that Uncle Ross butchered the rabbits cause Dad was afraid Sis and I would see him do it. At the same time we always had a meat stew called hasenpfeffer. I never did like that meal. When I was older and found out that hasenpfeffer is another name for pet rabbit stew, I knew why I didn't like it. I know that some people claim that rabbit is a delightful dish, but to this day I cannot bring myself to knowingly eat rabbit. Chickens on the other hand, as you will read later, were just critters that were meant to be eaten.

With that kind of a plane Jane dietary regimen as a youth, how did I turn out to be a gluttoness gourmand? Today I am fond of delicacies that I am sure mother never knew existed. Included in that list would be Sushi, octopus, squid, Sea Urchins, kelp, lamb, feta and a long list of other cheeses, crab, lobster, raw oysters, shrimp, crayfish, jambalaya, escargots, paella, fried grasshoppers and crickets, Alligator, Reindeer, Elk, Bear, buffalo, pheasant, quail, rocky mountain oysters, sweet breads and others to many to mention. Believe you me; I made up for lost time and tastes in a big way!

CHAPTER SEVEN
Some Good Trees and Some Trees That Were Not So Good

It truly is amazing how our thought processes can multi-task our memories from one experience onto another, seemingly unrelated experience or memory in the blink of an eye. You have just witnessed my love-hate relationship with food, especially some of Mother's concoctions and of course the ritualistic Thursday evenings supper of liver and spinach. One of my fondest memories of food starts with Cherry Pie. That sends my mind to recalling fruit trees that I not only spent a lot of time in, but trees that supplied me with a full belly more than once. Trees I loved soon gives way to trees that I hated. Be patient, before long, I hope this segue will make sense to you.

One of my favorite trees was the sour cherry tree that grew in our backyard. Mother hated it because not only did she have to pick and pit the cherries to bake a cherry pie, the birds would sit in the tree and eat their fill before flying to the bird bath for a drink and a quick cleaning of the cherry juice from their feathers before they flew to and perched upon the clothes line to digest their belly full of cherries. Of course, their favorite perching spot was directly above Mother's freshly washed bed sheets. You can imagine what came next. Yep, bird droppings streaked down the entire length of the sheets. Off the clothesline and back to the wringer washer in the basement the sheets did go, only to be returned to the clothesline in hopes that the birds had flown away. Mother used to call sour cherries, "poop fruit."

That reminds me of a story that my Dad used to tell. It seems there were three or four Sparrows feasting on the top of a manure pile. One by one, when they had eaten their fill, they would fly up to the handle of the pitchfork, rest a while and maybe sing a song of contentment or two. When the next sparrow flew toward the pitchfork handle, the sparrow already sitting there would fly away only to die after only three or four flaps of its wings. Do you know what the moral of the story is? "Don't go flying off the handle if you are full of s---!"

While Mother hated the tree, I, on the other hand, waited patiently, well maybe not so patiently but wait I did, until the cherries were ripe enough for human consumption. I would shoo the birds from their buffet and climb the tree. I had a favorite seat between two limbs about three quarters of the way to the top of the tree where I could comfortably sit and reach in a 360-degree circle. There in the seclusion of Dad's cherry tree I ate my fill. Gathering as much air in my lungs and in my cheeks as I could, I launched each cherry pit as far as I could. I considered it to be a good shot if I could clear the white picket fence about twenty feet away. One spring Dad found a bunch of little cherry trees growing in the flowerbeds near the picket fence, about twenty feet from the tree. I must admit, if I do say so myself, that was one heck of a spit. I cannot remember if I was as good with watermelon seeds or not. I don't think Dad ever found any watermelon vines growing in the backyard.

Eventually Mother nagged Dad so much about his blasted cherry tree, the poop fruit and the birds that Dad had no choice but to cut the tree down, that is, if he ever hoped to once again have a moment's peace. Mother had a bit of a professional nagging streak in her that she inherited from her mother. So off to the garage father went to retrieve Grandpa's old bucksaw. Who did he think he was, George Washington? What was I going to snack on now?

Mr. Dudeck's backyard was the home of my second most favorite tree. It was a gigantic apple tree, Granny Smith I believe, with the sourest green apples I have ever tasted. More than one bellyache came from the branches of that dear old tree. Of course they wouldn't have been so sour and I wouldn't have had a bellyache quite as often as I did if I had only waited until the apples were ripe. Quite a few succulent apple pies resulted from Mr. Dudeck's generosity and my climbing skills. Remember, "Apple pie with out the cheese is like a kiss without the squeeze."

The third, the tree that probably should have been listed as my favorite tree now that I think about it, a tree that I remember affectionately, is the tree that I carved my first girlfriend's and my initials (**D.N. + M.A.**) encircled by a heart pierced by Cupid's arrow high in the crotch of two large branches where I frequently sat to have a yet another tasty fruit snack. I don't think Marilyn ever saw the carving, although I am quite certain that she knew of its existence. I never told her about it, but I am sure that one of my fellow mulberry lovers spilled the beans. Climbing a tree just wasn't something that Marilyn did, but I knew that our initials were there until the day that someone cut the tree down.

It was a grand old Mulberry tree that stood in the lawn of Lincoln Junior High School. Every summer's day, after our baseball game and before we went our separate ways back to our homes, friends and I would shinny up the trunk of the Mulberry tree to eat the sweet fruit of the tree. Of course, the crotch between two branches where my girlfriend's and my initials were carved was my very own reserved seat, and everyone knew it. If I caught anyone sitting in my reserved seat, I would pitch mulberries at him until he was so stained by the ripe fruit and so frustrated by his inability to eat any of the treasured fruit that he couldn't stand it any more, calling truce and climbing down.

If you have never tasted a mulberry, you have missed out on one of nature's most delightful tastes. The taste of their sweet nectar lingers on the taste buds of my memory to this very day. The one bad thing about Mulberries is that they stained everything that they came in contact with. Our fingers and lips turned a deep hue of purple. My otherwise white tee shirts had stains from the mulberries that somehow missed my gaping mouth. I guess you could say that I had the tie-dyed look long before Woodstock and tie-died apparel became fashionable.

I am not finished with trees, not by a long shot. Eventually I will get around to telling you of the trees that I hated. I think you will agree, or at least understand, my hatred of the soon to be described trees.

Every December, my entire family would search the tree farms on the outskirts of town for the perfect Christmas tree. It had to be eight feet tall, deep green in color and most importantly symmetrical in shape. A straight trunk was essential. That hunt became as much a part of our family tradition as Oyster Stew and Pork, veal and beef BBQ's.

The major difference between our traditions surrounding hunting for the perfect Christmas tree and my uncle's tradition of the December hunting of deer that was so important to my uncles was that we could bring our Christmas tree inside and decorate it. The deer hunters sure couldn't do that.

Christmas and Santa Claus turned out to be a real passion for me. I won't trouble you with all of the details, but if you are interested in reading about the sometimes hilarious, sometimes tear jerking transformation of a young wanna-be Santa into the real Santa, may I suggest that you go to the library and borrow or better yet, go to your local bookstore and purchase "Childhood Dreams Really Do Come True."

For many years, we went on our traditional Christmas Tree Hunt. That is, until my sister was diagnosed as being severely allergic to tree mold, spores and pollen. Out went the real tree and in came the most awful recycling project in American history. The highly polished refugee of a supper polished aluminum can. Yes, an aluminum tree. I hope that you do not have that experience stored in your memory bank. What sort of twisted, depraved mind came up with the ridiculous notion of designing a Christmas tree from recycled beer cans? You couldn't even put lights on it. God how I hated that tree! In retrospect, I'd be willing to bet that the inventor of the Aluminum tree was the same person who thought it would be funny if the Grinch stole Christmas.

All we could do to decorate a tree like that was to put some glass ornaments on it and shine a bright light on it, a flood light that shined through a revolving disk containing sections of red, blue and green cellophane. Can you imagine, even in your wildest dreams, a red or blue Christmas tree? If I remember correctly, the year was 1950 when that tin can tree first made its appearance in our living room. I remember it very distinctly because that was the worst Christmas I had ever had.

Like most of my friends, that year I had asked Santa Claus for a Lionel electric train. Sure enough, Christmas morning there was a rather large wrapped gift with my name on it nestled below the branches, if you could legitimately call them branches, of the tin can tree. Ripping the paper off the box, I was devastated. I had asked for a Lionel Electric train and what did I get, some God awful wind-up train made in Japan. I may have played with it once or twice until I took it apart to see what made it tic and the spring sprang and I couldn't get it back together again, kind of like Humpty Dumpty! See why I hated that tree? I still have the abortion of a train on a shelf in my office to remind me never to deliver such a pathetic toy to any boy or girl again.

Hold on, you ain't heard the worst of it yet. As if the aluminum tree wasn't bad enough, a few years later the newest fad in non-allergenic trees was to take a real tree to a vendor who would spray the tree with a mysterious, synthetic foam, I think they called it Methylcellulose or something like that, in your choice of hideous colors to simulate a snow laden tree. The vendors called it "flocking." I, on the other hand had a different name for it. It was an embarrassment!

One year Mother came home with a pink-flocked tree with little pieces of metallic glitter imbedded in the fluff that covered a perfectly good tree. Can you imagine how hideous a pink flocked tree is that is adorned with big red bows and dark blue glass ornaments? It got even worse when she turned on the flood light to shine through that revolving kaleidoscope of red, blue and green cellophane. What do you suppose a green light shining on a pink tree looks like? I'll tell you by way of asking you a question. Do you remember what the contents of a baby's diaper looks like?

As if a pink tree wasn't bad enough, the next year Mother favored a flocked tree with Robin's egg blue flocking. A blue tree with a red light shining on it turned the darn thing purple. The only place I have seen a purple Christmas tree is in a child's coloring book if the kid had either broken or misplaced his or her green crayon. I don't think even Barney has a purple tree.

Don't misunderstand me. I really did love my mother, but sometimes her solutions to a problem were worse than the original problem. Know what I mean? To top things off, the flocked trees didn't soak up water as effectively as did a non-flocked tree. That fact increased the fire hazard. There you have just one more reason that they should never have been created.

Those hideous trees were almost reason enough to cancel Christmas all together. I was certain that when Santa Claus came down the chimney and saw what he would obviously see, that he would just shake his head and high tail it back up the chimney as quickly as he could. Who could blame him?

To be completely honest, there was one flocked Christmas tree that I thought was beautiful. It was almost eight feet tall and flocked with a thick coating of white flocking. It really looked like a pine tree in the forest after a snowfall of heavy, wet and sticky snow. It was adorned with nothing but large red velvet bows. The fact that it stood in the living room of my girlfriend's (Penny) home and the fact that she was standing next to the tree when I entered the house with her Christmas gift may have had something to do with my acceptance of that particular flocked tree. Amazing, isn't it, what the love for a pretty young lady can do to a fella's sense of priorities and propriety?

CHAPTER EIGHT
The Color Purple

As long as we have been talking about the color purple from the delicious mulberries, as well as the hideous blue tree with the red light shining on it, I might as well let you in on one of my most embarrassing memories. No, the memory has nothing to do with Oprah Winfrey and the movie, "The Color Purple."

Come to think of it, it is really two embarrassing memories, two separate incidents involving the color purple. Each of the two incidents contained its very own attributes of a most embarrassing moment. Had Candid Camera or America's Funniest Home Videos been around at the time, I think I might have been a candidate for some sort of monetary prize or at least reorganization as a real Sad Sack.

As a ninth grader, it was a special honor to be invited to march with the High School Marching Band at their annual homecoming foot ball game. I had been fitted with a band uniform, a little too large for me, but after all it was a high school band uniform. I had memorized all of the marches and show tunes that we were to play. I was prepared for the half-time show. I knew the patterns and routes of each formation that we would sprightly form, but not for the practice session at Strong Memorial Stadium the afternoon of game day.

It was two o'clock and all was well. Well, that is, until out of nowhere a bolt of lightning struck the ground just outside of the stadium. The bandleader screamed through his bullhorn, "Head for cover. Run for the locker rooms beneath the bleachers."

In a panic we all turned to run toward the protection of the locker rooms. I turned toward the bleachers and as I did, Charlotte Zick ran into me, the neck of her saxophone clobbering me just above my right eye. I was knocked out cold. First I lost the marbles championship in fifth grade to a girl, and now in the ninth grade yet another girl had decked me. Is there really a God in heaven? I know that there is, but I am beginning to question whether or not God is God the son or God the vengeful daughter.

The next thing I remember was waking to cold rain pelting me in the face. Opening my left eye, because the right eye was swollen shut, I could see a group of band members hovering above me and Mr. Cuthbert, the band director, kneeling down saying, "Give him some air, give him room to breathe." Needless to say, I was whisked off the field for medical attention, never again to grace the field or halftime show at Strong Memorial Stadium until I was a sophomore in high school.

That fateful day was the Friday before Thanksgiving Day. Traditionally, the day following Thanksgiving was the date for Beloit's annual Christmas parade down West and East Grand Avenues through the business district. You must know me by now. Of course there was more embarrassment to come my way. I don't understand. Why is God, why is she picking on me?

I was the Drum Major of the junior high school marching band my freshman year. There I was, strutting down Grand Avenue like a proud peacock in my red and gold jacket, white trousers with the gold braid on the legs and an extremely tall white rabbit fur Shako atop my head. A four-foot long chrome plated baton, complete with tasseled gold braid clenched firmly in my right hand. With back arched, head tilted back just far enough so that the Shako didn't fall off, strutting with my knees as high as I could make them go, and moving my baton rhythmically high above my head directing the band to maintain the proper tempo, I really was presenting a proud as a peacock picture to the town's people lining the parade route.

To emphasize the peacock persona to the "Nth" degree, I still had a tremendous lump over my right eye and much of my right cheek, part of my forehead and nearly my entire right ear were colored the most hideous shades of purple, green, yellow and blue. You see my friends; I really did look like a peacock. Wearing a brightly colored uniform, strutting with knees thrust high and my rainbow completion, I made for a most interesting spectacle. Oh well, at least my Mother and my girl friend were proud of me.

That pallet of hideous colors began to fade about a week or ten days before Christmas. By Christmas Day, I was back to normal and the rolls of pictures that my parents took of Sis and me opening Christmas presents gave no clue as to my previous gaudy complexion.

That year for Christmas, Santa Claus brought my sister and me our first pair of figure skates. Up until that time, I had to use a pair of my father's old hockey skates that were about six sizes too big for me. It is no wonder why my ankles kept turning over and I couldn't skate worth a darn.

You will recall that I said that I would relate two embarrassing events. Christmas Day afternoon, after the lethargy of the humungous turkey dinner and the chemical tryptophan had affected the adult members in attendance, casting many of them into a contented, peaceful sleep on the davenport or the many chairs in the house, Sis and I saw this as our chance to get acquainted with our new Christmas presents.

Diane and I seized the opportunity. We grabbed our new figure skates and ran to the local ice rink at Lincoln Junior High School's flooded and frozen baseball field. Fifteen minutes later, after lacing my sister's skates and then my own, Old Carl, pipe and all, opened the door for me and I negotiated the wooden stairs from the warming hut to the surface of the ice. I took one glide, caught one of the notches at the front of the blade, fell forward and cracked my head on the ice. You guessed it, another shiner on the very same right eye. The worst thing about the whole incident was the fact that I had to go back to school on January 2, looking like Rocky Marciano had pummeled me. Once more I would be sporting the color purple. I was certain that my friends would think that I was going to look like that for the rest of my life. I must admit, I wondered the same thing myself. (Now that I think about it, Purple and White are the colors of Beloit Memorial High School. Was this second shiner an omen of what I was going to be forced to endure for the next three and one-half years?)

Sis, on the other hand, just glided off into the sunset as graceful as a gentle breeze. By the time I got to my feet and was headed back to the warming shed, Diane had made a full circle of the rink. When she saw me all she could do was laugh. Now that wasn't very nice of her, was it?

I know that girls are much more graceful than we boys, but how could my younger sister skate without falling and all I seemed to be able to do was fall down, hit my head on the ice and blacken my very own eye? Go figure!

CHAPTER NINE
YMCA

My maternal grandfather, God bless him, gave me two memberships to the Beloit YMCA when I turned eight years old. There was one membership for me and a second membership for me to give to one of my friends. I gave the second membership to my friend, Richard Hinder. Every Saturday morning my father or Dickey's father would drop us off at the YMCA for a morning of athletic endeavors.

We were taught how to climb a rope suspended from the two-story gym. We learned the rules of basketball and even learned how to shoot free throws and to dribble correctly. Every Saturday we followed the instructor as he led us through a regimen of exercise, including running lap after lap on the second story oval track. Then, of course, came the exercise where we had to pass the heavy medicine ball from one to another, gaining speed with each successive pass. God forbid you dropped that medicine ball on your toe. That sucker was heavy!

Prior to taking a shower and dressing to go home, each workout was followed by a cold, but refreshing, dip in the unheated swimming pool. Back in those days, way back in the late 1940s, the YMCA was exclusively for boys. So, the instructors saw no reason for the young boys to bother with bathing trunks. We were not even allowed to wear our athletic supporters. We were au-natural and that's all there was to it.

I think I was pretty smart. I figured that if I were the first person to jump into the pool and the last person to climb out of it, not many people would see me in my buck nakedness. Modesty, you know.

Dickey on the other hand was afraid of the water. But, he didn't want anyone to look at him in his state of undress. So, he just sat on the tiled edge of the pool, shivering uncontrollably, his arms clenched tightly around his knees that were pressed tightly to his chest. Now just picture that in your mind. His knees were pushed against his chest and his arms clenched tightly around his knees. Dickey had no idea that what he thought was a position of modesty was in fact completely revealing. For the duration of the thirty-minute swim, there sat Dickey Hinder, exposed to everyone who swam past him. I never could understand how sitting naked in front of God and everybody was less embarrassing than conquering his fear of diving into the cold water. After all, there was a shallow end of the pool so he didn't have to be afraid of putting his head under water. He could have stood in the corner and just waited out the thirty-minutes,

When it came to attending the YMCA summer camp, Dickey had already given me the membership back, but unfortunately, the membership was non-transferable. Off to camp I went, just me, myself and I.

One of the first things we learned how to do at camp was the art of making a real Indian bow and arrows. It is a good thing that I was not born to a real Indian family back in the 1800s fore when I had notched my first arrow and pulled back on the bowstring, my bow snapped in half. I didn't hear war whoops. All I heard laughs, snickers and giggles.

I had the opportunity to learn how to ride a horse, something I have never done to this day, but the first time I stood next to a horse and saw how big it was, I decided that I would rather ride a bicycle or walk around camp or maybe find a raspberry or blueberry bush and have a snack. I am glad that I didn't take a chance on the horses because William, a friend that I made at the camp, was thrown off his horse and broke his arm. Not only did he have to have a plaster cast put on his arm, poor William had to go home. Before he went home, we all signed his cast so that he would remember us.

I had a great time at camp. It was nothing like Alan Sherman's "Camp Granada." You remember, "Hello Muddah, Hello Faddah…" The next summer I got real serious about baseball and never did go back to the YMCA camp. A boy just outgrows things, you know? Baseball, and of course girls, took on a much higher priority.

Other than the square dancing lessons that we were forced to participate in when we were in elementary school and the less than enjoyable dance lessons at Jack Wolfram's Studio of Dance, the first time I actually got to dance with a girl was at the YMCA on Valentines Day. I did not have a girlfriend at the time. I hadn't yet met my junior high school sweetheart yet, so the dance promised to be a big yawn. Most of the time the girls sat on one side of the dance floor while the boys congregated near the table where the snacks and punch was located. The boys did lots and lots of eating, but very little dancing.

My mother and father were chaperones at one dance. Every once in a while, mother escorted a girl by the arm to where I was busily stuffing my face with chips and dip and suggested that I dance with the young lady. Sometimes Mother picked a winner. Other times, I wondered if Mother needed new glasses. What's a boy to do in circumstances like that? Sometimes mothers can be a real hemorrhoid on the ass of life, can't they? More than once that night I wished that my parents would just go home.

The next several dances I was permitted to attend without my parent's constant supervision. Eventually I worked up enough courage to ask a young girl to dance, or was it the result of a double dog dare? Anyway, I finally danced with a girl of my choice and must admit that I really liked it. She smelled as sweet as a flower and had hands that were as soft as a cloud. Sadly, I don't think I ever caught her name, but I sure did enjoy the slow dances with her, even if the chaperones constantly checked to make sure each couple stayed an appropriate distance apart. I never did master the faster, more popular dance steps. My version of the Jitterbug looked more like a squashed bug. When I tried to dance to one of the faster pieces of music, all of the kids laughed at me. That did it, no more modern day, fast dancing for me. That experience left an imprint on my psyche that lasts with me to this day. I still cannot master anything faster than a fox trot or a waltz. I can do the "Mashed Potato," but it is with a fork, a plate, salt, pepper and butter.

Much before I was ready to go home, one of the chaperones announced, "Donny Nelsen's father is here to take him home." How I wished Dad would just go home without me and come back later, much later. No such luck. So it was goodbye, Miss what ever your name is. Hope to see you at the next dance. As luck would have it, or the lack thereof, I never saw the young lady again. It has been said, "If you are lucky at love you are unlucky at cards." Well, I can tell you I can't play cards worth a damn.

CHAPTER TEN
Automotive Engineering

Recognizing that the membership to the YMCA didn't really kindle an overwhelming response from me, especially from my friend, Grandpa never did offer the memberships again. He did, however, offer to sponsor me in the Soap Box Derby races the summers following fifth and sixth grades.

My father used to recite a funny little saying, "I see said the blind man as he picked up his hammer and saw." I think that little ditty was subconsciously my father's way of admitting his total ineptness with tools of any kind. I knew what a hammer and saw was, but I had never used either of them with the exception of a hammer that I'd use in our basement as Dad and I cracked the shells of dried Hickory nuts and Black Walnuts that we had gathered the previous fall. How in God's name was I going to build a Soap Box Derby racecar? Anyway, weren't soapboxes made of cardboard?

The book of rules that came with the hardware necessary for the car to be legal stated that an adult could advise the young builder, but under the penalty of expulsion from the Derby, the boy had to perform one hundred per cent of the work himself. Yes, no girls allowed. There was one exception to the rules. An adult was permitted to wind the steering cable onto the shaft of the steering column. Just how many fathers do you think actually let their sons do all of the work? If any of you believe that even one father, with the exception of my father, stood idly by, I would like to talk with you about purchasing the Brooklyn Bridge or some ocean front property in Death Valley.

I can honestly say that my father did not help me, not even one little bit. I loved my father, but when it came to woodworking, the only wood he knew was, "I wouldn't have the foggiest idea how to do that." Dad had fewer skills with tools than he had with knitting needles and yarn.

Fortunately, Mr. Smith, our next-door neighbor, was a retired carpenter. Mr. Smith built almost every house on our street. When he saw Dad and me unload the parts for the racer from the trunk of Dad's car, Mr. Smith walked through their Privet hedge to investigate. He was kind of a nosey old man, but likable. Immediately, he offered to advise me and told me that I could use all of the tools in his workshop except the table saw that he hand built and the drill press. I could see and hear a sigh of relief emanating from my father. So, Dad and Mr. Smith carried the parts to Mr. Smith's workshop and Dad gave him twenty-five dollars to purchase the wood and other necessities that Grandpa had given to him. Twenty-five dollars was the maximum limit that we were allowed to spend for materials and such to build our Soapbox Derby Race Car, so sayeth the official rulebook.

The next Saturday, Mr. Smith and I piled into his old, really, really, rusted black Model A Ford pick up truck and headed for his favorite lumberyard slash salvage yard where he knew we could get a real good deal on used and salvaged lumber. There we found two old salvaged maple heart planks, each of them eight feet long, fourteen inches wide and an honest to goodness two inches thick. Along with the salvaged one hundred year old maple heart planks, we searched the scrap piles for broken two by fours, several pieces of three quarter inch pine boards that had once been ten or twelve feet long before they were damaged in shipment. The broken two by fours we were given to us free of charge, inasmuch as they were destined for the burn barrel. The maple heart planks were four dollars each and the three-quarter inch pine boards were priced at twenty-five cents a board foot. If I remember correctly, Mr. Smith told me that we had spent a whopping total of ten dollars and fifty cents. That left fourteen dollars and fifty cents to spend on the car for paint, (the paint I got free from my grandfathers paint store—Case's Paint Shoppe), screws and nails and a yard of fake leather to be used to upholster the rim of the cockpit and the driver's seat. Not bad for an old scrounger and his nine year old sidekick.

On the way home, while driving up West Grand Avenue, Mr. Smith said, "There is one more place we need to stop. We'll be able to get some free wood there. If you are exceptionally nice, I will buy you a plum." Mr. Smith parked his old rust bucket behind the Meat and Vegetable market owned by Maier Putterman. Mr. Smith explained that we needed thin slats of wood to form the underlayment of the body of the car, something that would be easy for a young lad to plane into a curved surface." Mr. Putterman chuckled and pointed to a pile of orange and apple crates, "Take as many as you want. The more you take, the less I will have to pay the junk man to take them away." As we piled the last crate into the back of the old Model "A" pickup truck, Mr. Putterman said, "You make a pretty racer Donny. You listen to old Fred and you will have a fast race car worthy of the record books." I graciously thanked Mr. Putterman, and true to his word, Mr. Smith bought each of us a gigantic purple plum to munch on as we drove back to the workshop.

I won't bore you with the details of the construction other than to tell you that I had great difficulty cutting a straight line with a handsaw. Have you ever tried to cut hundred-year-old maple heart planks? Mr. Smith insisted that the rulebook says, "I can only advise," but as my tender muscles were obviously waning, Mr. Smith put is strong right hand atop of mine and provide the muscle power needed to cut off the unwanted wood.

Now that I am as educated as I think I will ever be and having scores of years in marketing and sales management under my belt, I can't help but wondering if the Soapbox Derby organization hadn't broken some little known law regarding Child labor.

I remember being awakened one hot and humid morning by a scratching sound on the screen of my open bedroom window. At least this time, the sirens of an ambulance did not awaken me as had happened a year or two before on just such a morning. I looked at my alarm clock. It was 5:13 A.M., that's in the early morning hours a long time before breakfast! Who or what was making that racket at my screen at that ungodly hour? It was Mr. Smith.

We had come to the point in the construction of the racer that wood braces needed to be attached to both sides, front and back on both the right and left side of the bulkheads forming the cockpit. Four braces on each of the twelve bulkheads had to be cut and installed to make sure the frame would remain rigid when I put all of my seventy-five pounds in the cockpit.

The previous day Mr. Smith had taught me how to use a coping saw. By the time I had cut the last of the forty-eight braces, the last two or three actually looked pretty good. Over all, it was a good thing that slats of wood from the orange crates and apple crates would cover all of the braces.

"Pssst, Donny, you know those bulkhead braces that you cut yesterday? Well, I screwed all of them to the bulkheads last night before I went to bed. Then as I lay in bed I got to thinking about the rules. So, I got myself out of bed and went out to my workshop and unscrewed all of the braces. It'll be real easy for you to put them back on because all the holes are already there. Besides, the holes will make screwing the screws into the bulkheads as slick as butter on a doorknob. You might have to put a little glue on the screws before you screw them in so that they are sure to hold fast."

Once the orange and apple crate laths had been nailed to the bulkheads giving the racer some semblance of really being a race car, Mr. Smith patiently guided my hands to teach me how to use a block plane effectively. In addition he taught me the finer points of using a wood rasp and file to smooth the gentle curves of the body of the car. Then came a layer of a foul smelling hide glue to attach a skin of contractors building paper to make a smooth surface which would be painted with at least three or four coats of exterior enamel.

My beautiful green racer had at least four coats of paint on it. Mr. Smith insisted that I apply the paint inside my father's shaded garage so that the paint wouldn't dry too quickly, leaving unsightly brush marks. Once a coat of paint had been applied, Mr. Smith would attach a rope to a large eyelet hook I had screwed into the floorboard at the front of the car and pulled the car outside into the sunshine to insure a good drying of the paint. Eventually the last coat of green paint was applied over the contractor's paper. One of my grandfather's sign painters lettered the side of the racecar to look just like Grandpa's delivery truck.

Wax on, Wax off, wax on, wax off. I waxed that car so many times with Butcher's Paste Wax that I used every bit of the wax in the can. I think I must have added at least a pound to the car's total weight.

In an attempt to break in the wheels so they would run smoothly and as fast as they could, Mr. Smith and I lifted the car and rested it on four left over orange crates. With a squirt or two of liquid graphite between the wheel and the axel, with an old towel I would spin the wheels faster and faster. I guess you could say I looked like a bootblack putting a lustrous shine on a pair of boots. Hour upon hour I would spin those wheels.

I thought I had conditioned the wheels as well as I could. The air might have slid swiftly over the highly polished surface of the car, but that is all that was swift. Mr. Putterman's prediction of the fastest racer in the history of the event was not to come true, at least not this year and certainly not by me. I lost my very first race by over three car lengths and was eliminated from the competition. No more runs down Liberty Avenue hill for me that year. Two months of daily blood, sweat and cheers it took to construct that car and it was all over within ninety seconds from launch at the top of Liberty Avenue hill to the finish line and the railroad tracks at the bottom of the hill.

I was very proud of the work I had done on my Soap Box Derby racecar. Happy that is until I saw the car that David Faust had made. It was beautiful. It was sleek with a mirror finish and was as fast as the wind. Thank God I didn't get paired with him. He probably would have been three quarters the way down the hill before I left the launching ramp.

In later life, as I drove my real car down that hill, my mind slipped back to the cockpit of my soapbox derby racecar. Without any intention of breaking the law, I inevitably pushed a little harder on the accelerator in an attempt to win that race that was flashing back and forth in my mind like a neon sign.

The reality that faced me that, even though I had no desire for such a career, deep down I knew there would never be a career in Automotive Engineering for me. The plus to the story is that as an adult I have an avid interest in wood working, especially hand carving ducks, fish, geese and birds of prey. Thanks, Mr. Smith, I think of you often, especially when I hear the rhythmic pulse of a hand saw cutting through wood, smell the fragrance of fresh sawn sawdust or the putrid smell of hide glue.

CHAPTER ELEVEN
Should Have Read the Instructions

Most of my relatives who attended my confirmation party when I was in eighth grade gave me money to put toward the purchase of a new bicycle and newspaper basket to aid me in delivering the one hundred newspapers that I delivered six days a week. I had a little over $105 in my wallet at the end of the festivities. The next day Dad and I drove to the bicycle shop and looked at all of the bikes. A black Schwinn with white pin striping on the fenders, and three speed gears caught my eye. The red price tag attached to the handle bar indicated that the price had been cut from ninety-nine dollars and ninety-five cents to ninety-five dollars. I thought that was a pretty good deal and coaxed Dad into letting me purchase the bicycle. After paying the shop owner for the bicycle, I still had ten dollars and some change left over. I rode my new chariot home while dad followed ever so slowly in his 1949 Chevrolet Coupe. I guess he wanted to be certain that I could make it the almost two miles to our home before I became plum tuckered out. I guess Dad didn't remember that I was accustomed to riding my bicycle much further than that through sleet, rain, and six months worth of snow six days a week.

My paper route was interesting because of the people. There was one old spinster who had an eighteen-year-old Angora cat. One day when I went to her door to collect the thirty-five cents for the week's newspapers. She came to the door crying. She invited me in and then excused herself as she went to the kitchen cupboard and took down a bottle. The label on the bottle revealed it to be a bottle of Brandy. She said that Fluffy, her cat, had just had another heart attack. She poured a teaspoon full of Brandy and fed it to the cat. For a minute or two, the old cat just lay there on her sofa, licking his chops. Then off he ran. I don't think her cat really had a heart attack. I think the cat was just telling her that he wanted a shot of Brandy.

There was another elderly couple that lived on my paper route. The old man could always be found on their front porch swinging to and fro while reading the newspaper I had delivered the afternoon before. Back and forth he would rhythmically glide sitting on the swing that was attached to the ceiling rafters of their front porch. His wife, a real grandmotherly sort of woman, was probably the bestest cookie maker in the whole town. Her oatmeal raisin and peanut butter cookies were to die for. But, her chocolate chip cookies with pecans were even better. More than once she gave me a brown paper lunch bag filled with cookies to take home to my family. I must confess, I don't think I ever made it home with anything but crumbs in the bottom of the bag, inasmuch as I would stop at Hart's grocery store on St. Lawrence Avenue, purchase a pint of chocolate milk and gorge myself with the cookies.

To show my appreciation, I took thirty-five cents out of my change purse that contained the money I had left from the previous week's profits, and paid their paper bill myself. I thought that was an excellent trade. It most certainly was a delicious trade.

I had one particular young couple on my paper route that appeared to be away from their home every time I attempted to collect for the papers that I had delivered. I was close to stopping delivery to their house when I decided I would ring their doorbell and pound on their front door the next Saturday morning at seven o'clock. After two or three minutes of ringing and knocking, the door opened. It was the young lady who answered the door in a white, flimsy see through robe and nothing, that's right, absolutely nothing on under the almost non-existent robe. I think my eyes must have popped out of my head like Jerry Colona's.

I stammered for what seemed to be an eternity and finally said, "I'm-I'm-I'm here to collect the $7.35 that you owe for the last twenty-one weeks worth of newspapers that I have delivered. She gave me a Ten-dollar bill and told me I could keep the change, smiled, turned and closed the door. Did she do that on purpose? I don't remember which I was more excited about, seeing what I had seen or the $2.65 tip. It probably was the tip. I think if Mother had known about what I had seen that she probably would have made me stop delivering papers.

I kept that experience to myself, hoping that I would see her again in another twenty-one weeks, but alas, they moved. It was my very own private secret. I don't remember having sex education in Junior High, but I had my first lesson at that young couple's front door. How I loved that paper route.

Of course, one of the highlights of the route was stopping at Bob Gilmore's home. Bob's mother always had a glass of lemonade at the ready for a thirsty paperboy on a hot summers day.

Riding a three-speed bicycle was a totally new experience for me. The instructions explicitly stated in bold red lettering, "Be certain to peddle backwards when shifting gears." Well, like with so many things, I didn't always follow directions. After all, I was a smart kid. I didn't need no instruction book to tell me how to ride a bike.

Riding up hill on a particularly steep street, I shifted from third gear down to first gear to make the peddling a little easier. Oh how I wish I had followed the directions. As soon as the shift lever hit the number one position, the sprocket slipped and I came down on the cross bar, one leg on each side of it. I saw stars that no astronomer has ever seen. Stars that I hope I never see again. You know what I mean?

By now, you know what is coming next. Yep, the kicker, the real coupe de gras! Of course, you already suspect the worse. Was it a tornado, a dust storm, a deluging rainstorm? No, it was just a rather windy day. I was aching big time from my bar straddling experience and could hardly stand, but I had to chase the papers that went flying from my basket when I fell. Some of them had been jarred unfolded and the separated pages of the newspapers were being blown by the gusty wind.

This was not a good day, not a good day at all! Wouldn't you know it; my fall had put a dent and a big scratch in the front fender of my new bicycle and gave my new newspaper basket a well-worn look. Some days it just doesn't pay to get out of bed!

Then there were those winter days when I had to deliver papers in the midst of a snowstorm. The paper bag filled with one hundred papers was too heavy for me to carry on my shoulder so I had to use my bicycle in spite of the snow. Try peddling a bike laden with newspapers through the snow, stopping at each house to put the paper between the storm door and the inner door, only to return to a bicycle that had tipped over with newspapers spilled all over the ground. I sure earned my money in November through February and early March.

CHAPTER TWELVE
Interesting Folks About Town

I have already introduced you to Mr. Fred Smith, our next-door neighbor. I forgot to tell you an interesting story about him. Mr. Smith used to purchase nails for his carpentry business in bulk. They came in small oak kegs. Being frugal as he was, when the nails had been used, old Mr. Smith had another use for the empty oak kegs. Before he securely fitted the top in place he laid the keg on its side. With a large hand auger he drilled a bunghole in the side and made a large tapered peg to be pounded into the hole. Sometimes he would spend two bits and purchase a wooden spigot to plug the bunghole and provide a vehicle for easy sampling. Next he would clean all of the wood shavings from the keg and sand any stains left by the nails before he securely attached the lid to make an airtight nectar chamber. Then he began to make Dandelion Wine by scavenging the neighborhood for the most tender, the most succulent Dandelion greens.

First he would wash the Dandelions to rid them of dirt or insect pests. Then in the attic of his wood working shop, using those oak kegs to ferment his "nectar of the gods," as he called it, Mr. Smith would baby each keg, turning it periodically. If he was no where to be found, a quick climb up the ladder to the attic of his work shop would usually find old Fred sampling the nectar of those colorful lawn denizens. When the alcohol level had reached the desired level and his taste buds indicated that it was palatable, old Fred would filter the wine before he bottled it and sealed the bottle with a cork or even a whittled down corn cob. My mother, the strict prohibitionist that she was, forbade me from going up to the attic. Mother wasn't going to allow her little boy to be subjected to the evils of hard liquor. What she didn't know didn't hurt me. But, if I got caught, or Mother even suspected that I had been in the workshop attic, Katie bar the door.

My maternal grandfather had a sister named Kitty. She was married to an older gentleman of German ancestry. Uncle Mert was an imposing hulk of a man who was missing the tips of the three middle fingers of his right hand.

Uncle Mert's passion was making homemade sauerkraut, an art that he learned back in the old country from his father and his grandfather. Uncle Mert must have had at least fifteen or twenty large earthen crocks in his basement with German lettering on their sides and heavy oak lids. Each fall Uncle Mert purchased hundreds of heads of cabbage from local farmers and shredded them to make his delicious Sauerkraut. Oh how I loved his fried sauerkraut and Aunt Kitty's thick cut pork shops with mashed potatoes and a big dollop of sweet Wisconsin butter.

As I said, I loved Aunt Kitty's pork chops and fried sauerkraut with caraway seeds until one day I asked Aunt Kitty what had happened to Uncle Mert's fingers. She told me a most gruesome story.

"Every year when your uncle Mert shreds the cabbage, he somehow shreds just a little bit of his finger tips into the crocks as well. He claims that little bit of flesh, and blood are what makes his sauerkraut taste so good. I've told him, I said, Mert, you gotta start using your left hand. Pretty soon you ain'ta goon have any fingers left on your right." She laughed that cackle type laugh that so many older women do.

I have not eaten sauerkraut since hearing that gut-wrenching story. Can you imagine, eating Uncle Mert's fingertips? I don't care if they were pickled or not, none for me, thank you! Uncle Mert has been dead for well over fifty years, but each time I smell sauerkraut, I am reminded of his pickled fingertips.

Then there was Mr. Lafky, one of our senior English teachers. He was a tough taskmaster with a quick wit and a rapier like mind. Other than William Shakespeare, the Bard of Avon himself, I believe Mr. Lafky knew more about Shakespeare than anyone that I knew.

He took delight in peering at his students over the black horned rim glasses (I am pretty sure he wore glasses) that were always perched at the end of his nose. He once said to me in front of God, the whole class and everybody within earshot of his bombastic voice, "Donaldo Nelsenovitch (Deep down I think he was calling me a Son-of-Bitch) you are without a doubt the most verbose, the most exasperating individual it has been my misfortune to have enrolled in any of my English classes." In spite of his sarcasm, and the occasional thrust and parry of his rapier like wit, Mr. Lafky turned out to the most influential teacher in my academic career. To give the devil his due, it was Mr. Lafky who encouraged me to express my passions through writing. "Be certain that your words are well chosen, young man, be terse and succinct! Do not use ten or twelve poorly chosen words when three or four well chosen words will suffice." As I have told many people, Mr. Lafky encouraged me to write about something that I was totally passionate about. He added a qualifier to that encouragement, "Make sure that your topic of passion is not your current girlfriend!" I am still verbose, aren't I?

Whistling Pete was a moderately mentally challenged man who walked the streets of downtown Beloit whistling and either tossing and flipping a yo-yo or batting a little rubber ball attached to a long rubber band and a wooden paddle. Sometimes he would stand in front of my Grandfather's Paint Shoppe on East Grand Avenue and put on a show for the passers by. I remember that Grandpa would always give him two bits and a Wolfe Brothers Crook cigar for drawing people toward the shop. Whistling Pete could make that yo-yo dance. He'd do tricks like Walk the Dog, Around the world, Over and back, to name a few. I don't think I ever saw him miss a stroke with that paddle and rubber ball. He was a gentle man who constantly whistled either popular songs of the day, or more impressively, the songs of robins, chickadees, cardinals, meadowlarks and the like. One day, Whistling Pete just up and vanished. I don't know if anyone knows what happened to him. If any of you readers know what happed to my friend, will you please let me know?

Then, who could forget Roaring George? Roaring George was one of the more colorful and interesting people in town. Roaring George visited my grandfather's Paint Shoppe every day around noon to play poker with Grandpa using the serial numbers of dollar bills as the cards in their hands. Roaring George always smoked a cigar and smelled of Bay Rum after-shave lotion. Roaring George was always impeccably decked out in the finest of suits, complete with vest, a white shirt with French cuffs and gold cuff links and a heavily starched collar, a bow tie and sporting a Hamburg hat atop the head. Roaring George usually carried an Ebony gentleman's walking stick reminiscent of Fred Astir. Oh my, I almost forgot to tell you the most important thing about Roaring George. I forgot to tell you that Roaring George was a woman. Katie, bar the door if you ever addressed her as Sir.

I cannot write about the influential and memorable people in town without mentioning my first band instructor, Mr. Eugene Bohrnstedt. Mr. Bohrnstedt was a kind and gentle man, an extremely talented musician who could play just about any woodwind, brass or percussion instrument known to man. He was of similar size, and stature as Fred Rogers with a demeanor to match, expect, if I remember correctly, Mr. Rogers had a little more hair than I remember did Mr. Bohrnstedt.

My memories of Mr. Eugene Bohrnstedt started way back in September of 1953 at the start of my fifth grade year. At that time, almost every child wanted to play a musical instrument. Some wanted to play band instruments, some wanted to play a stringed instrument like a violin of a cello, while others wanted to play an accordion, guitar or a banjo. It was the cool thing to do and the coolest club to say your were a member of. All children were encouraged were to participate in the band or the orchestra when we entered junior high school.

To get us off to a good start, the junior high school offered music lessons to fifth and sixth graders. When the band and orchestra instructors came to our elementary school to discuss the various opportunities to play different musical instruments, I was excited. I had always wanted to play the saxophone since hearing the saxophone section of the Glenn Miller orchestra featured on a radio program.

Our fifth grade teacher was a stickler for proper spelling and punctuation. Of course, I had not done my homework on the subject of musical instruments the night before, so when the question of what type of instrument I wanted to play was asked, I searched my memory bank of words that I knew how to spell. I had not the foggiest idea how to spell Saxophone. "Does it start Sex….,(No, I don't think that could possible be how it started) or was it sacks-o-phones?" Like I said, I didn't have the foggiest idea. Not knowing how to spell saxophone, I wrote down Cello inasmuch as it was spelled similarly to my favorite desert, Jell-O. I wonder if there is such a thing as a Raspberry, Lime or an Orange Cello?

Imagine the surprise on my face at the enthusiasm the orchestra leader showed as he or she (I honestly do not remember whether the director of the orchestra was a man or a woman. It didn't really matter. I was not going to play a fiddle!) sat in our living room and told my parents that he was truly excited about having a young boy express such an avid interest in playing the cello. He opened the large case that was lying at his feet and pulled out this monstrosity of wood and strings. He began to play. "Well, young man, what do you think? Do you like the sounds of a cello? Do you want to try, I'd be happy to show you how to play it?"

"Unh, unh, that ain't what I want to play. I want to play the saxophone."

"Well then, why did you write cello on the questionnaire? This is your hand writing isn't it?"

"Yes, Sir, that is my name and my writing, but I, I, I didn't know how to spell saxophone and I did know how to spell cello, so…."

"Never mind, son," he said as he packed his overgrown fiddle back into its case and left our home muttering to himself. Mom and Dad understood, but that orchestra director sure didn't.

That month I started taking saxophone lessons once a week from Mr. Bohrnstedt and lessons twice a week from a member of the Beloit College Orchestra. To this day, I still do not know how Mr. Bohrnstedt tolerated the squeaks and squawks, toots and honks that emanated from my saxophone in those early days.

The E flat Alto Saxophone was a very popular instrument at that time. In spite of the fact that I was purchasing the best professional grade saxophone on the market at the time, a Paris Selmer E flat Alto saxophone which cost me Eight hundred and ninety three dollars in 1953, there were so many boys and girls wanting to play the alto sax when I entered the seventh grade that Mr. Bohrnstedt coaxed me into playing the Baritone Sax.

The Baritone Sax was nearly as big as I. I think it weighed almost as much, too. It was so big that I had to support it in a special stand on the floor on the right side of my chair. The mouthpiece was so large that it literally filled my mouth. How in God's name was I going to be able to breathe? It took a lot of hard blowing to get the reed to vibrate. Once started, boy did it ever vibrate. It vibrated so much that I quickly found that many of my teeth had in fact been loosened. All of that huffing and puffing did help me when it came to holding my breath under water at the local swimming hole. I wish my muscles developed as quickly as did my lung capacity. Lugging that monstrosity home to practice was a real pain in the butt, not to mention the arms, legs and back, too.

As it turned out, I played the baritone sax from seventh grade all the way through my junior year in high school. I still took lessons and practiced on my E Flat Alto Saxophone, but in Concert band and Symphonic band as well as the dance band, I was known as Mr. Baritone Sax man. I actually grew very fond of old Barry. Mr. Bohrnstedt once told me that I would know when I had come close to mastering the Baritone sax when I could make beautiful music on it at a volume just above a whisper. Our junior year I played in a Saxophone quartet in the state music contest. I played my old friend Barry and my three colleagues and I were awarded an unprecedented double stared first rating. Was I getting close to mastering Barry?

Thank God and Mr. Bohrnstedt for giving me the opportunity to be the Drum Major of the junior high school marching band. I don't know how I would have ever been able to march down the customary two or three-mile parade routes carrying the baritone sax. I guess we could have put it in its stand in a little red wagon and have one of the majorettes pull the wagon. Wouldn't that have been a sight?

As drum major, I had several responsibilities. The first was to lead the marching band down the parade route marching erect and looking as regal as was humanly possible for a six-foot two-inch gangly teenage boy to look. The drum major had to be certain that the band was marching at the proper pace, and that they were following the tempo of the music as set by Mr. Bohrnstedt. To do so, sometimes I would have to turn around and walk backwards as I gave signals to the band or attempted to get them back on the proper tempo.

I remember one particularly cold Saturday afternoon on the parade route. We had just hit the intersection of Grand Avenue and State Street when a mighty gust of cold winter wind from the north blew through the intersection like a runaway freight train. I looked to my left to see Mr. Bohrnstedt holding his hat on his head with his right hand, but walking ever so proudly to the music that his students were playing. I am certain that he had goose bumps on his arms and the back of his neck, but I'd bet the goose bumps he was experiencing were not from the cold blast of winter wind, but rather from the pride that I am certain he was feeling. If I remember correctly, for group of half frozen kids, with cracked lips and numb fingers, and sniffling runny noses, we sounded pretty darn good.

Thanks, Mr. Bohrnstedt. You gave me, and many students like me, the opportunity, the go-ahead signal, to begin a most rewarding and satisfying musical trip that lasted for many of us through High School and College. For me, it even lasted through a tour of duty with the 84th Division Army band.

Even as a young Army SFC, goose bumps rose from my arms every time we played the Star Spangled Banner or one of the spirit lifting John Phillip Sousa marches like Stars and Stripes Forever. God Bless America always brought a shiver that ran down my spine and brought a tear or two to my eye. Thank you again. My life was greatly enriched by your tutelage, your patience, your love of band music and your understanding.

Over your career you challenged thousands of us neophytes to express ourselves through music, whether it be beating on a drum, playing a slide trombone, blowing on a licorice stick, a flute or fife or blasting away on a mouthful of baritone saxophone. You gave each of us an appreciation for all genres of music and taught us the work ethic of "practice makes perfect." By the way, what ever happened to that behemoth we called a baritone sax? I wish I could afford to purchase one. What do you think, would a good blast from Barry send the field mice that invade our home each fall back to their homes in the woods at the rear of our property?

I have always wondered how many aspirin did it take to overcome the headaches you must have suffered from listening to us squeak and squawk our way through the beginnings of our musical journey? Did we ever play anything that was remotely close to being in tune?

There is another memorable character in my life, even though he lived just across the Wisconsin, Illinois state line in Loves Park, Illinois. He is my cousin Neal who is nine years older than me.

When Neal was about eighteen and I was about nine or ten, I always thought he looked just like James Dean in "Rebel Without A Cause." He even rode a motorcycle, as did James Dean. I have vivid, yet scary memories of riding on the back of Neal's motorcycle from his home, over pastures, through the woods, across creeks until we came to Rock Cut, his swimming hole. Just like the swimming hole that I would frequent in the Turtle Creek at the Shopiere dam, we had to contend with the blood-sucking leeches in Rock Cut as well.

What an experience. As Neal would lean to the left, my sense of balance told me I should lean to the right. Wrong? I damn near flipped us more than once until Neal stopped and explained why when he zagged I should not zig. "You don't want to tip us over and break our asses, do you?"

Talking with Neal the other day, I asked him if he remembered the experience with as much emotion and excitement as I do. His memory was not quite as detailed as is mine, but then again he wasn't being bounced around in back of him with only his flapping tee shirt to hang on to. Of course, in the true James Dean style, we both had our hair slicked back into a DA, wore blue jeans and white tee shirts. Sometimes I wish I had an old motorcycle like the one B.J. in MASH drove off into the sunset on in the closing scene of MASH, you know, the Indian Motorcycle with the sidecar, but then better sense prevails and I just drive away in my Mustang convertible.

During my sixth grade at Cunningham Elementary School (Miss Daisy Chapin's dungeon of corporal terror, Home of rump warming swats of her wooden ruler), Emmet Smelser, Pete Peterson and I made a volcano for our science project. This was just one of the many projects that Mr. Arnold Lee employed to make learning fun.

Miss Daisy Chapin was Principal of Cunningham Elementary School. The teachers did not appreciate my precociousness, bordering on insubordination and teetering ever so closely toward the precipice of insurrection, as my teachers proclaimed. At the time I was absolutely certain that they were all just old fuddie duddies and that they were incapable of conjuring up so much as one molecule of a sense of humor. So, Miss Chapin and I spent a lot of time together.

At the end of sixth grade, I am sure she was relieved to know I would not be back the next fall. I'll bet that she missed me, though! If you believe she ever gave Pat Reed or me a second thought, I'd like to sell you some ocean front property in Kansas. I can hear her now as she watched Pat and me walk off into our futures and into another principal's office. Long before Martin Luther King said the famous words, I know that Daisy was standing there on the steps of Cunnihgham Elementary School singing, "Free at last, Free at last, Thank God almighty, I am free at last."

Take a careful look at the photograph in the Photogravure section found in the middle of the book. Do you see what I mean about Miss Chapin's crazy straw hats? Do you suppose they really were stylish in the late 1940s? How many teachers or even principals wore a corsage to school? Take a look at those sexy shoes!

Pat Reed called my attention her left hand. Is sweet old Miss Daisy Chapin flipping us the bird? Maybe. I didn't notice her hand as I took the photograph on the last day of sixth grade, her last day as a teacher and principal. She then retired. I remember singing the following little ditty when Daisy was well out of earshot. **Daisy, Daisy, Give me a scolding, do. You drive us crazy, you and your ruler, too!**

I don't recall seeing it, but I would be willing to bet that in her closet or hanging behind her office door, the proverbial "Hickory Stick could be found. If you question my veracity, just ask Pat Reed. He tells me that he felt the sting of her wooden ruler more than once. Right, Pat? Pat and I had a lot in common, especially our love for Daisy Chapin.

Folks, permit me to introduce you to my Father, Leonard Christian Nelsen, the best Dad a boy could ever hope to have. Dad always had a Parker fountain pen in his shirt pocket, no matter what kind of shirt he was wearing. As far as Dad was concerned, if he didn't have that old Parker in his shirt pocket, he just wasn't fully dressed. I remember on more than one occasion when Dad discovered he had left his fountain pen at home, he would turn the car around and go back home to secure his trusted friend.

Dad promised that pen to me upon his death, but alas, Mother insisted that his good and faithful Parker fountain pen be buried with him. He is probably using it today in heaven to construct one of his infamous Ben Franklin Tallies, or keeping score of the daily Chicago Cubs baseball game. Or, perhaps, he is writing a letter to Mike Melass to get city council to do something about a problem that Dad wanted corrected in Beloit. The long and the short of it is I never did get the fountain pen.

That's O.K. I have my very own fountain pen. My fountain pen is a Levenger, not a Parker. My wife bought it for me as a birthday gift. I, like my father, never leave home without my fountain pen. I guess the apple doesn't fall far from the tree.

Let me tell you a bit more about my father and how poorly I treated him during my high school years. Dad was born to an emigrant couple from

Denmark in 1903. He, as did so many farm boys of his time, went to a one-room schoolhouse through the eighth grade when it was his time to work full time on his parents' dairy farm.

My father was not a highly, formally educated man and I do not ever remember him stressing the importance of education, even though he expected and accepted nothing but good grades on my report cards. He stressed honest relationships and the virtue of sticktoitiveness and the rewards of hard work. He may not have had a degree or an alphabet soup splashed behind his surname, but I swear he learned more in his eight years of formal education in that country one room schoolhouse than I did through twelve years of public school and well into my college years. Dad had his Masters Degree in Reverse Psychology and a PhD in Common Sense.

I am ashamed to admit it, but I feel what I am about to share with you is one of the most poignant things I can say about my father. Inasmuch as I knew Dad hadn't even graduated high school, let alone got a college degree as did so many of my friends' fathers, I was a little ashamed of his failure to become, what I naively considered to be educated. Ashamed, that is, until my sophomore year in college when I was working on a calculus problem at our dining room table.

I guess I must have gone through three or four sheets of paper trying to figure out a troublesome problem, The sounds of crumpling of paper and my cursing at the dining room table prompted Dad to turn off the Packer's football game that he was watching on television and come to the dining room and sit at the table next to me. "Let me see if I can figure that problem out for you." He said.

Out of my mouth came the most stupid, the most self-serving and without doubt the most ignorant sentence that I wish I had never uttered. (Believe you me; I have said some mighty stupid things in my time) "Dad, this is college calculus. You didn't even go to high school."

"Well, son, I did learn how to read. Doesn't this text book do anything other than give you a list of problems to solve?" He took the book, read parts of the preceding chapter and the chapter that I was working from. Pencil in hand and a fresh piece of paper, Dad scribbled for a few minutes and said, "There, I believe you will find that to be the correct answer."

I flipped the pages of the textbook to the very end where the answers to all of the problems were listed. "I'll be damned," I said, "How did you do that?"

"I told you son, I really do know how to read instructions, you know."

That Sunday afternoon, seated at the dining room table, this snot nosed kid was taught a lesson in work ethic and more importantly, the value of self-determination and stick-to-itiveness. From that day on, I realized that the older I got, the smarter my father became.

The most valuable lessons that my father taught me were what it takes to be a good, honest, God loving man, husband and father. I learned by his example every day that I was fortunate enough to be in his presence. He was one hell of an instructor.

Sometimes my father would frustrate me to the point of exasperation. If I was working on a problem, now matter what type of problem that it was, if I asked Dad for his advice, the answer was always the same. "What options have you come up with on your own?" If I had not thought the problem through, I could always count on his fallback response of "Well, Don, seems to me that you aren't trying to solve your dilemma, you are an integral part of the problem. Now go sit down and do the Ben Franklin Tally. When you have exhausted your ideas for possible solutions, you come back to me and we will discuss them." Dad rarely offered a suggestion that I hadn't finally worked through myself with the help of a Ben Franklin Tally.

One lesson that Dad tried to teach me was that of frugality, not purchasing anything unless I had saved the cash prior to making the purchase. Unfortunately, Dad, I didn't learn that lesson well enough. I sure wish that I had!

All throughout my youth and even well into my college years, our dining room table was the lectern that Dad presided over as he tried to teach me the facts and parameters of a good and Godly life.

I wish that I could claim to have learned his dining room table lessons well. I've tried to be a good friend, a good husband, father and grandfather, but alas, in all honesty, I know that I am not half the man that my father was. Pop, I hope as you look down from on high on your grandchildren that you might see at least a glimmer of the lessons that you tried to teach me. I'll see you in another thirty or forty years, the Good Lord willing. Thanks Pop for being my dad. You are the best. I love you.

CHAPTER THIRTEEN
Did You Ever? Do You Remember?

Places and things, even smells and tastes can and do evoke vivid childhood memories as do people. So let's see where Memory Lane takes us. Sit back and relax as I share with you key memories of landmarks and events in my hometown, Beloit, Wisconsin, that brings a smile to my face or a thoughtful scratching of my bald head. Even though your memorable landmarks, events, people and tastes and smells may differ from mine and those of my classmates, I'd be willing to wager that they linger in your memories as vividly as they do in mine.

I am sure that each of the readers, no matter where you were born or where you grew up, you all have memories of your own that are unique and special to you, even today. I hope one or more of the brief memories that I am about to share with you, or the questions I will raise for you to ponder, will evoke your very own special memories and will encourage you to rekindle friendships with friends from your youth or maybe even take a trip back to your roots on your next vacation. It may not look the same. Familiar buildings and such may have been raised for whatever reason, but your memories are still there and will remain there until the end of time.

Coming up are several special places, events and questions for you to ponder that may evoke a memory or two. A bit of a warning, some memories may be welcomed and perhaps some you would just as soon forget. Memories are just that, memories, and no matter how hard you try to forget them, they will always be memories, they will always be a part of who you are, so read, remember any perhaps laugh or even cry.

I seem to remember there was a popcorn wagon that stood on the sidewalk in front of Chester's Department store, or was it the little popcorn and nut shop on West Grand avenue just before the curve to cross the Rock River? Every Saturday morning as Dad, my sister and I drove through town, I would beg for a nickel bag of popcorn. Some times, Dad would stop and buy us each a nickel bag. Other times he would say, "Not today, just roll your window down and I'll drive by real slow so you can get a good smell." Was that mean, or what?

Do you remember the Fluoroscope machine in McNeany's Department Store that stood next to the wooden stairway that led to the second floor? Every chance I got; I would stick my feet into the opening at the bottom of the Fluoroscope machine to see the bones of my feet as I wiggled my toes in my shoes. I guess it is no wonder that my wife says that I have the ugliest feet she has ever seen.

Do you remember the pneumatic tubes that ran from each sales counter in McNeany's department store that sent your purchase payment to the accounting department and via the same tube returned a receipt for you?

Do you remember where Santa Claus sat in the back of McNeany's Department Store? Do you still believe in Santa Claus? You can bet that I believe. I have been Santa Claus for the past forty-two years, so you had better watch out because Santa knows a lot more than you might think he does or more than you would like him to know. Ho-ho-ho.

Do you remember, as do I, hearing your grandparents or your older aunts and uncles discussing the younger generation, our generation, and lamenting that we didn't know what hardship is. We didn't live through the great depression like they did. "They're soft, they don't know the meaning of work. They won't amount to a hill of beans," my grandfather was fond of saying. Well, Grandpa, if you can see us now, how does it taste, that humble pie filled with a scoop or two of crow that you should be eating right about now? It was members of your children's and your grandchildren's' generation who helped land man on the moon. We invented the transistor, the computer, the video camera, the Internet, the microwave oven, the cure for and elimination of chicken pox, open-heart surgery and organ transplants. We fought in Vietnam, served in the Peace Corps and raised some of the brightest great grandchildren you have ever seen. Need I go on? I love you, Grandpa, but you were ever so stubborn, opinionated and ever so wrong!

Who could forget that terribly bitter, twenty-five below zero night, January 31, 1951, when the historic Masonic Temple burned to the ground? The temperature was so low and the winds were blowing so fiercely the brave firemen who tried desperately to extinguish the fire, found themselves in the position of fighting a blazing inferno with the water from hoses that froze almost as quickly as it came pouring out of the high pressure nozzles. "It was as if they were spitting ice cubes at a forest fire," the fire chief later said in an interview. There was the ever-present danger that the gigantic icicles that formed on the superstructure and girders of the building would crash to the ground and cause possible injury to one or more of the heroic firemen. Look for the photograph, curtsey of the Beloit Historical Society, found in the photogravure section.

How about the Ben Franklin five and dime and Woolworth's Dime Store with their famous greasy and salty cashews roasting at the counter? Twenty-five cents would buy a quarter pound of the salty delights. Just such a bag was my Saturday mornings' treat after I'd paid my bill for the week's papers that I had delivered at the offices of the Beloit Daily News.

You guys who delivered The Beloit Daily News, weren't the movie passes we got for having no customer complaints great? Did you save them up until you had enough to take several friends to the movies? Did you give them a free pass if they would share their box of popcorn with you?

Did you ever sneak through the backdoor into the Smoke Shop on the corner of Fourth and West Grand Avenue? You remember, the store with all of the girlie magazines. How many magazines did you look through before the owner booted you out, threatening to call your Mother? Did people really play volleyball with no clothes on?

Speaking of magazines, how many of you will admit to thumbing through the National Geographic magazine at home or at the library to see the photographs of naked natives in Africa? You may have fooled your parents by saying. "I'm doing research for a term paper." But you can't fool me. I've been there and done that.

How old were you when you could first tie your own shoes? Did you use the rabbit around the tree and down-the-hole method to learn how to tie your shoes? Did your parents give you a heavy cardboard cutout of a boot with holes in it so you could learn how to lace a shoe and on which the made you practice tying a proper bow?

Did any of you have an Erector set? How about Lincoln Logs or Tinker Toys? Guys, did you play War with little lead or plastic replicas of soldiers and tanks? Did you ever have a cap gun or one of those guns that burst a hole in a paper ribbon? How about a bow with a red, white and blue braided string and arrows with rubber suction cups at the ends of the arrows?

Boys, did your mother make you play Jacks with your sister? Girls, did you have a Betsy Wetsey doll?

Do you remember the long crepe paper whirly gig that was attached to a long string and was spun round and round your head? Do you remember the children's book "Squirt"? Do you remember when everyone enjoyed reading Little Black Sambo? No one that I knew saw any racial overtones to that story until many years later when political correctness plundered our society.

Do you remember Old Mrs. Schwallenbach's little grocery store in her home in the 900 block of Moore Street?

Remember Fairbanks Morse and the diesel locomotives they made. How many of your parents worked at Fairbanks? Did you know that Fairbanks had an award winning baseball team? Did you know that they also had a rather respectable orchestra?

Who could forget the old train station and the puffer bellies that used to drop mail off every evening as it puffed, hissed and belched black smoke as it chugged its way north toward Janesville? Did you ever put a penny on the railroad track to see what would happen to it? How many of those pennies were never to be found? Did you for one minute ever believe that a well-placed penny on the railroad track could de-rail a train?

Did you enjoy the concerts in Horace White Park as much as I? Do you remember when Harry James came to town? I've been told that Tony Scodwell joined the Harry James Band after he completed college and later in his career played and managed the Doc Sevrenson (Of Johnny Carson's Tonight Show fame).

When you were a kid did you ride your bicycle in the Memorial Day Parade? If you were as anal as I, I feel sorry for you. In preparation for the parade, I would take the wheels and fenders off of my bicycle and wash then thoroughly in an old galvanized tub that Dad had in the garage. (Yes, the very same tub that Sis and I used as our swimming pool when we were younger.) With an old toothbrush and a discarded bottlebrush, I would scour each spoke and the spaces between them where they attached to the chrome-plated rim. Then I'd soak the fenders in the tub to loosen all of the dirt and manure from the underside of each fender, especially the rear fender. Once cleaned to my satisfaction I put coat after coat of automotive wax on the bicycle, attached new handle grips with red, white and blue streamers at their ends, shine and oil the lever activated bell, clip a playing card to the upright support of the front wheel so that it rubbed against the spokes when the wheel went round and round. Lastly, a new battery in the taillight mounted atop the rear fender. I told you that I was anal retentive, didn't I? God forbid that it would rain on the parade.

How many hours did you spend watching Saturday afternoon matinees at the Rex Theater, the State Theater or the Majestic Theater? Have you ever tasted popcorn as delicious as what we purchased at the concession stand? What was the first 3-D movie that you saw? For me it was Fort Apache. The opening scene was of a cannon pointed directly at the audience. Then the cannon was fired and the cannonball came screaming off the screen headed straight for our heads. Do you remember the red and green glasses that we had to wear to get the full benefit of the 3-D technology?

Did you and your mom ever make homemade popcorn balls or homemade candy? Did you ever butter your hands to pull taffy? Did you ever burn your mouth by sneaking pieces of taffy that were still too hot to safely eat?

Did you ever stick out your tongue and touch it against a cold metal pipe in the schoolyard? Don't you wish you had heeded the warnings not to do so? Didn't you feel stupid as the teacher had to pour warm water on you tongue to loosen the pipe's grip? Didn't you feel really, really dumb and embarrassed in class after recess when all of the kids were making fun of you and how funny you sounded when you tried to speak? Why did the teacher keep calling on you for a verbal answer?

Did your mother use yesterday's Beloit Daily News to wrap the garbage in? Was it your chore to take the wrapped garage out to the garbage can? Periodically, like me, did you have to pour some bleach and hot water into the garbage and using an old broom, scour the insides of the can? Why? Did you ever see a garbage can inspector? My mother had some strange ideas. I guess she believed next to clean garbage can and clean underwear came Godliness.

Do you remember the warming houses that were moved to Lincoln and Roosevelt junior high schools and placed at the edge of the flooded athletic field? Do you have any idea who battled the frigid winter nights to flood the athletic fields so we could ice skate? As you read on, you will discover whom we should all thank.

Do you remember the cast iron potbelly stove in the middle of the warming house and the wonderful heat that it gave off? Do you remember the aroma of Juicy Fruit gum or Bazooka Bubble Gum sizzling on the stove that some kid had thrown at it? Did any of you have to walk home in your skates because while you were skating on the rink some thieving felon stole your shoes and galoshes?

Those of you who skated at Lincoln, do you remember old Carl, the attendant in charge of the rink and warming house? Do you remember his wool hat and the pipe he puffed on continually? Was it Half—N-Half or Prince Albert tobacco that he smoked? What ever it was, it sure did smell good.

For those of you who were students at Cunningham Elementary School, do you remember Principal Daisy Chapin? Do you remember those hilarious straw hats with the flowers on them that she wore all of the time? How about those God-awful ankle length dresses and the old-fashioned tie shoes with the squat heel? For those of you who don't remember, if you will turn back to chapter twelve you will find her photograph. Do you remember catching grasshoppers in the fields surrounding the schoolyard?

Did you ever get sent to the principal's office? I became quite well known by my elementary school principals. Did you ever get a swat across your behind with the principal's ruler? The teachers said that I was a precocious child, bordering on insubordination and even nearing insurrection at times, what ever that means. Were those good things, or were they not so good? Unfortunately the excursions to the principal's office did not stop in elementary school. One day during our senior year, my girlfriend's mother was substituting for Mr. Haglund. George Whaley and I were not paying attention in class, so my girlfriend's mother, can you imagine Mrs.

Rowbottom, sent George and me to the Mr. Everill's office. If I remember correctly, Penny and I had a difference of opinion as to her mother's actions that evening during one of our lengthy telephone calls.

Did your parents put a limit on the length of time you were allowed to talk on the telephone? Did you lay on the floor beneath the wall phone with your legs stretched out on the wall? Did your parents complain? Did it make any difference to them that you were not wearing shoes?

How many of you remember eating a stack of pancakes drenched in rich Wisconsin butter and wild clover honey accompanied by four or five thick-cut slices of crisp bacon at the Little Bungalow?

Did you ever have a greasy double cheeseburger with pickles and ketchup, a heaping order of French fries dripping in oil and a glass of mud at Al's Snack Shop? Do you remember how they cooked the hamburgers at Al's Snack Shop? Sure you do. The hamburger was contained in a rather large stainless steel rectangular pan at the side of the grill. Ice cream scoop sized balls of hamburger were tossed onto the greasy grill and flattened with a heavy blow of the cook's spatula. They were so thin that at least a double was required in order to be able to taste the meat. Good Wisconsin cheddar cheese melted on top with pickles and ketchup and a culinary masterpiece was ready to be served. Periodically the Public Health Department would make an unannounced inspection and Al's would inevitably be closed for a day or two to give them an opportunity, as the inspecting officer said, to scour the grill and eliminate what ever other Health Code infractions he had found. Little did that inspector care that by scouring the grill with Brillo or S.O.S. pads and Bon Ami, that the wonderful, lip smacking flavor that the greasy grill imparted to the meat would be destroyed and would take a long time to build back that deliciously distinctive Al's flavor. Each time they were sited, the closed sign remained in the window for a day or two more. We always waited a week or two after the re-opening to go back to Al's so the well-seasoned grill had an opportunity to regenerate itself.

Did you avoid having onion on your double cheeseburger just in case the opportunity to see your girlfriend so that your breath would not reek of onion?

How about the taste of aged cheddar cheese or aged smoked Swiss cheese from Baumgartner's Cheese Shop in Monroe. I remember in 1980 you could still get a two inch thick aged smoked Swiss cheese on rye bread with dark mustard on it for $1.00 and a nickel beer in the old saloon in the back of the cheese shop. I wonder what that sandwich and nickel beer costs today. Old classmates and I intend to find out when we attend the reunion in 2010 if the good Lord is willing and the creek don't rise. Want to join us? The more the merrier. We'll just have two reunions in one.

Do you remember the aroma that confronted you when you walked through the front door of Cox's Feed and Grain store on State Street? What about the spring day that we awoke to the Rock River overflowing its banks and inundating much of the downtown area? There were dead and rotting Carp everywhere. What redeeming social value does a carp have anyway?

Have you noticed that many of my memories have been stimulated by smells or by taste? I wonder what Sigmund Freud would say about that? Maybe, by some psychological twist of fate, I was destined to be a fat man, the perfect Santa Claus. Ho-Ho-Ho!

How many of you parked in the parking lot of the Municipal Natatorium on the west side of town with your best girl to spoon after the sun went down? How long has it been since you've heard the term "spoon" used that wasn't related to a teaspoon, a tablespoon or a soupspoon? Did a local policeman ever shine his searchlight in the window of your parked car and scare the be-Jesus out of you? Were the windows of you car all fogged up? Did you ever stop to think that the fogged over windows might have been the impetus of the police officers investigation? Do you remember the large stone map of the state of Wisconsin in the woods near the swimming pool? Did you know that the stone representing the size and shape of each county was carved from a stone native to each individual county? Did you just learn something?

Who was the first girl or boy that you ever kissed? I'll never forget my first sweetheart, Marilyn Rae Ahrens. When I sneaked my first kiss, we were seated in the back seat of her father's car that was parked in the garage. We were holding hands and listening to music from the car's radio while one of her girlfriends, Sandy Tuller, kept a watchful eye in the rear view mirror as she chaperoned from the front seat. At the time, I never thought about the possibility of draining the battery. Boy, would Mr. Ahrens have been angry.

Even though Marilyn is happily married to another gentleman and I have been married to the love of my life for over thirty years, how could I possible forget my first sweetheart and our first kiss? Even though we only recently reconnected via telephone, as a result of a "guess my identity" game that I initiated to generate interest in our fiftieth class reunion, we sometimes talk on the telephone, but more often than not, we keep in touch through the wonders of E-mail. We have exchanged many messages about our lives since graduation, our families, our careers, our memories, what we have done with our lives and what we hope to accomplish in the future as well as our hopes and dreams for our children and grandchildren. She always signs off, Hugs, Marilyn.

Now that I think of it, Marilyn gave me more than just my first kiss. Marilyn's parents took Marilyn, her brother and me to the first professional baseball game I had ever seen in person. The Milwaukee Braves playing against the Chicago Cubs. What a thrill it was to watch Warren Spahn, Eddie Mathews, Red Schoendiest, Hank Aaron and Ernie Banks play ball. On the way home we stopped for dinner in the nicest restaurant that I had been to up till then. The Ahrens family introduced me to the gastronomic delights of Fillet Mignon and Thousand Island Salad Dressing. And to top it off, I got to sit in the back seat with Marilyn, smelling her perfume and holding her hand all the way from Milwaukee to Beloit. What a trip!

Do you think that the first girl that you kissed, and for you girls, the first boy that you kissed, remembers? Wouldn't that be a kick in the seat of the pants if you remembered but he or she did not? How long did it take you to realize that the old wives tale about French Kissing causing pregnancy was just your mother's way of scaring you into behaving yourself?

Did you ever go to the Pop House? What was so great about that experience? What was the attraction? My mother and my grandmother forbad me from crossing their threshold. So, the whole Pop House thing is a mystery to me. I hope one of our classmates will enlighten me.

Nancy Bue, do you remember playing Post Office during a party in the recreation room in your basement? Help me remember, what was the difference between Parcel Post and Special Delivery?

Do you remember the Forever Yours candy bar or the Seven-Up candy bar with bites of seven different kinds of filling? Do you remember the five-cent bag of potato chips that was actually filled to the top? Today that same sized bag costs ninety-nine cents and it is only filled half way. That must be the results of new math, less for twenty times more. Expressed Algebraically, $\$TB = < 1/5 \ PC \ (20) \ \$$.

Can you remember the Geritol or the Hadacol advertisements on the radio? No wonder those tonics were so popular with the elder citizens. I seem to remember reading about an analytical assessment of both products. The report stated that each of them was ninety proof. Care for another shot? Make mine a double, straight up. Do you remember, "You'll wonder where the yellow went when you (... ....?")

Remember when you could get enough penny candy for a nickel to insure at least one or two cavities? Do you recall the long strips of white paper with three or four rows of little pink, yellow, blue and green dots of candy attached? Can you recall your stained index finger from wetting it and sticking it into a package of Kool-Aid only to lick it off, thereby wetting your finger for the next plunge into the package?

Did you have or did you ever play with a top that as you pushed faster and faster the spinning top made more and more noise? How about an Erector Set or maybe a set of Lincoln Logs? Could you keep together the Tinker Toy windmill long enough to get the wheel to spin? Did you by any chance have a Charlie McCarthy doll? Could you throw your voice without moving your lips? Did the noises that you made come anywhere close to sounding like human speech? How about it, did any of you have a Howdy Doody marionette? How about a Raggedy Ann Doll? Do you remember playing Old Maid, Hearts, Go Fish or War with a deck of cards? Did you ever tie a string around a loose tooth and tie the other end of the string to a doorknob and then be too chicken to slam the door?

How many of you stud muffins bought a corsage for your favorite girl at Emmanuel The Florist's for Prom Night? Try buying a Cymbidium Orchid today for just ten dollars. Gentlemen, did you actually pin the corsage on your girlfriend's strapless formal or did you chicken out and pass the corsage off to her mother? What were you afraid of, as if I don't know? Come on now, fess up, deep down you were secretly looking forward to the experience, perhaps an accidental slip of the hand so to speak, now weren't you? To be safe and to avoid the temptation, I always bought wrist corsages. (My Mama and Daddy didn't raise no fool.) I had absolutely no problem slipping the corsage onto my girlfriend's wrist. Alas, that very special girl whom was my steady all through high school, the recipient of all of those Cymbidium Orchid corsages, Penny, and I went our separate ways after graduation. She went to school in Florida while I went to school in Milwaukee. That ended that romance!

Did you have a part time job while you were in high school? I had several, including, mowing lawns, shoveling snow and raking leaves in the spring and the fall. My main job, however was as a "Soda Jerk, all around store manager at the Portland Avenue Confectionary when the owner was not there. You may remember the store as the "PX."

The PX was a little like Ike Gotsey's store on the Walton's. It was a grocery store, an over the counter pharmacy, a soda fountain complete with sodas, malts, any flavor phosphate you could dream up, hamburgers, cheeseburgers, chips—no French fries! In addition to the above-mentioned amenities, the PX also was a newsstand, a bookstore for mostly trashy novels and a Postal Sub-Station.

On evening, just about closing time at eleven P.M. one of the city's finest a policeman came bounding through the front door. Looking around to see if anyone else was in the store, he came over to the soda fountain where I was making simple syrup and said, "I need a box of prophylactics."

"I don't think we sell what you are asking for, sir."

"Sure you do, sonny. Come with me, I'll show you where Phil keeps them." He put his hand on my shoulder and walked me to the area of the store where the Postal sub-station was located. "There," he said pointing to the bottom drawer of the filing cabinet where the stamps were securely locked away. I pulled the key for the file cabinet from its secret hiding place and opened the bottom drawer. Sure enough, there was an array of five or six different kinds of those things as big as life. "Well, I'll be," I said. What kind do you want and can you please tell me what Phil usually chargers?" That was a bit of knowledge that I learned outside the hallowed halls and classrooms of Beloit High.

What did you do after Commencement Capers? John Drager and I took our dates home early, changed and went to Lake Whitewater and were fishing about an hour before sunrise. I had much more fun fishing with John that I did with my date at Capers.

Did you ever use Bazooka Bubble Gum on a fishhook to catch Catfish in the Rock River? How about baiting your hook with stale marshmallows or Ritz Crackers with a dollop of peanut butter to hide the hook? You didn't believe your grandfather when he told you the only thing that would catch Catfish was that stinky catfish dough; did you?

How many of you long for the taste of a Spudnut from the Spudnut Shop on the corner of Fourth Street and Liberty Avenue? Was there anything that came close to the mouth-watering taste of a warm glazed Spudnut as you walked the last block to school in the morning? Did you know that Janice Witte's father and uncle owned the Spudnut Shop? Do you know what the secret was to the light, tender donut? It was made with Potato flour.

Right about now, couldn't you go for a tall frosty mug of root beer and an order of freshly deep fried onion rings from Showers A&W root beer stand. Did you ever notice the strange phenomena of how much better the root beer tasted from the heavy frosty mug than it did from a plastic or cardboard container?

Who could forget the Friday night Fish Fry of either Perch or Walleye Pike? I think it was about that time that my arteries started to fill with cholesterol. What is that old saying, "Sin in haste, repent in leisure?" There are a lot of things that I miss from my life in Beloit. High on the list you will find just such fish fries, six year or older aged cheddar cheese, aged smoked Swiss and of course Limburger cheese, Al's hamburgers and grandma's spicy pumpkin and minced meat pies. Even though grandma was a devoted prohibitionist, she did put a dollop or two of Brandy in her minced meat. Of course, I miss my friends whom I have not seen in thirty years or more.

What do you suppose was going through the mind of the first person to eat a raw oyster? In the book, "Chesapeake," the author, James Michener never said. Do you suppose that courageous individual had a spicy cocktail sauce on the side? Did John Rockefeller invent Oysters Rockefeller? Were Clams Casino first served in a gambling casino?

Were you or are you now one of those nuts that dipped French-fries into mayonnaise, or even worse, mustard? How about beef gravy? Did you ever have a sandwich with the French fries inside the sandwich?

What did you call a soft drink? Was it Pop or was it soda? Did you prefer Coca-cola, Pepsi or Royal Crown cola? How about root beer? Which did you like better, Hires, Dad's Old Fashioned Root Beer or A&W? Make mine a tall frosty mug of A&W from Shower's A&W Root Beer Stand any time!

Wasn't a "Soda" a fountain concoction made with ice cream, flavored syrup and injected with pressurized carbonated water? Did you ever order one soda with two straws so that you could share it with your girlfriend? As you sipped the soda fountain delight, looking deeply into each other's eyes, did you rub noses? Were you brave enough to sneak a kiss? Do you remember what color your girlfriend's or boyfriend's eyes were? I'll bet that you don't.

What did you call a round piece of hard candy on a rolled paper stick? Was it a sucker, a lollipop or taffy? Could you lick the hard candy off a Tootsie Pop, resisting the urge to bite through the outer coating of hard candy to get to the Tootsie Roll center? If you could, how many licks did it take?

Could any of you finish eating one of the three-quarter pound or even the one- half-pound California burgers at the Toot and Tell Drive-In out on route 51 between Beloit and Janesville?

Do you remember how delicious the cheese and sausage pizzas were at Florieo's in South Beloit? Was Florieo's your post Friday night game rendezvous? Do you recall the first time you ate pizza?

How many ears of roasted sweet corn in the husks could you eat at the fair in South Beloit? I think my gluttonous record stood at thirty-three ears of butter-drenched sweet corn devoured on one Saturday afternoon and evening. All of the sweet corn you could eat, all day long, for the reasonable price of only one dollar. What a deal! Needless to say, my digestive tract was a mess for several days. Add the cholesterol found in the melted butter to the cholesterol from the fish fries, and you should readily see why at the age of sixty-three I had to have a Roto-Rooter job done on one of the arteries that feeds my heart. Knowing then what I know now probably would not have deterred me from those gastronomic delights.

Were you ever stupid enough to park with your best girl and leave the heater on without the motor running? What happened when you tried to start the car? Did you have to get out and flag down a passerby in the hope that he or she had a jumper cable? Kind of reminds one of the song, "Wake Up Little Suzie," doesn't it? I must admit that I was one of those stupid individuals.

Do you recall the songs, "Pennsylvania Six Five Thousand or The Little Brown Jug?" How about, "I've got A Lovely Bunch of Coconuts, Green Sleeves, Bernadine, or Too Pooped to Pop ?"

Do you remember when they wouldn't show Elvis Presley on TV below the hips? Wasn't it kind of freaky-scary the way girls behaved when they saw Elvis? How many dabs of Wildroot Cream Oil do you think it took to keep Elvis's hair in place while all that shaking was going on?

Who were Topo Gigo and Senior Wenches?

Do you remember when moms and dads in the old family situation comedies were required to sleep in twin beds? Do any of you know who the first husband and wife shown in bed together were? Fred and Wilma Flintstone, honest.

How many of you old geezers have resorted to twin beds, or even separate bedrooms because your mate snores?

Do you know what the difference between Memorial Day and Veterans Day is? Is there a difference between Veterans Day and Memorial Day? Did you know that Memorial Day is a day for remembering and honoring military personnel who died in the service of their country? Veterans Day was a day set aside to thank and honor all those who served honorably in the military—in wartime or peacetime. Veterans Day is largely intended to thank living veterans for their service, to acknowledge their contributions to our national security are appreciated, and to underscore the fact that all those who served—not only those who died—have sacrificed and done their duty for God and Country.

Were you one of the kids who decorated his or her bicycle with red, white and blue crepe paper? Did you attach a playing card to the frame of your bike in exactly the right place so that when you rode your bike the flap, flap, flapping of the card as each spoke passed over it that it would make a sound like a motorbike? Do you remember how loud the sound was when you went really, really fast?

Do you remember when the Veterans of Foreign Wars sold paper poppies for us to wear proudly on our shirts, blouse or jackets? Did you know that the wearing of a poppy in honor of America's war dead is traditionally done on Memorial Day, not Veterans Day? Do you know that the origin of wearing of poppies came from the poem "In Flanders Fields" written in 1915 by John McCrae, a Colonel in Canada's First Brigade Artillery? If you are interested in more information, check out the many sites on the Internet. Just type in Veterans Day Poppies and prepare to have an interesting, thought provoking read. Do you remember what color they were? Remember, there were two colors, red and white?

Do you recall what each color poppy signified? The blood red colored poppy signified the honoring of those who died in the service of their country. The white poppy, on the other hand, is a divisive, protest symbol if you will, in that it honors the victims of war, not the heroes. Do you think our children or grandchildren have any idea of what Memorial or Veterans Day is other than a day off from school? I can almost guarantee you that they do not know the meaning of the word armistice, let alone know that Armistice Day was later renamed to Veterans Day. Did you know that not all schools close on Veterans Day? Do you know why? There is no legal requirement that schools close on Veterans Day. The decision to hold class on that day or to close is left up to each individual state or school district. I'll bet you didn't know that, did you? Well, perhaps those of you who are or were teachers knew.

As a little girl, did you march in the parade wearing your Brownie or Girl Scout uniform?

How about you boys, did you march wearing your Cub Scout or Boy Scout uniforms with the sash over your shoulder adorned by all of the merit badges that you had earned? How many of you made it all the way to Eagle Scout?

Do you remember the big family gatherings and picnics we all had to honor our relatives who fought, and possibly died in WWII and the Korean War?

Remember when the circus came to town? Do you remember how horrible the elephants smelled? How about the midget walking next to the bearded lady and the giant? Do you remember the warnings to be ever watchful for pick pockets? Did your parents or friends tell you to stay clear of the Gypsies because they were known to steal children? I snuck in under the flaps of the big top, did you? Do you remember the hot roasted and salted in the shell peanuts at the ball part or at the circus? How many dollars did it cost you to win a fifty-cent prize for your girlfriend at the carnival?

How many will admit to waiting until the night before a term paper was due to actually write it? Did your parents ever catch on to the fact that all those nights you claimed to have spent at the Library doing research were bogus?

How about you night owls like me who did our homework late at night to the voice of Earl Nightingale on WGN, or was it WBBM radio broadcasting station from Chicago, Illinois? Do you remember how he started each program? I believe he was quoting Elizabeth Barrett Browning when he said, "I love you not only for who you are but for what I am when I am with you." I sincerely hope that each of you has found that very special person. I have, her name is Judy.

Do you remember what paste tastes like? Not the flour and water version like Mom made at home, I mean the real stuff. The sweet smelling paste that came in a small jar with a twist off lid with the little brush attached to the underside of the lid. Remember the Le Pages liquid glue in the brown bottle with the brownish-red rubber applicator on top with the horizontal slit in its beveled edge?

How many of the Sloppy Joes could you eat in the high school cafeteria at lunchtime? Each Monday I would purchase seven lunch tickets for the week. I'd then have three lunches on the days that we had those delicious Sloppy Joes. Do you remember how much each meal ticket cost us? How about thirty-five cents per ticket? Do you remember the political conversations we had sitting around the lunch table? We were so serious, weren't we?

Wouldn't you like to go back to the Rock County Fair in Janesville, ride the Ferris wheel and have a corn dog, a juicy Bratwurst with sauerkraut and mustard, a fluffy cotton candy or one of those gigantic waffle ice cream sandwiches with freshly churned strawberry ice cream?

Did you ever get sick while atop the giant Ferris wheel? How about the roller coaster?

Did you and your parents ever go to Door County and partake in a fish boil followed by a slice of Cherry pie? Were the Green Bay Packers your favorite football team? Do you remember what Vince Lombardi said about being on time? He said, "If you are ten minutes early you are already fifteen minutes late." Did you worship God on Sunday morning only to go home, turn on the Packers game and worship Vince Lombardi like I did?

Do you remember your mom giving you two pennies every day for milk money? Did you ever purchase white milk? I always went for the chocolate milk myself. Do you remember Tuesdays as being Bank Day? Each of us would bring our nickel or dime to school and the teacher or the student banker would enter the amount in our bankbooks? Did you have one of the chromed metal barrel banks from one of the local banks to save your money in? Did any of you have the blue, Flash Gordon style rocket bank that shot a penny into the slot at the front of the bank?

Did any of you have the courage to ski off the ski jump near the old hospital or better yet, the even taller ski jump at the Big Hills? There was no way in Hades I would even climb the ski jump let alone strap a couple of planks of wood to my feet and descend the jump to an almost certain death! How about in the springtime, were any of you crazy enough to climb that one hundred twenty foot ski jump located at the Big Hills to catch the winds that were constantly blowing down the river into which you launched you kite? Watching that spectacular sight, it looked as if the kites were just mere dots in the sky. If you were one of those individuals who did just that, I have one question for you. Were you nuts or did you have a death wish?

How about tobogganing down the landing slope at the foot of the giant ski jump at The Big Hills? The first run down that mammoth hill for me was about the most dare devilish thing I ever did.

You must remember who the junior high school class bully was. You weren't that bully, were you? I am not going to mention any names, but to this day, I would still like to beat the snot out of him.

You must remember, D., Santa Claus sees all, knows all and remembers everything. As Santa Claus, I have become very skillful, proficient and deadly accurate with a whip myself. I can slap a tick off Rudolph's rump with one flick of my wrist at twenty paces. So, you had better watch out! Know what I mean?

I'm not going to reveal his name, but Mr. Junior High Bully, do you want to confess? Well, Mr. D? Rather than reveal your identity, I am going to wait and see if you will fess up on your own.

I believe we were in seventh grade. Young Mr. D. didn't really like to have any competition. He did not like the fact that I had a crush on Carol McCarville inasmuch as he also had a crush on her. Rather than woo her with kindness and fawning affection to gain her attention, young D. apparently decided it would be easier to frighten his adversary into submission via means of physical intimidation. He chased me all the way from Lincoln Junior High School through backyards, down alleyways all the way to my home after school. In his hand he carried a long braided leather bull- whip with which he was trying to hit me. It was a good thing D. couldn't run very fast. It is also a good thing that his mastery of the bullwhip was thankfully inept at the best. I knew where the openings in the fences were and where I could push my way through the hedges.

I must be honest and tell the rest of the story. By the time we reached the hallowed halls of BMHS, ironically, D. and I became quite good friends. It's a damn shame what the favor of a girl can do to the relationship between two otherwise sensible young men is, isn't it?

Did you have to take a nap when you were in kindergarten on a rug laid out on the classroom floor? Do you suppose the teachers really thought that cold, hard asphalt tiled floor was conducive to sleep?

Do you remember your first train ride? Where did you go? Was it a puffer belly pulling the train or was it one of those newfangled diesel powered trains?

Do you remember who Buffalo Bob and Clarabelle were? Do you remember when Groucho Marx's television show was taken off the air? Do you remember why? He was taken off the air during the middle of his program when he asked one of his female contestants what she attributed her thirteen children to. Her response was, "I guess my husband likes me." To that Groucho said, wiggling his cigar between his thumb and index finger, and moving his bushy black eyebrows up and down, "Hell, I like my cigar, but I take it out once in a while." Instantly the TV screen went blank and on came an advertisement for Desoto followed by a repeat of the 5 O'clock news.

Before the advent of color television, did any of you have one of those multi-colored plastic screens that were held to the TV screen by static electricity? Remember, blue on top and green on the bottom?

When and where did you ride your first roller coaster? Mine was at Riverview Park in Chicago. I rode the Bobs, at that time the world's tallest and fastest roller Coaster in existence. Never again, NEVER AGAIN! While my Uncle and I were descending the steepest drop he leaned over to me and said, "I wish I had gone to the bathroom before I got on this damn thing."

Did you ever try milking a cow? Did the cow ever kick over the milk bucket or stomp on your foot? Did the cow turn to look at you as if to say, "Hey, Buster, warm them cold hands first, if you please." Can you remember what fresh milk straight from the cow's teat tasted like? What? You never tried it? You must have been a sissy city slicker, right? I suppose you thought that chocolate milk came from a brown cow, didn't you, just like brown eggs come from brown chickens? How about how awful milk tasted if it was left outside in the milk box and it froze? Surely you must remember that. Did you ever see a calf or a lamb born? Did you ever help churn butter, help make cheese or make homemade ice cream? Did you ever fall through the trap door in a haymow or play hide and seek between the bales of hay?

Do you remember the old electric refrigerators we had that contained a very small metal box attached to the inside top surface that was to be the freezing compartment? Do you remember how quickly the frost built up on the walls of that little box that made it almost impossible to put anything into the freezer? Do you remember the defrosting process?

Do any of you remember going from door to door in your neighborhood collecting scrap metal to aid the war effort? Like I said before, trading old pots and pans to make bombs seemed to be the patriotic thing to do.

Do you remember how much faster you could run after you got your first pair of PF Flyers?

How many of you experienced swinging on the thick-knotted rope that hung from the branch of the large maple tree that overhung our swimming hole in Turtle Creek at the Shopiere dam? Do you remember picking leeches from each other before riding your bicycles back home? Weren't those leeches just about the most disgusting things you have ever seen? Can you imagine that leeches are many times used in hospitals today to debride burns and other infected wounds?

Did you ever tip a cow off its hooves or play catch with a Bovine Frisbee? You do know what a Bovine Frisbee is, don't you?

Did any of you ever get caught soaping windows on Mischief Night or throwing rolls of toilet paper high into your neighbor's treetops? Even dastardlier than soaping windows or TP'ing trees, you weren't one of those cruel hearted individuals who smashed children's Jack-o-lanterns on the streets or sidewalks were you? Did you ever scoop up some of your dog's droppings and put them in a brown paper bag, delicately place the laden bag on someone's front porch, set it afire, ring the door bell and run like the wind to a hiding spot where you could watch the resident open the door and stomp out the blazing bag? Did you hear words uttered that you had never herd before? Did you get caught?

Does anyone still have his or her class ring, or did your girlfriend keep it? Do you remember whom you first pinned? Didn't the pin come before the ring? Do you still have your pin?

Where does the white of the snow go when the snow melts?

Speaking of picking, (going back to the leeches) how many of you remember picking wild raspberries and winding up with chigger bites or worse yet, ticks in you hair or around the tops of your socks or the top of your trousers?

Do you remember having to analyze Sir John Suckling's poem "Why So Pale and Wan, Fond Lover?" (Why so pale and wan, fond lover? Prithee, why so pale? Will, when looking well can't move her, looking ill prevail? Prithee why so pale?

Why so dull and mute, young sinner? Prithee, why so mute? Will, when speaking well can't win her, Saying nothing do't? Prithee, why so mute?

Quite, quite, for shame, this will not move: If of herself she cannot love, Nothing can maker her: The devil take her!) Just think, that little poem was written sometime in the early part of 1642. I guess the games men and women play are just as they were 400 years ago.

How about "The Death of the Ball Turret Gunner?" At the end of the poem, can you imagine the ball turret gunner being washed out of the turret with the water of a high-pressure hose? Didn't reading that just about turn your stomach? Did you have the foggiest idea what James Faulkner was saying in "As I Lay Dying?" What's with the chapter with only one sentence? "My mother is a fish?" Do you remember where the line, "This is the forest primeval, the murmuring pines and hemlocks." came from? Did you ever have to read "The Flowering Judas?"

How many of you took Mr. Lafky's after-school class on the Iliad and the Odyssey? Do you remember that Homer in the late 9th century BC or the early 8th reportedly wrote it? Who the heck was Homer? Does anyone know? Was he more than one person?

Do you remember the words to "If you want to be a Badger?" Did you ever see a Badger who could pass by a saloon? Given that Wisconsin was known at the time as being the dairy state and given that there is a plethora of breweries in the state, how do you explain the exceedingly excessive per capita consumption of brandy? Could it possibly be the boilermakers, the shot of brandy followed by a beer chaser?

Can you recall the words to "Hail to Our Alma Mater?" You should, it appeared on one of the first pages of this book!

Who were "Les Petit poufs et les Fille faries?" (Spelled phonetically) The only thing I remember from French class is Parlez-vous francais, and "Mon tant et sur la table." I think the lattert means, "My aunt is on the table." Get off the table, Mabel; the quarter is for the beer!

Do you remember the words to the song "Give a Cheer?" Allow me to refresh your memory: Feel free to sing along if you would like. "Give a cheer;

Give a cheer for the boys who drink the beer in the cellar of old Beloit High. They are brave, they are bold, and the beer they drink is cold, in the cellar of old Beloit High. So, it's guzzle, guzzle, guzzle as they pour it down their muzzles and if Royal should appear they'd say, "Sir, have a beer." So no matter where you roam, you will always know it's in Beloit High where they're drinking the beer." Now do you remember?

I don't believe that the following could be considered a fight song, but do you recall singing this little ditty? "Cheers, Cheers for old Beloit High. You bring the whiskey; I'll bring the rye. Send the freshmen out for gin and don't let a sober sophomore in. Juniors never stager seniors never fall, they sober up on wood alcohol while the loyal faculty lay drunk on the bar room floor yelling More, More."

Do you remember the song, "Too Pooped To Pop?" How about Banana Boat or Yellow Bird?

Were your parent's music snobs like mine who would not let you listen to rock-N-roll, you know, the devil's music?

How many of you remember getting poison Ivy while playing in the woods of the Big Hills? Did the stinky soap and Calamine lotion help? I must confess, neither of those remedies ever worked for me.

How many different species of insects were you able to collect for your seventh grade science project? Did you cheat by having relatives from other states send you their local pests? Could you identify them by species and genus or were they just little bugs and big bugs? Did you glue them to a board or did you stick a pin through their thorax? When you were catching them did any of them bite or sting you? Did you catch a Praying Mantis or a Walking Stick?

Did you do any better in the Botany project when we had to collect leaves and seed pods and correctly identify them? None of you were stupid enough to pick poison Oak or poison Sumac, were you? How did you explain the inclusion of a leaf from a banana tree, an orange or lemon tree or a eucalyptus tree in your collection of local species?

Did any of you have a Sylvania television set with the halo light? Can anyone tell me what was that halo light was supposed to do?

Hey guys, do you remember when we all wore black or blue leather jackets with the upturned collar in an attempt to look like James Dean, or the Levies and a spanking white Tee Shirts that some wore with the sleeves rolled up? Did you ever roll your package of cigarettes up in the sleeve of your tee shirt? Do you remember slicking your hair back into a DA, or more politically correct, a Duck Tail, with the help of a dab of Wildroot Cream Oil? Remember the jingle. "Get Wildroot Cream Oil, Charlie…just a little dab will do ya." And they say that vanity is a girlish trait. But on second thought, guys, in our defense, we did it to impress the girls, now didn't we?

Did you have to use Butch Wax to get your limp hair to stand up in a flat top? How many of you had courage enough to get a Mohawk haircut the week after school let out for summer vacation and then had to go home and face your mother? Did she want to scalp you as my mother threatened to do?

How about attempting to smoke dried corn silk in a handmade corncob pipe behind your father's garage? Did you think you were going to die when you inhaled the first and probably the last puff of smoke like I did? How many of you purchased a Kaywoodie, a Dr. Grabow, a Yellow Bowl, a Medico pipe with the paper filter or a Missouri Meerschaum corncob pipe and a pouch of Half-n-Half or Prince Albert pipe tobacco when you were in college just to impress the girls with your collegiate persona. It never worked for me. Did you have any better luck?

Can you explain why the aroma of burning pipe tobacco seemed to turn the girls off? What's that you say? They loved the smell of burning pipe tobacco. Are you telling me that they must have been repulsed by me? It was me, not the pipe and tobacco? Well, I'll be damned!

Did you ever pull the telephone prank of calling a store and asking if they had Prince Albert in the can? If the proprietor answered affirmatively, do you remember telling the proprietor not to flush him down, or to rescue him before he drowns? Did you ever order a pizza over the telephone and ask that it be delivered to some poor unsuspecting person?

Remember how big Denny Lee's feet were? My dad always said that Denny's feet were so large that he could get a job with the Fire Department stamping out grass fires in the springtime.

Did your father ever complain about how much you ate by saying, "I'd much rather pay for your room than for your board?"

What was your first car? Did you ever have enough money to fill the tank? Did you ever attempt to chop and channel the body? Who owned the '49 or '50 chopped and channeled Mercury that was painted purple? Did raising the rear wheels of your street rod make you feel like you were always going down hill? It didn't increase gas mileage, did it?

Do you remember Dan Taylor's red 1953 Mercury Convertible? Who had the little Isetta? You remember, the little blue and gray car with just one door that was located in the front of the car? No, it was not Steve Erkel. Can you imagine surviving an automobile accident in a car like that? Did you know that the Isetta was made by BMW?

How many of you Cool Cats had a pair of fury dice hanging from your rearview mirror? Did you have a statue of Saint Christopher affixed to your dashboard? Did Saint Christopher protect you from getting a speeding ticket? How many times did you have to try before you were granted your permanent driver's license?

How many of you remember the little mint green and white Nash Metropolitan convertible that Tony Scodwell drove?

You must remember Rick Ramsey's 1949 Studebaker. You know, the car that looked like a corn picker. If I remember correctly, I believe it was a light manure color brown. Appropriately colored for a corn picker, don't you think?

How many of you bookworm types now wish that you had taken woodshop? You may know how to read instructions, but can you cut a straight line with a hand saw? Are you a do-it-yourselfer or do you have to hire it done?

Guys, do you remember how grown up you felt when you were finally able to buy clothing in the men's department from George Brothers or Dunick's Men's Shop? Do you remember when you rented a tuxedo for the first time? It was amazing how even the most ugly of us looked pretty darn good. How many of you got sent home from school because you tried to get away without wearing a belt?

Do you remember how you felt as though you were a big fish in sixth grade only to realize you really were a guppy the first day you walked into junior high?

Could anyone get a piece of liver past his or her nose?

Did anyone like peaches? I did, "Peaches McCarville."

Were you frightened when you heard the news about aliens' crash landing in Roswell, New Mexico? Did you, or do you believe in UFO's? Come on, are you sure you don't know someone whom you suspect is from another planet?

Do you remember the smooching sessions in the car at the local drive in movie? Did anyone ever really watch the movie? Were you ever one of the poor slobs who were secreted into the drive in Movie Theater in the trunk of a friend's car? Did your trip to the drive-in theater include a stop at the Toot and Tell for a tasty California burger and fries on the way home?

Does anyone recall the delicious taste of the Elephant Ears or the Terds (crullers) from the City Bakery? How about the smell of fresh baked bread that came pouring out of the exhaust fan?

How many of you guys were forced to endure dance lessons at Jack Wolfram's Studio of Dance? I assure you it was nowhere near as enjoyable as watching "Dancing with the Stars" today. Inasmuch as I was the tallest kid in the class, I was the poor individual that Mr. Wolfram always chose to be his partner as he demonstrated steps to the class. I always wondered if maybe he wasn't just a little bit light in the loafers. I remember Ann Marie Kernland and Sharon Putterman took lessons from Mr. Wolfram. Did you? Sharon told me that he kicked her out of the class because she talked too much.

Do you remember when you could get a bag of five hamburgers, an order of fries and a small Coke at Mc Donald's for just one dollar? Do you remember the gasoline wars around town and being able to buy a gallon of gasoline for eighteen cents? How many times did you stop at a filling station and purchase a quarters worth of gasoline? Can you remember Gerry White and Dan Taylor's fathers' gas stations?

Who was your favorite teacher? Mine was James Lafky. While there were times that we hurled sarcastic witticism each others way, I remember one day in the front of the class he said, "Donaldo Nelsenivich, you are the most verbose, the most exasperating individual it has been my misfortune to have enrolled in any of my English Classes. You must learn to be terse and succinct, young man, terse and succinct." To that I responded, "Sir, your vocabulary is too copious for my diminutive apprehension, therefore, please elucidate more explicitly." Classmates roared as if they were at a boxing match, Mr. Lafky got red in the face and I stood next to my desk waiting for the next shot to be fired. In spite of our clashing with epees of sarcasm, it was Mr. Lafky who influenced me the most of all the teachers I have had in my academic career and it was he whom encouraged me to find something, other than a girl, to be passionate about and to use the written word to express that passion.

Do you remember sand lot baseball games before the advent of little league and official uniforms? Who was your favorite baseball player when you were growing up? Mine was Roy Campanella. I actually cried that December day in 1958 when I learned that Campy had been in an automobile accident. Was paralyzed and would no longer be able to play catcher for the Brooklyn Dodgers.

For you fellow Concert Band and Symphonic Band members. Do you recall the day before our big concert when Mr. Cuthbert told us that we would know when we were playing perfectly because he would put his baton down and direct with the tiniest of movements with his index finger? Do you recall what happened the night of the concert? Yep, you got it. During our playing of "The Love Death of Tristan and Isolde," Mr. Cuthbert lay his baton down on the podium and directed the remainder of the concert with just his index finger. What an experience that was. Do you remember playing at the Music Educators conference in Chicago during the very same week that The Al Capone Story opened in the Chicago movie theaters?

Was there so much as just one girl in high school that did not have a crush on Mr. Bernie Barkin? Sharon Wheat, that question is for you. Come on guys, how about it, will any of you man up and admit to having had a crush on Miss Bostetter or Miss Sobola? Remember how neat Mr. Ralph Whipple, one of the custodians, was? Guys, wouldn't you have rather had Miss Joan Whitby for a Physical Education instructor than George Wittic or Harry Pohlman? Does anyone have any idea what Mr. Haglund was trying to teach us? The other day I found my old report cards going all the way back to Kindergarten. I was shocked to see that I received straight B's in Physics class with the exception of one C. How the hell did I do that? I guess I must have learned at least a quark's worth of what ever it was that he was teaching. Do you think any of you could use a slide rule today for anything other than a straight edge if your life depended on it? Why do you think it is that those of us that did so well in Geometry had such a difficult time understanding even the simplest concepts of Algebra? 7x (4x+2) = 3B+ 5(C-2)—A What in the name of everything that is holy does that mean? Why is it that teachers never went on strike when we were in school?

How many of you young studs wore pink and gray saddle shoes, white buck shoes, dirty buck shoes or blue suede shoes? Are any of you ladies willing to own up to wearing a poodle skirt, white socks with ruffles and saddle shoes? Careful now, we have pictures! Remember the wool plaid, pleated Pendleton skirts and the cashmere sweaters your best girl wore? Didn't she look great? A question for you male fashion mavens. Do you remember the button down collar shirts we wore with a button on the back of the collar as well as at the collar tips? How about the Dickeys that had the little belt and metal buckle on the middle of the backside of the trousers, just below the belt loops? What in God's name was that midget belt for, anyway? Does anyone recall the name for that slack?

Remember how steep we thought the hill on Liberty Avenue was? Did you ever notice how much steeper it was going up than it was going down? Do you remember your father telling you that he walked two miles to and from school, uphill in both directions? How about making that trek in snow that was chest high?

Did you ever fish for catfish in the Rock River? Can't you still smell the foul odor of Catfish Dough? Did you ever catch anything but carp and suckers? If you had caught anything worthwhile, would you have eaten it knowing that it came from the Rock River? Do you remember the motor boat races held on the river? Do you remember the tall rooster tails of water the boats shot up into the air? Do you remember how you could hear the boats roaring up and down the river from just about anywhere in town?

Speaking of bad smells, will anyone finally own up to setting off the stink bomb in Mr. Aubrey Wood's Chemistry class?

Did you catch the Mumps or the Chicken Pox when you were a kid? If you had the mumps or the measles, did your mother make you stay in bed in a darkened room? Did your parents have to put that big red sign with black lettering on it warring of a quarantine situation on the front door of your home? Did your physician really make house calls? Do you remember how bad Ether smelled? Do you still have your appendix? Did you ever buy the argument that you could have all the ice cream you wanted after you had your tonsils removed?

Does anyone remember who "Señorita Lotta Bull" was? A bit of a clue: She appeared briefly at a high school football game halftime show.

Does anyone remember the Friday night football game at Strong Memorial Stadium during our sophomore year when the police arrested a man for smoking a reefer in the bleachers? Did you have any idea what a reefer was at the time? Who could forget the football game when one of our defensive linemen put such a ferocious hit on an opposing player that the opposing player had to be taken out of the game because he had literally had the digested stuffing knocked out of him? At our junior year homecoming football game, who was the nut that wore the full length, Raccoon coat and a freshman beanie with the propeller on his head? It was my brother-in-law's brother, Ron Hamilton.

Weren't you surprised by the commotion there was in the auditorium during an assembly the day Rick Ramsey refused to be inducted into the National Honor Society? What was that all about? He was one of the smartest kids in the class, wasn't he?

Do any of you remember driving just south of town on a cold Friday night or a wintry Saturday night to a farm where the farmer was waiting for us with a hay wagon filled with hay or sweet smelling straw to take us to the frozen pond on his farm? Can't you just hear that old John Deere tractor chugging and sputtering as it pulled us along the long dirt path? Do you remember building a bonfire at the edge of the pond and skating away the hours in the moonlight? Do you remember snuggling with your best gal while buried under the straw and then enjoying a mug of steaming hot chocolate and the S'mores made of Hershey's chocolate, marshmallows and graham crackers around the bonfire?

Does anyone know of the evil that lurked in the hearts and minds of the four depraved vandals whom, wielding post hole diggers and shovels, erected various scavenged, and/or stolen traffic signs in the front lawn of Sue Howell's home in Turtle Ridge under the cover of darkness? **THE SHADOW KNOWS, BUT HE AIN'T TELLING!** I ask you esteemed, learned but heartless attorneys in the class, has the statute of limitations on vandalism run their course yet? If we are still in jeopardy, I won't fess up. Neither will Rick Ramsey or Dick Blakely, that is, if it was any or all of us plus one. Is any one of you depraved vandals finally willing to man-up and admit to the absolutely most brilliant, enviable, most hilarious and long kept secret prank ever to be enacted in the history of BMHS? What kind of pranks did you pull? Is it true, John M. that you had the unique experience of being held hostage by a bunch of girls?

Can you remember when the tornado came roaring through town and ripped up half of the golf course? Have you ever seen straw imbedded in a tree or a telephone pole? I have. It was on a Good Friday.

Was there anything worse than having gym class in the first period of the day? Was there anyone in the class that didn't hate the communal showers in gym class? The girls didn't take communal showers, did they? Weren't the girl's gym uniforms just about the most hideous, the most asexual garments that you ever saw? Who do you think was the fashion designer responsible? Was the girl's locker room as smelly as was the boy's locker room? Wasn't it fun when the boys' gym class joined the girl's gym class to play volleyball? Guys, don't you wish you had taken your gyms clothes home the previous Friday to be washed?

As a child, did you ever ride a horse? Was it a horse or was it a pony? Did you ever ride on a fire truck or in the cab of a locomotive?

Other than not working up to your potential, do you have any school related regrets?

Do you remember your favorite Halloween costume, radio program or game that you, your siblings and neighborhood friends played? Remember playing Red Rover, Hide and Seek, Hop Scotch, Monopoly or with Lincoln Logs?

Do you remember being afraid to drink from a public water fountain because of the Polio scare? Did you know any kid who had Polio? I did. My friend and classmate in elementary school, Rex Millheam. Luckily, Rex fully recovered.

Remember making little construction paper baskets and filling them with little candies and delivering them to classmates on May Day? Did you ever learn how to dance around the May Pole? Did you ever sell flower and vegetable seeds for your class to raise money for your school?

Why was it that the boys could not master the art of Double Dutch jump rope when the girls were so good at it?

Did any of you young studs take home economics? How many of you same studs now really enjoy cooking and baking in addition to the manly art of BBQing? Who cleans up the mess in the kitchen after you have prepared a dish or a meal?

Do you remember the Portland Avenue Confectionary, better known as The PX?

Did you ever eat pickled pig's feet? Weren't they gross?

Did you prefer Ucher, Canasta, Samba or Cribbage? How about Checkers, Chinese checkers or Chess? Which was your preference, The Big

Band sound, Calypso or Rock-N-Roll? Were you a fan of Elvis, a Rick Nelson fan or a fan of the Everly brothers?

Do you believe in Deja Vous as Yogi Berra said, "Deja Vous all over again." What was Fibber McGee's nemesis? Who was Kayto? Who was Dennis Day and what did he do? Did you ever have a Secret Decoder Ring? Do you remember the name of the talking mule of movie fame? Do you remember the "Ma and Pa Kettle" movies? How about the movie, "County Fair or the Blackboard Jungle?"

Weren't the steaks at Bill Lucas' father's restaurant the best steaks in town? Did you go to the Coral for dinner before or after the prom? Didn't you about choke when you got the bill?

Did you leave your finger impressions in the soft acoustic material on the walls of the auditorium at BMHS? Why?

Do you remember who the Rockford Peaches were?

Do you remember the Amateur Hour on WREX-TV in Rockford, Illinois? I appeared on that program when I was in fifth grade and completed against a girl who later became my high school sweetheart. Small world isn't it? Do you have any idea who she was? Do you remember what her talent was?

Were you one of the unlucky souls who had to mow the lawn with an old-fashioned push reel type lawn mower? Did your father insist that you catch the clippings? Did you have to first mow the lawn from north to south and then repeat the process from east to west?

Did you have enough courage to drink a beer while you were in high school, or were you scared to do so as was I? My mother had placed me under the curse of sure death if I was ever caught with beer on my breath. Did you make the trip to Brodhead to guzzle 3.2 beer?

Girls, how many of you, as a little girl, walked in the Easter Parade wearing your Easter Bonnet? Did the bonnet really have "all the frills upon it?" If I recall a conversation I had with Janice Witte, I believe she walked in just such a parade.

Did anyone other than my sister and me receive three or four colored chicks at Easter time? How about a little bunny?

Did you consider them to be your pets, or were they just critters that would eventually grace your supper table? Did they grow to adulthood? Didn't you just want to strangle the rooster as he crowed loudly at the crack of dawn each morning? Were you forced to eat them?

Guys, did you have a pair of black Wellington boots? How about a white silk scarf to wear with your blue or black leather jacket? Did you have kidney bean shaped metal plates put on the heels of your shoes so you could make a metallic clicking sound with each step you took down the school hallways?

Do you remember when a penny postcard actually cost one cent or when the postage for a one-ounce first class letter was three cents? Did your dog ever bite the postman? Do you recall how quick mail delivery was? Two or three days, to cross the country, right? See what government intervention has done. The postage for a basic first class letter today is forty-two cents and it takes as long as thirteen days for a letter to travel between Philadelphia and Irvine, California. What happened? Why can we go to the moon and back in a fraction of the time that it takes a one-ounce letter to travel three thousand miles?

Can you remember where Mr. Oswald Tobit came from? Wasn't it Lucknow, India? Can you recall the last assignment we were given in Civics class? It was an assignment to look forward ten years, describe our lives and to prepare a household budget for the year 1970. My prediction and household budget contained the following: I would be married to my high school sweetheart. We would have two children, one boy and one girl. We would live in Beloit (probably on the East side) in a two-story house with a picket fence. I would be a Mortician looking to create the Nelsen Funeral Home. My projected income would be $10,000 per annum and I would have the world by the tail on a downhill pull. So much for plans and predictions. My high school sweetheart married another man. I never did become a mortician, In 1970 I earned significantly more than I had predicted, but I had to move to Pennsylvania to do so. My wife and I wound up with seven children (No, not by the year 1970). We lived in a four bedroom Pennsylvania Colonial with not even the slightest inkling of a white picket fence until 2005.

Do you recall the night of the infamous "Panty Raid" at Beloit College when the fire department was summoned to the campus to hose down the overly enthusiastic participants? Remember how angry the guys got when the girls threw their unmentionables out of their dorm windows denying them access to their rooms. If I remember correctly, during the near riot on campus, one of the city's fire trucks was severely damaged by rocks and beer bottles that the youthful transgressors hurled at it. Now, I ask you, is that or is that not something that you would like to write home to mom and dad about, or worse yet, telephone home asking that they send bail money?

I'll bet you cannot recall what the theme song of the high school dance band was? Does Deep Purple ring a bell? Purple; get it, purple and white, school colors?

Did you ever sneak off for a smoke during a fire drill? Did you ever play hooky? Who caught you? How many hours detention did you get? Did you ever get caught going up the down stairway? Why was it when we had to climb up the stairs to the second or third floor on the north side of the building that our next class was always on the south side of the building? Who was the mental midget who thought up that concept of traffic control?

How did Art Wienke get the nickname "Punch?" Was it from the British puppets, Punch and Judy? You know that Art had a sister named Judy. I'll bet that is how he got the nickname. Did Punch ever become a professional thespian? What was Punch doing when the photograph on page 91 of the 1959 Beloiter? Was he demonstrating the intricate moves of the Hookey Pookey?

As a kid, where did you hang your Christmas stocking? We didn't have a fireplace so I hung my stocking on the bedpost at the foot of my bed. Do you know who Belsnickel is? What did you get in your stocking when you woke on Christmas Day? Did you ever get coal? Were you allowed to open a present when you returned home from church on Christmas Eve or did your parents make you go to bed right away so Santa Clause could come to leave your presents? Did you go to Grandma's house for Christmas dinner? Weren't you proud when you went back to school after New Years wearing the new clothes you got for Christmas?

Were you by any chance a medal winner at the Silver Skates Derby? Guys, did any of you play hockey on the frozen Lagoon? Even though Carl forbad playing "Crack the Whip" on the ice at Lincoln, did you play it anyway? Were you ever at the tail end of the whip? Do you remember old Carl and his ever-present pipe? Didn't the tobacco he smoked smell great? Do you remember how romantic it was to skate hand in hand with your boyfriend or girlfriend to the strains of The Skaters Waltz?

Did you attend the summer festivities at the local elementary schools? Do you remember the smell of banana oil? Did you make those four-strand bracelets and lanyards? Do you remember how to play Swiss Navy? How about Zell-ball? Did you participate in the playground talent shows? What was your talent?

Did you get sick as a dog after you smoked your first cigar? What kind was it? Did it cost more than five cents or did you swipe it from your father?

Do you remember the first time you had a Tasty Freeze and the inevitable brain freeze from eating it too quickly so that it didn't melt all over your shirt?

Were you successful in removing the brain and spinal column from the frog that we had to dissect in Biology class? Were you the one who flung little bits of frog innards at the girls two or three tables in front of you?

Did you ever get caught passing notes? Was it worth taking the chance, knowing that if caught that it was almost a certainty that the teacher would make you read the note aloud to the entire class?

If you were asked to sum up your life's story in just six words, what would they be? Mine would be: "Stud Muffin, went stale, crumbs left!" My second choice, definitely more accurate and descriptive, would have to be, "Was skinny, got fat, now thinning."

Ladies, did you ever break a boyfriend's heart? How about you guys, I ask you the same question; did you ever break a girl's heart? Aren't you sorry now? You should be. I know from personal experience what it is like to be a jerk. While you were in high school, did you have an unrequited love? Who was he or she?

Did you ever get your finger slammed in a car door? Did you ever break a bone? Did you like to climb trees? Have you ever fallen out of a tree?

Girls, how many of you still cannot boil water? How do you prepare for dinner, make a reservation?

Do you think the Chicago Cubs will ever win a World Series? In your lifetime?

Do you remember having a party line telephone and an actual operator you would give the number that you wanted to be connected to? Do you remember how neat it was to get a dial telephone? Do you remember your old telephone number? Mine was Emerson 2—4102.

Did you engage in a sibling rivalry? If you had a little sister as I did, did she create a problem and you always got reprimanded for it? My sister was a great instigator.

Did your parents believe every word that your teachers wrote in your report card? Did your parents ever tell you that if you got in trouble at school you would face even more serious consequences when you came home?

Will someone please tell me what an "Opera Cream" is. What is the meaning of "Is"? I still need to know where the white of new fallen snow goes when the snow melts. Why isn't there a white residue left on the lawn?

What special traditions did you and your family observes at Christmas time? Did you and your family purchase a tree from the local tree lot or did you go to a tree farm or into the woods and cut your very own tree? Did you put tinsel on your Christmas tree? Did you lay it on each branch one strand at a time or did you stand back and just throw it at the tree? Did you string popcorn and cranberries for the tree? How about making chains of colored construction paper and paste for your tree? Do you or your folks still have all of those God-awful ornaments that we brought home from elementary school? Did you make a candleholder out of one-half of a Birch log?

Did your parents try to allay your fear of thunder by telling you that it was just Rip Van Winkle and his friends bowling in heaven? Did you believe them?

How much wood could a woodchuck chuck?

Did you ever attend one of Gary Fawcett's boy-girl parties?

Did you ever have to eat Scrapple or headcheese? Was there anything that tasted as good as a bratwurst steeped in beer and fried on a griddle at a Braves game in County Stadium? What was your favorite kind of cheese? Don't tell me it was American or Cheeze Whiz.

I plan on making it to the sixtieth class reunion, how about you? How about the seventieth? We'll only be damn near ninety at that time. We can have a parade down Grand Avenue in our walkers and wheel chairs.

Come on folks, one more chance, I am dieing to know where the white in the snow goes when the snow melts.

Do you think your grandchildren will be able to look back on their childhoods with the same reverent and nostalgic memories as we? I sure hope so, but I shudder to think what their lives will have been like in today's society with its plethora of litigious attorneys and political correctness. What will it be like and what will they remember as they prepare to attend their fiftieth class reunion? Will they be lucky enough to be able to look back and say, "Those were the Good Ole Days?"

To you readers who are or were residents of my hometown, Beloit, has this list of questions, places and observations tweaked your curiosity about what happened to so and so? Has it been tweaked enough for you to try to reconnect with an old friend? I hope so. Ask the reunion committee for a current listing of classmate's addresses, telephone numbers and E-mail addresses and dive into catching up with old friends. You won't be sorry.

For those of you who grew up in another town, whether it be a large or small city, in the East, South, North, the Midwest, the Great Plains States or the beautiful West Coast, I hope these questions and observations have prompted you to not only remember the good old' days of your childhood and adolescence, but that they may also encouraged you to re-connect with your old classmates and friends. Honest, folks, this trip down memory lane is shaping up to be a real hoot. I hope that you have enjoyed the reconnecting with classmates and the process of sharing your memories, as have I.

Who knows, maybe even you will be able to relive those Good Ole Days (at lest in your mind) and share them with your families, especially the younger generations. You will be surprised at how good reconnecting will make you feel and how fascinated the younger people are to hear about the olden days. Five will get you ten that your grandchildren will be jealous of the freedom to do what we took for granted as a kid. Those days may be long gone, just a Fig Newton of our maginations, (Yes, that is the way I wanted to spell it) but that doesn't mean that we can't share our memories, now does it?

Start writing your own journal of memories. I guarantee you that once you get started you won't be able to stop and you will recall things that you hadn't thought about for decades.

Photogravure Section

Eugene Bohrnstedt—The Music Man

**Daisy Chapin—Notice the shoes,
the hat and her left-handed commentary**

Original Beloit High School

The charred remains of the Masonic Hall after the fire

On your Mark…

A view from the top

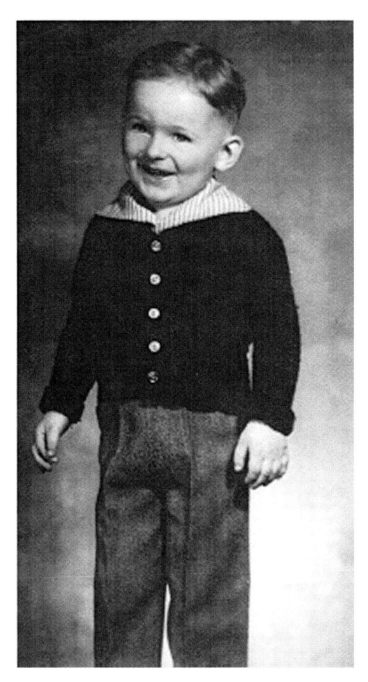

My first pair of long pants

The tattle tale sweater

Recognize anyone?

Confirmation Day, May 20, 1957
St. John's Lutheran Church

Front Row: Ron Skallerud, LaVonne Schroeder, Mickey Guetzke, Karen Wolfram, Pastor Walter Baese, Karen Grenier, Bob Hessler, "Cant remember."

Second Row: Norman Kopp, Jim May, Joan Kimbrell, Ronald Lee, Al Edwardson, "Cant remember," Gerald Menne, David Peacock, Guenther Neuman.

Third Row: John Drager, Nancy Pearson, and Joan Aney. Helen Mitchell, "Sorry, can't remember," Diane Worsley, "Once again," Tom Marx, "And still once more"

Top Row: Linda Short, Karen Guines, Gloria Ahrens, Ray Woltors, David Gums, Donald Nelsen, Steve Hemmis, Linda Nelson. Please help fill in the blanks.

The Peacock and his lady

James Lafky, Teacher extraordinaire, mentor and friend

Ventrographics II

Jim Lafky

An example of Mr. Lafky's quick wit and rapier-like mind

CHAPTER FOURTEEN
Memories of People, Places and Events

The photographs in the photogravure section as well as the commentary that follow are intended to evoke memories of both good times and even the not so good times of when we were growing up in the 1940's and 1950's.

Many of the photographs on the previous pages have been provided courtesy of Mr. Paul Kerr of the Beloit Historical Society, many of which are the artwork of Mr. Stuart D. Klinger. I hope they remind you of our hometown the way it was in the good old days, the days of our Hometown Memories, long before the demolition, renovation and modernization that has taken place since we graduated.

In the top center of the first photograph are the original High School and the second High School that was built in front of it. Directly across West Grand Avenue is the Beloit Public Library, built with a grant from the Carnegie Foundation. Immediately to the left of the Library is the Masonic Temple that suffered a devastating fire on January 31, 1951. At the far left hand side of the photograph stands the North Western Railroad Station. Between the railroad station and the high school stands St. Paul's Episcopal Church.

Term paper after term paper was researched in the dusty stacks of this of the Carnegie Library. Some papers earned good grades while others undeservedly did not. When the wrecking ball of so called progress leveled the Carnegie Library, leaving nothing but a pile of rubble and dust, I'll bet old Andrew Carnegie rolled over in his grave when he saw what they had done to his beautiful library.

It's no wonder we don't have any sense of history today when someone destroys institutions in the name of change. The Masonic Temple burned to the ground long before the Library was destroyed. Why didn't the city purchase the Masonic property and expand the existing Library? Politicians! Perhaps we have to thank an influential Brother-in-law?

What is it in the American psyche that dictates "Down with the old" and up with the new"? Isn't that contrary to our ancestral heritage to preserve and revere old structures for the ages? I guess our beautiful old buildings suffer the same fate as do we senior citizens; how many young people respect, let alone revere their parents and grandparents. I am sorry to say the answer to that question would be a very few.

Can you remember receiving a Penny Post Card from Grandma? Yes, people sent postcards every day, not just from some vacation spot. Three copper pennies could carry your innermost sealed thoughts from coast to coast in less than a week. Special delivery meant that the postman actually delivered your letter to the door and handed it to the addressee. Remember how the mailman greeted everyone as he walked his route? Did you ever know of a mailman being bitten by a dog?

The Beloit College Science Building referred to by Fred Kitto no longer stands. It is yet another historical treasure that became a victim of progress. I understand, however, that many pieces of furniture in the new Science Building are made from wood salvaged from the old Science building. Thank God. Perhaps a sense of history still exists, even if only in a desk or a chair.

Ah, the splashing fun we had at the Public Swimming Pool as kids.

When you were old enough to drive, did you ever park with your best girl in the parking lot atop the hill at the Municipal Natatorium? Did the fuzz ever catch you? Why do you suppose the police picked your car out of the many parked there to investigate? Could it possibly have been the fogged up windows? Dah!

Do you remember what it cost to swim? How about fifteen cents for the entire day, or $1.50 for a summer pass?

As you will read in later chapters, classmates like Cathy Kitto and Penny Rowbottom spent many hours as little girl's ice skating on the frozen lagoon and competing in various skating events such as the Silver Skates Derby and talent show presentations. How about you?

It was on the football field at Strong Memorial Stadium that the infamous knockout and shiner occurred. Yes, I was K.O.'d by a girl. "Hey Miss Charlotte Zick, you turned a reasonably confident young lad into a laughing stock. Thanks a lot!" Besides the embarrassment and humiliation of being knocked unconscious by a girl, it hurt like the devil.

I always knew that I would never be sprawled out on the turf at Strong Stadium wearing a Football jersey and pads. At 170 pounds and afraid of my own shadow, there was no way that I would be put in the position of being tackled by a guy the size of Larry Bond, Dick Thomason or David Weaver. Little did I foresee, however, that my repose on the turf at Strong Stadium would come at the hands of yet another girl! First it was Roxanne Russell in the fifth grade in the marbles championship and then it was Charlotte's turn to humiliate me. I heard about my loss to Roxanne until I reached Junior High. Was I destined to spending the next three years being reminded that a girl had knocked me out cold? The humiliation it would be more than I could bare.

Who could forget awaking the morning of February 1, 1951 to learn that the Morningstar Number 10 Masonic Temple had burned to the ground during the middle of the night?

The temperature was minus twenty-five degrees Fahrenheit. Interviews with the fire Chief the next day related that the water froze almost as quickly as it came from the nozzles of the high-pressure hoses. "It was like spitting ice cubes at a forest fire," he said.

The YMCA was the site of the unbelievable story about my friend Dickey who would rather sit on the edge of the pool in his birthday suit than go swimming naked. It was also the place where Cathy Kitto and her girlfriends tried to sneak peek at the naked boys in the swimming pool. The Y with its memory filled recreation room was the site of the parent-chaperoned dances that both Fred Kitto and I will tell or have told you about.

Please tell me that you remember the old steam engine trains that puffed and belched smoke as they waited for the last bag of mail or the last passenger to board the train. I was a train nut and remember vividly the last time the Chicago and Northwestern Dakota 400 pulled out of the old railroad station in Beloit on its last runs before it, too, was relegated to the trash heap of progress. What an eerie, yet pitifully lonely cry its whistle made as it slowly inched its way north toward Janesville. Sometimes I have to wonder if there will be anything that we remember from our childhoods in another fifty years. Probably not, not even Al's Snack Shop. No longer does the smell of sooty smoke from the smoke stacks of the puffer bellies fill the air. No longer does the plaintiff Wooooo—Woooo of the train's steam whistle make the hairs on the back of your neck stand up in anticipation of seeing that powerful iron horse come rolling through town. The kids of today will just have to be content with the honk of a car horn or watch the jet's contrails in the sky. Who knows, by the time our grandchildren are our age, what will be left to give a little hint that we once existed.

Beloit Winter Fun in the 1940s & '50s
(Courtesy of the Beloit Historical Society)

Fred Bull of the Beloit Historical Society remembers Carl, who was caretaker of Lincoln Junior High School's ice rink wouldn't allow "Pom Pom Pullaway," or "Crack the Whip" to be played on the ice because he considered it unsafe for the kids. (Author's note: If I remember Carl, as I believe I do, he was a small man of advancing years who always wore a wool German style Tyrolean cap, a heavy wool car coat type jacket, big mittens that reached nearly to his elbow and continually puffed on the apple shaped pipe that he held clenched tightly in his teeth. The smell of his pipe tobacco was as much a part of the ice-skating experience, as was the ice. He ran a tight ship but we kids were safe. Safe that is except for an occasional minor scrape or a bump here and there, and of course, my Christmas Day shiner.)

There was probably a like scenario over at Roosevelt Junior High School's ice rink. Kids and tomfoolery on ice went hand in hand as part of the winter fun in Beloit during the 1940s and 50s. It was a time when ice-skating was a big part of winter recreation in the city for kids and adults alike.

Notice the warming hut in the background and Lincoln Junior High on the left side of the Photograph. Tie them tight, please.

It wasn't always just fun and games either; there was real ice skating talent in this town. Who can forget those wonderful annual performances by the Ice Skating Club of Beloit at the Riverside Lagoon? Those fourteen years of dazzling shows on ice?

At the Riverside Lagoon the Ice Skating Club would hold competitions and produce shows that attracted thousands. The skating club was founded in 1944 and it spotlighted area talent. Original members were William and Evelyn Kitto, Marcella Westbrook, Clarence "Baba" Lynch, Martin Redmond, Harold and Adeline Delaney and Ervin Keller. The first performance of the club was on February 10, 1945. It was a cold day and a big, wonderful event for two thousand spectators who banded together in a ring around the ice.

Many people throughout the years braved cold afternoons to see proficient Beloit skaters parading their talents. The ice shows were marvelous productions. Like so many other annual shows, the one in 1958 was typical: It consisted of clowns and acrobats as well as dance numbers and ballet. Some of the stars were Adeline and Howard Delaney (Adeline directed most of the shows), Howie Westbrook. Marty and Mary Redmond, Clarence Lynch, Bill Kitto and Oscar Wentland. Some of the acts were "Twins on Ice" (Barbara and Beverly Ernst), "Twin Time" (June McDonald and Howie Westbrook), "Twirling Miss" (Miss Penny Rowbottom) and "Two Alike" (Bill and Cathy Kitto).

They glided, jumped, danced and twirled in an extravaganza delightful to the eyes. There are many Beloiters of today who remember those days. The Beloit Daily News provided medals and ribbons and these were presented to the winners by City Manager, Archie Telfer. The winter days passed with ice skaters skating, but also with sledders sledding, skiers skiing and tobogganers tobogganing.

Ice attracted the skaters, but snow attracted everybody else. They all seem to have met with their toboggans and sleds at the popular Hospital Hill on Olympian Boulevard. Olympian was the location of Beloit's hospital and the hill provided years of fun and competition.

The Toboggan Club held races there, which attracted competitors from Delevan, Williams Bay, Lake Geneva and Milwaukee. Orville Haas, Sid Renir and Art Couts were important club members in this sport. The Sledding Club also raced on the hill, and the Jaycees were instrumental in managing the sledding events. Jake Jacobsen, the city Recreational Director, also officiated at many of these races. There was even a mini ski jump erected at Hospital Hill for those less hardy souls unwilling to tackle the giant one at Big Hill.

The photograph on the left with the bird's eye view from atop the one hundred-twenty foot tall ski jump shows just how high the ski jump was.

You had to either be crazy or have a death wish to strap wooden slats to your feet and willingly plummet down this man made slope only to fly for a brief moment and them come crashing to the ground.

The ski jump was 120 feet tall and the longest jump ever recorded was a flight off 65.0 meters made by J. Running from Eau Claire in 1951. In 1955 the ski jump was dismantled, moved to and erected again in Westby, Wisconsin. According to Mr. Paul K. Kerr of the Beloit Historical Society who graciously contributed the above commentary and photographs, "the Big Hills ski jump was a magnet for competition from all over the world."

I hope the the side view photo gives you a better perspective of just how tall that beast was. Would you be crazy enough to climb to the top let alone willingly slide down on a couple of sticks? The landing slope beneath the large ski jump at the Big Hill was an ideal place to test your courage and mettle. In a young boys mind, if you could belly down on your sled or hold on for dear life as you grasped the side ropes of your toboggan and launched yourself over the precipice to engage the near vertical slope, you could do anything. You could deal with whatever came your way, even the steep walk back to the top of the hill. I don't recall a warming house. I don't remember hot chocolate; all I remember is going lickety-split and then thinking I was going to die before I reached the top of the hill.

There is a lot more to say about winter sports in Beloit. There are numerous other kids who skated where they could find a frozen pond river or creek, (for example, Cathy Kitto told me that she and her friends would ice skate from Beloit to Shopiere and back on the frozen Turtle Creek. Talk about being devoted to ice-skating. I used to ride my bicycle to Shopiere in the summer to fish or swim at the base of the dam. It never occurred to me to skate all the way to and from Shopiere.) or a slope other than the one at Hospital Hill that kids and adults could tackle with their saucers and sleds. I hope this has given you a brief glimpse into the organized winter sports in Beloit, both for those involved as wells as the spectators during the 1940s and 50s.

Please permit me to share one of my fond memories as humbly expressed in my attempt to use poetry to express my feelings. I hope you will remember and that the following little ditty will bring a smile to your face.

FROM BASEBALL FIELD TO RINK OF ICE

When the autumn nights got colder,
But no snow lay on the ground,
A crew of school workers
Leveled the pitcher's mound.

Using just rakes and shovels
They flattened it real nice,
Then got out the hoses
To make our rink of ice.

Each year from out of nowhere
A warming house did appear,
Resting on large wood skids
As we children clapped and cheered.

Inside of that warming house
Stood an old potbelly stove,
Adults kept it burning hot
To warm our chilly toes.

Benches lined the old oak walls,
Racks hung to hold our shoes,
And on the wall there hung
A list of Don'ts and Dos.

Every night if cold enough
After the rink had closed,
Some kind man from our school
Spread water with a hose.

On our way to school,
We'd all check out the ice.
Oh to be out here, not in school,
Would be really, really nice.

Crack the whip, tag and hockey,
Just to name a few,
Lovers skated to the Skaters' Waltz
And do what lovers do.

Then came the worst day,
The worserest day of all,
The day the temp went up
And our skating rink did thaw.

Back will come the pitcher's mound,
Be sure you build it high,
So that baseball we can play,
Beneath the bright blue skies.

Let's go back to winter fun in Beloit in the 40s and 50s. Organized fun is great, but for me it was the spontaneous, the impromptu fun that I enjoyed the most and subsequently remember most fondly. What kid didn't engage in a friendly snowball fight with the neighbor kids or throw snowballs at passing cars? What about building a snowman, a fort or an igloo. What about the greatest winter conditioner of all, snow shoveling? Wasn't making snow angels a part of winter fun, too? Wasn't building a bonfire on the bank of a frozen pond and drinking hot chocolate to wash down the hot and gooey S'mores a part of winter fun that went along with ice skating or hay rides?

Do you remember the old Beloit Memorial Hospital on Olympia where many of my classmates and I came into this world? It was a time when a mother and baby spent at least a week or ten days in the hospital after the joyous event. Those were the days my friends when fathers waited out the labor and delivery in seclusion of the waiting room, destined to pace back and forth as we were taking our first breaths.

Upon hearing the good news, the fathers would hand out the customary White Owl, King Edward or John Ruskin cigars.

How many of you had your tonsils yanked out in the operating room? Wasn't that story about eating all the ice cream you wanted after the surgery just a lot of crap? Who wanted ice cream? Somehow the smell and taste of

Ether and Ice cream didn't mix well. The smell of Ether that lingered in the nose and the awful taste that engulfed our taste buds certainly was not conducive to eating ice cream.

Are any of you gentlemen man enough to admit that you snuck in the side door of the Smoke House on Fourth Street and West Grand Avenue to take a peek at the girlie magazines with the pictures of naked ladies? "Get out of here, kid, or I'll call your Ma!"

Gentlemen, I'd be willing to bet that as did I, you saw your first Playboy centerfold in the smokey backroom of the Old Smoke House, correct?

If you can put your hands on a copy of "Century of A City," published by the Beloit Historical Society, look through it, especially the photograph on page 65. Just look at what our parents did. Look at that mess they left after the V-J Day celebration. And they had the nerve to scold us if we so much as threw a candy wrapper on the ground. Can't you just hear them say, "Hush, you do as I say, not as I do?" Sound familiar? Shame! I wonder if anyone got a ticket for littering? Double standards go a long ways back, don't they

Photographs of the cars that will be mentioned on the next page or two will be on display at the reunion in 2010 for your amusement. For those readers who will not be at our reunion, log onto Wikipedia and search for automobiles of the 40s and 50s. I promise you, it will be a memorable ride through those two decades. Were any of you guys in the class of 1960 the proud owner of a 1949 or 1950 chopped and channeled Mercury? If I remember correctly, one of the upperclassmen had just such a car that he had painted Purple, complete with white furry dice with purple spots hanging prominently from the rear view mirror. Do you remember the roar of the big V-8 engine amplified by the Hollywood Glass- Pack muffler and duel exhaust? I remember how hot the car looked and envied him for owning it.

Did you ever go to the drag races on either Madison Road, Shopiere Road or on the road to Afton? Did you ever drive or ride in a car and play "Chicken" with a speeding oncoming car?

I did not own a car when I was in high school. Hell, I didn't turn sixteen until the middle of November of our junior year. I did however have a fantasy car. It was a 1950 MGTD that originally sold for $1,650. Unfortunately, I could never afford to own one then. For that matter, I still cannot afford to own one now! I would have given my left arm for a 50 MGTD with racing green paint and saddle leather interior and ragtop.

Dream on Don. Maybe you will in your next life. Don't hold your breath. If I could purchase even a wreck of a 1950 MGTD today for $1,650, I'd buy one, maybe two or three, combine the best parts and have a cheerio good time.

As the years have passed and the pounds have piled on, I am no longer able to sit in such a car, so why even dream about it? I'd give the same answer to that question as I would give for my reason of daydreaming of a date with Christine Laage. I knew there was no way in hell that it would ever happen, but I still hoped that it would.

Do you remember the 1955 Chevrolet Belaire Convertible, V-8 Version which sold for a whopping $2,305.00. My girlfriend and I had many dates in a 55 Chevy Convert. I painfully remember a trip we took to the Wisconsin Dells. By the time we realized that we were both sunburned beyond belief, it was too late to put the top up. What a price we paid for being cool. At least when the sun went down the cool breeze felt good.

Next to Judy Reynolds, Norman Kopp's Street Rod was Norman's pride and joy. The Street rod was Norman's "Love Machine." I understand that Norm's beauty was the second fastest car on the drag strip in Beloit. I wonder if Norman was as fast in the car with Judy as the car was on the strip?

Who could forget the farm implement that Rick Ramsey drove to and from home with his girlfriend, Cathy Kitto seated next to him in the front seat? I think his 1950 Studebaker was probably the ugliest, most disgusting looking car I have ever seen, that is if you rule out the Henry J. There were two original price tags, depending on what agricultural implements you wanted included in the deal. The Studebaker ran from $1,419 to $1,519.

When we double dated with our girlfriends, Cathy and Penny, we were fortunate that Ricks father would let us drive his 1956 Buick Roadmaster four-door hardtop. Of course there was a price to pay. We had to put gasoline in the tank and we had to wash and wax the car as well as polish all of the chrome with Brasso. Do you remember how much chrome there was and that old Buick?

Dan Taylor had a '53 Mercury convertible that looked just like the 1953 Ford Convertible, color and all. I was very fortunate that Dan would stop at my house and gave me a ride to school. We rode in style. What a cool car to ride in and to be seen in. Appearances, you know! Dan's red Mercury cost $2,043 when it was new.

Tony Scodwell's littler Nash Metropolitan was just about large enough to accommodate four average size teenagers, I remember riding in his car with Tony and two other passengers, all with cases that held our musical instruments. For a person under five- foot, eight inches this was a nice little car, but for anyone over five foot eight or so, the back seat was a real knee breaker. Sometimes those of us relegated to the back seat would sit on the folded down convertible top with our feet between the guys seated on the seat. The originally price of the Nash Metropolitan was $1,696.

Someone in our class owned a one-door Isetta, you know, the Steve Irkel car. Do you know who it was? Can you imagine ever getting in an accident in this? God forbid you got hit in the front because that is where the only door is located. I keep harping about how good the good ole days were, but this automobile is a classic example of things that were not so good! Can you imagine making out with your best girl in the back seat? There was no back seat! 1957 Isetta, Original Price $1,093 with a whopping top speed, 43 miles per hour.

Richard Lovaas owned a Street Rod that he made. It started out as a 1932 Chevrolet Coupe. Don Marske said that Richard let him borrow the car one night. Don told me that the first time he gingerly let out on the clutch, the car bolted forward, snapping his head back while burning several miles worth of rubber tread from the tires. What a car!

Was there one guy in the class who wouldn't have given up a girlfriend to own a 1953 Corvette? I had a cousin, Bob Warren who purchased a 1953 after he retired from Professional Golf. The wire mesh headlight covers, the rich read leather upholstery and the rock your head back acceleration made the Corvette the most outstanding, the sexiest American made sports car for its time. Can you imagine the girls you could have picked up if only you had a car like that? Just think, if you made an investment of just $3,498, you could have would parked a '53 Corvette in your driveway and would find scads of girls clambering to go for a ride.

Just so you ford enthusiasts don't get offended, I must admit that Ford tried to compete with the Corvette with the Thunderbird. That didn't work too well for Ford. It wasn't until Ford came out with the Mustang that they even came close to mimicking the Corvette's performance. That's it! You have hitched a ride down memory lane long enough! Let's leave cars in the dust and concentrate on people and other common experiences.

My sister and I had a little red wagon. Our little red wagon was advanced for its time. While most wagons were pulled or were gravity powered, but our little red wagon was powered by a 160 pound Uncle Roy. He usually pushed my sister and me in the very same red Radio Flyer wagon that mother pulled me in up and down the streets of our neighborhood as she collected old pots and pans from which bombs were made to be dropped on the Nazis in France, and western Europe. I guess in some sort of way, Mother's junk collecting was her way of saying, "Achtung, Here Hitler, this bomb is for you, you ***@$#&%^(#& murdering Nazi.**"

As you have already read, Mother's pressure cooker would have been a good addition to the war effort. All the Army would have to do is to send Mother to Germany and have her prepare a meal for the German troops in her infamous pressure cooker. I wonder if she knew how to make Sauerbraten or winerschnitzel?

My uncle Roy always had a Raleigh cigarette in his mouth. Years after the wagon pushing had faded from my memory, I asked him why he smoked so many cigarettes. His reply was, "Donny, this ain't just any cigarette, it's a Raleigh! I get a coupon in each pack of cigarettes and five extra if I buy them by the carton. When you have collected lots and lots of coupons, you can trade them for a free gift. I'm saving up to get your Aunt Evelyn a new fangled washing machine. I only need 29,853 more coupons."

If I remember correctly, Uncle Roy died from Emphysema; leaving behind a shopping bag filled with Raleigh coupons. I don't think Aunt Evelyn ever got the washing machine that Uncle Roy apparently was willing to die for. If I know my Aunt Evelyn, she probably burned the coupons, bag and all.

Yes, folks, the young dude in the long pants is none other than yours truly, decked out in my first pair of long pants. Mother made them from an old wool suite my grandfather was going to throw away. I don't know why I am smiling in the photograph because those pants were about the itchiest things I had ever worn.

Mother insisted that her little boy be dressed properly. Mother was so anal retentive that she ironed my underwear, my socks, and my handkerchiefs. I was not allowed to wear blue jeans to school until my senior year. By that time, I wouldn't be caught dead in a pair of jeans. Girlfriend influence, you know.

Note the infamous green sweater I was wearing the day I got caught throwing a snowball at the wall of the school, but hit the principal's windowsill instead. That damned safety patrol, that snitching tattletale. I never wore the sweater again until the next year when Mr. Tattletale went to junior high. By that time it was really too small for me, so Mother donated it to the Salvation Army.

I know it may appear strange to you, but I get so nostalgic when I see that photograph that I search department stores, men's haberdasheries and even the internet in search of a sweater like that, a much larger size, of course. So far, no luck, but one day I will be successful even if I have to knit it myself.

For those of you who were in our graduating class, I invite you to grab your annual yearbooks from 1958 through 1960 and search for the photographs that go along with the following descriptions. I came to the realization that you would have a much more rewarding experience if searched through your own yearbooks or if you walked around the 50th Reunion and try to figure out what which wrinkled, balding and generally more Romanesque attendee is the person I will describe for you

To test your referencing skills, turn to page 71 of our senior yearbook. The photograph on the lower left-hand side of the page consists of eight elementary school thespians. Are you able to name any of all of them?

Recognize anyone? I'll give you one little clue; one of the handsome dudes in the picture is my brother-in-law. No, it is not the person at the left in the first row! Does anyone know where Eugene Kunde is?

There was a young man in our class by the name of Harry E. Hamilton. I had a sister who was three years behind us in school. So when Harry penned the message, **"Don: Well, we made it. Take good care of your sister for me." Harry E. Hamilton** in my yearbook, little did we know that my little sister, who was in the ninth grade at the time, would eventually become Mrs. Harry E. Hamilton? Yes, as time went by, Harry dated my sister, Diane. Eventually, they were happily married, the parents of three children. Unfortunately my sister died as a result of multiple ruptured aneurysms just before their youngest child graduated from BMHS. Harry is a good man; He has always been a dedicated husband, father and a doting grandfather.

Inasmuch as Harry and I knew each other since we were in first grade, do you suppose he knew when Diane was four years old that some day he would ask her to be his wife? Well, Harry? If you knew back then, who is going to win at the Kentucky Derby this year? Harry was hairy then!

Were any of you gentlemen of such good fortune that you were born into a family that would permit you to own a Red Ryder BB Gun with a compass in the stock? I wasn't! If you were one of the fortunate few, were you constantly nagged about not putting your eye out? Pat Reed's daughters found an original Red Ryder BB Gun with a compass in the stock at a flea market and gave it to their father when he was in his early fifties. Better late than never. As you will read a little later, at least one of our female classmates not only got an air rifle for Christmas, she got a whole lot more with her gun.

Did your father ever want to enter a contest with a grand prize like Ralphie's father's lamp? You remember, the lady's leg with lampshade. My mother would not allow Dad to enter such a contest, and Dad was smart enough not to ever try.

I'd like to make a wager right now that many of you young boys who had a grandmother like mine who thought those hand made bunny pajamas were the cutest thing, wished that she had worked as hard to convince your mother and father that you could be trusted handle a Red Ryder BB Gun, Right? Get used to it kid, no one ever said that life was going to be a bed of roses, or would contain a Red Ryder BB Gun with or without a compass in the stock.

Were you ever so stupid as to stick your tongue to a cold metal pipe? Unfortunately, yours truly experienced all sorts of lapses in good judgment; including sticking my tongue to the upright of the metal swing set in the schoolyard on a cold December day. Just like in the movie, "A Christmas Story." When the bell rang bringing recess to a close, I was left stuck to the metal pole by the tip of my tender tongue until the teacher realized she was missing one of her chicks. Then and only then did one of my classmates tell her of my mindless plight.

If you weren't lucky enough to get a Red Ryder BB Gun with a compass in the stock, but you did get grandma's homemade bunny suit, did Santa Claus take pity on you and at least bring you an O Gauge Electric Lionel Freight train?

You were lucky if you did. Let me tell you what Santa brought me instead of an electric train. I got a cheap piece of Japanese junk that looked like a crumpled tin can with a sardine can key stuck in its side. I hated that train with a passion. I quickly broke it. It was made in Japan and broke with very little effort on my part. I don't know why, but I saved it and it is now displayed in my Santa office to remind me of what not to bring a kid when he asks for an electric train.

The annual Soap Box Derby was a major event for boys in fifth grade through junior high. Many of our classmates entered the competition. Eugene Kunde, David Faust, Don Marske, Vance Johnson are just a few of the wannabe racecar drivers. Vance now lives in Chiba-Ken, Japan. I doubt seriously that he will be able to attend the reunion. Does anyone have an E-mail address for Vance?

Look through your Beloiter and find young Don Marske as she stands holding his Kodak Brownie camera as he waits to board the bus for our trip to the Zoo in Madison.

After the many months of Saturday morning instruction, Confirmation day was upon us. Not only did that ceremony mean that we were considered to be adult members of the congregation, that we could partake of Holy Communion, that we were expected to tithe, but in a lighter vane, we now had our Saturday mornings free!

You have already read about the peacock strutting down East and West Grand Avenue in the chapter called, "The Color Purple. Look for the photo of me in the monkey suit that I strutted my stuff in and the pretty young lady to my left is my ninth grade sweetheart, Marilyn Ahrens. The large tree behind us is the Mulberry tree where I carved our Initials (D.N. + M. A). Of course I encircled our initials by a heart and cupid's arrow piercing it high in the top of the tree where I would climb to eat my fill of the succulent mulberries. Mother cursed that tree every time she tried to wash the stains out of my clothing.

At the end of our sophomore year, Marilyn wrote the following in my yearbook:

> *Don:*
> *Best of luck to a swell guy. I hope you and Penny have a wonderful summer and don't forget our crazy homeroom and our Junior High days.*
> *A friend,*
> *Marilyn Ahrens*

Then at the close of our senior year Marilyn wrote:

Don:
Best of everything to a long time friend. Thanks for the memories and
remember our crazy homeroom periods. I hope you have success in the business
you want, but I hope I don't meet you there for a while.
Bye for now,
Marilyn

I was happy to read that Marilyn remembers our junior high days. As I have confessed, she was a very special girl to me in the ninth grade, and she continues to be a very special lady to this day, even though she nags me to walk every day and to eat just one cookie, not twelve. Yes, I had another steady girl in high school other than Marilyn, but I never lost those special feelings that I had for Marilyn. Thanks, girlfriend. You were very special fifty years ago and now that we have reconnected via "Guess Santa's secret identity," you still are a very dear friend. The business Marilyn is referring to was my short lived intreest in becoming a mortician and owning my own Funeral Parlor. No, that pipe dream never did come true. I'll bet people would have died to come to my business. Yes, Mother, I remember, "Just put one foot in front of the other," right? Just because we used to listen to the song "Lost Beneath The Streets of Boston" and the MTA, doesn't mean that I am a walking devote. But, "I will Just Keep Walking."

Do you remember the Budweiser or Hamm's beer can Christmas trees that came out in the 50s? Just think, in a past life those monstrosity were once a beer can! Does a tree made from a recycled aluminum can have even the slightest bit of a redeeming social value? BURRRRRRRP! Just imagine the horror of a Christmas tree of alternating red, green, yellow and blue as a floodlight shown through the panels of the abomination, the most disgusting Christmas prank ever foisted on traditional tree Christmas lovers. "@%&*! $#&?~!!"

You know what I am talking about! The hideous contraption was the spawn of some depraved, anti-Christmas nut. It must have been someone who wanted to scare poor ole Santa into a heart attack. Shame on you, sir, shame on you! I hope when you try to sleep at night that you are kept awake by alternating red, green, blue and yellow lights.

What would you think if your mother came home with a tree that was covered with some sort of plastic foam instead of a real Christmas tree? What if instead of white snow, she had chosen a pink or a robin's egg blue tree? Would you have thought your Mother had lost her mind as I did? If you said yes to my last question, you would be right. If God intended Christmas trees to have snow on them inside the house, wouldn't he make it snow inside?

Thank God that artificial Christmas trees today at least look like the real thing. My wife is a Christmas nut and has a total of seven theme oriented Christmas trees that she puts up every year. She'll probably come home this year with yet another. The Philadelphia Electric Company loves Judy.

Turn to page 100 of your 1958 Beloiter, please. Why the frown, Art Wienke? Watch out Pat. It is a well-known fact that Miss Bostetter spits when she lisps. Larry Bond, that is no way to treat a lady. Is that you Phil Plautz and Sandy Jones making out on the sofa?

On page 91 of your 1959 Beloiter you will find several interesting photographs, For example, how about the photograph of Art "Punch" Wienke doing the Hookey Pookey? Yours truly with a saxophone stuffed in his mouth. Janice Witte and Pat Sheehan laughing at something that Pat must have dropped on the floor. What do you suppose it was?

You will find, on the next couple of pages, the scribbling of classmates found in my senior yearbook, The Beloiter. You will note comments about two influential teachers that everyone seems to remember. Some of their memories were fond memories. Then again, some were not. Nonetheless, they're memories and you cannot fault either.

Mr. James Lafky was one of those teachers that you either loved or you hated with every fiber of your being. For me, Mr. Lafky was an outstanding instructor. An objective critic and an honest to God mentor. When Mr. Lafky was asked his favorite color; his sarcastic response was, **"Black Crepe."**

As you read our classmates memories, you will quickly understand why Mr. Lafky is so revered by many of us. I wish I could sit down with him now, share a cup of coffee or tea and just pick his brain clean. What a mind! What a man!

Richard Lovaas wrote in my 59-60 yearbook the following:

Best of luck, Don,
You were a riot in English Class. It wouldn't have been the same without
you.
Richard Lovaas

Dave Meeker wrote:

Donaldo:
Best of luck to another one of Comrade Lafky's peons. His class was enough
to send anyone to an early grave. Hope you have a lot of fun after graduation and
maybe I'll see you around this summer.
Dave Meeker—1960

Mr. Lafky probably knew more about the Bard On Avon than the Bard
himself. Do you remember the hand-constructed replica of the Globe
Theater that Mr. Lafky was so proud of? Can you imagine what Gloria
Steinem would have said about men playing the roles of women? She would
have burned more than her bra. Maybe that is how the original Globe
Theatre burned down.

Speaking of upset women. Miss Sue Howell penned the following
message in my 59-60 yearbook. What in the name of God is she talking
about?

Donaldo Nelsonavitch:
First of all I must clarify one thing—I am not a h-----, bless it all! I don't
think you're very nice. Usually though, you're a pretty good guy. I'm glad I was
in English and Physics with you. You're really kind if a lot of fun, sometimes.
Seriously, I know you'll be a success in whatever you do. You have a nice outgoing
personality. Keep up the good work.
Sue Howell

Mr. Lafky had a way about him that made studying the Classics almost
enjoyable. I don't know what he is pointing to in the photograph. As he
pointed out various features he would probably have told the girl students in
attendance that there were no ladies rooms in the Globe Theater. Like many
of our classmates, I even took an after hours class from him on the Iliad and

the Odyssey. Was Homer a real person or the penname for "Anonymous" or a host of unknowns from the the latter part of the Ninth century B.C. or early Eighth century B.C.? How about it, Mr. Lafky, got an answer for that question?

Yes, James L. Lafky was an unrelenting critic of our written words. The way he went through red ink, he must have bought it wholesale or had a brother-in-law that could get him a sweet deal on case quantities. Richard, David and I, just to mention three, were Mr. Lafky's most frequent victims of his sarcasm and embarrassing scolding. That withstanding, Mr. Lafky was the best teacher I ever had! He is and was my respected mentor. If he remembers me, I know he would be shocked to hear that, but it is true. It is because of Mr. Lafky's prompting that this sixty-five-year old retiree has taken up writing. Thank you sir, I owe you one.

After reading Sue Howell's message, I feel that now that fifty years have lapsed that it is safe to make a confession. Yes, confession time, time to take a load off my shoulders and the shoulders of three of my closest friends! If you do not remember reading about the incident in The Beloit Daily News, permit me to fill you in. Perhaps then you will understand my compulsion to confess. Confess, not only for myself, but also of two of the remaining three pranksterish vandals that struck Sues Howell's front lawn, using all the stealth learned in R.O.T.C., while under the cover of darkness.

Rick Ramsey's father would let us use his 1956 Buick Roadmaster for our double dates if washed and waxed the car, including using Brasso polish on all of the chrome. If you remember anything about the cars in the late 1950s, you surely remember they were laden with lots of shiny chrome. After all that work washing and waxing the car just to be able to drive Mr. Ramsey's car. We were determined not to put any more gas in the tank than we thought we would burn. So, each of us would kick in twenty-five or fifty cents.

Confession is good for the soul, correct? So. Here it goes: The ringleader, the genius whose brain child we carried out that night under the cover of darkness was none other than General Rick Ramsey, one of the smartest kids in the class.

Second in command, Rick's go to man, if you will, was another one of the intellectuals in the class of 1960. At the time he was known as Dick, but now we respectfully call him, Dr. Richard Blakely, M.D. That is Dick in the bib overalls in the picture found on page 100 of the 1958 Beloiter. Do you suppose the large book Dick is holding in his hand is a copy of Grey's Anatomy?

The third prankster, the man we referred to, as the First Sergeant cannot be identified, at least not by me, inasmuch as I do not remember his identity. So far, no one has fessed up to being the First Sergeant.

Closing the ranks, the poor devil that sat in the back seat of Rick's father's 1956 four-door hardtop Buick Roadmaster with a million pound cement ball at the end of a ten-foot Stop sign resting in his lap. He held the Stop sign out the rear window of the car, holding on for dear life and praying the Fuzz wouldn't see them. Private Donald E. Nelsen reporting for duty, Sir! I would like Sue to purchase this book, but I hope she skips this part, at least while I am still in town.

The following day, Saturday, my family and I were seated at the dining room table eating Saturday night's supper. Dad was reading the Beloit Daily News as he usually did. All of a sudden he folded the paper in half and laid it on my plate. There it was, a photograph of the Howell's front yard where road signs had mysteriously sprouted and grown to ten foot heights during the night. "I don't suppose you know anything about this, do you?"

"Sure don't, Pop, I'll bet Mr. Howell was really mad when he went to work the next morning." Twenty years later on the occasion of our twentieth reunion of our graduation, Jim May and his wife and my wife and I were seated around my parents' dining room table. Mother served coffee and cake as Dad, Jim and I talked about the days we were in high school. Jim, the Rat Fink, said. "Hey Don, do you remember the night you and the guys planted all of those road signs in Howell's front yard?"

My father's exceptionally large ears perked up and he asked, "What did you say, Jimmy?" Of course, good old Howdy Doody repeated what he had said.

"I knew it all along, you S.O.B., I knew you were in on it. If I remember correctly you claimed you were playing poker. You even showed your mother all of the dollar bills, quarters and four bit pieces you had in your pocket. I'll be damned, I didn't think you had it in you."

We all had a good laugh and went on to other topics. Thirty years later I thanked Jim for ratting me out to my father, but he claims to not remember. Very convenient, probably not truthful but very convenient, wouldn't you say?

Sue, did you or your parents ever know who did what? Would you ever have suspected Rick and Dick? Surely you would have never suspected one of the sign gardeners could possibly have been **moi**. See I did learn something after two years of French classes.

Reading through the hand written messages in my senior yearbook, I think many of my classmates were too harsh and, yes, even deliberately unkind to Mr. Haglund. While I found his monotone lectures to be a bit on the boring side, those of us who appreciated a dry, a very dry, almost aired sense of humor, got a kick out of his delivery and actually learned, at least a quark's worth of Physics. Yes I can still use my slide rule. Not as a Straight edge, so there. How about you? Do you even know where your slide rule is?

Richard and I were like two peas in a pod, at least academically. Out of a class of 423 students, Richard and I had the same class ranking. I wonder if Richard's teachers said the same thing about him as they said about me, "Doesn't work up to his potential. Now, I ask you, wasn't having fun equally as important as achieving stellar grades?

Richard wrote the following in my yearbook:

> *Don,*
> *I know we are of equal status in the class but please excuse the grammar in this entry. In future years we can look back on this senior year and say, "Why couldn't we have had a better physics teacher? With this exception, 1959-1960 has been an outstanding year to remember. I wish you all kinds of success in college.*
> *Richard Lovaas*

Mr. Fruzen is a real Beloiter. After teaching seventeen years at BMHS he became an associate principal at the high school then the principal. In 1990 he retired, but as of this writing, after fifty-two years in the Beloit school district, Mr. Fruzen is currently doing special projects for the school district in the Office of Safe & Drug-Free Schools. Now that is dedication to our old alma matre, isn't it? Look for Mr. Fruzen's memories of trying to teach us blockheads. He may have a story or two to tell about you. When you read his commentary, you may be surprised at the historic event that took place at Beloit Memorial High School when we were Sophomores.

Now to one of the most interesting entries ever to be penned into my yearbooks.

> *Don:*
> *Best of luck to a "real fun guy." I'll take you on wrestling any time that it is not too obvious. See ya this summer.*
> *Love ya,*
> *Chrise L.*

Christine's comments as penned in my yearbook went over my head like the Goodyear Blimp. How the hell could I have been so stupid not to recognize what an opportunity had been laid in my lap? If I had only known then what I know now, that wrestling match might have been a whole lot of fun. I don't honestly remember what prompted Chrise's message. I wonder? Jell-o wrestling? If it is Jell-o wrestling, I sure hope it is Lime flavored. The price a guy pays for being naïve and non-worldly. Oh to be young again! Oh to be a little more observant and a whole lot less stupid.

Chrise, if the offer still stands, I'll be waiting for the opportunity to wrestle with you at the reunion. Would you prefer Jell-O, Molasses, honey or baby oil? You name the time, the place, and your preference of slippery substance and I will be prepared for a whooping. My wife, Judy has volunteered to be your cheerleader. She is hoping that you humiliate me.

Please turn to page 168 of the 1958 Beloiter. Reference the bottom right corner photograph. Do you think Christian Dior designed those sacks? Have you ever seen the opponents in a jump ball situation pose with a hand on the hip? Hey, girly, stop pandering to the camera. What totally, fashion oriented, non-sport innovation will you come up with next, high heel sneakers?

Come on girlie, quit posing for the camera. A basketball player does not pose at a jump ball with hands on hips like you are doing the Cha-Cha. What next, high heel sneakers to go with your Dior togs?

I'll always have fond memories of Peggy Goetzke even though she rejected my invitation to dance with me at a ninth grade dance, leaving me stranded on the dance floor. There I stood, humiliated by the rejection and embarrassed by all of the eyes that watched me shuffle off the dance floor.

That was the first of many ego-shattering rejections that I suffered through junior high school and especially in senior high school Slugger, as she was affectionately known, was one heck of a second baseman. I think the "Slugger" comment in the greeting that Peggy wrote in my yearbook had something to do with a softball game we played in at a school-sponsored picnic, or did it stem from the fact that in elementary school all of the boys were afraid of her because she hit or kicked the boys? I, for the life of me, cannot imagine that I was brave enough to try to get to second base any other way than in a baseball game.

> *Don,*
> *Best of luck to a real swell guy. I haven't seen much of you this past year but I'll never forget the Latin picnic last year. Please quit calling me Slugger you big slob!! Remember the Ninth grade party? I should have danced with you. Next time I will. Best wishes and keep smiling.*
> *You've got such a cute smile. Lots of luck,*
> *Peggy Goetzke*
> *'60*

Once again, turn to your 1959 Beloiter and turn to page 40, the top left hand corner picture. I don't recall ever seeing anything like this at the BMHS event that I went to. I may have been a geek, but I wasn't dead or destined for a monastic way of life. Believe you me; I would have remembered if I had witnessed a sight like the one in this photograph. I guess I must have been absent that day. This photo came from the senior section of the 1959 Beloiter. Drats, I always seem to be a day late and a dollar short. What are they looking down at, any way? Were they looking at the girls or were just pretending to be coy? How could they possibly have been trying to be coy standing there in their "Baby Dolls?"

I must confess that I don't remember anything about Student Council. What did we accomplish? Did we get anything out of the experience other than getting out of class? Why do we look so bored? If you want to see a bunch of bored individuals, turn to page 150 and 151 of the 1959 Beloiter.

Moving on to more important subject matter. FOOD! There were many favorite haunts for Friday and Saturday night dates and delectable gastronomic delights. While the Spudnut shop was not a date night destination, for many of us, especially those who lived on the west side of town and who passed it each morning on the way to school, how could we pass the aromas wafting from the exhaust fan without purchasing at least two or three to eat the remaining block we had to walk to school?

Unfortunately I am only aware of one of our favorite eating hangouts that still exists today. Al's Snack Shop is still alive and well, but it isn't the same since the Sauers family sold the restaurant. I guess the new owners are trying to stay on the good side of the Public Health Department by scouring the flavor out of the grill each evening. Why the hell don't they just leave well enough alone?

How many date night tales do you suppose could be told of friends gathering at any or all of the following hang outs?

SPUDNUTS
America's Finest Food Confection.
Take a Dozen Home Today
1101 Fourth Street

---

* * *

Of the many varieties of Spudnuts, which did you favor? Does anyone know if they are still available? If they are, I'll take two-dozen to go. Mix em up, please. To think that the folks who today make "Krispie Kremes" think their doughnuts are soooooo good. You and I know that Spudnuts had them beaten twelve ways to Sunday as far as I am concerned. Did you know that Janice Witte's father and uncle owned the Spudnut Shop? Did you know that Spudnuts were made with potato flour?

I did a little research and discovered that there are still thirty-five Spudnut Shops in business in the United States. Most of them are in California. If any of you fellow classmates drives past a Spudnut shop, will you please stop and purchase a couple dozen for me?

```
┌─────────────────────────────────────┐
│                                       │
│              A & W                    │
│          DRIVE-IN GRILL               │
│         1007 Eclipse Avenue           │
│          Emerson 2-5419               │
│                                       │
└─────────────────────────────────────┘
```

* * *

Was there ever anything as thirst quenching as a tall frosted mug of A&W Root Beer? I'd be willing to bet that Shower's A&W Root Beer Stand was where you were introduced to a California Burger. Who had ever heard of putting lettuce, tomato and mayonnaise on a hamburger?

How many of you were carhops at the A & W? Did you wear roller skates or were white Keds more your style?

As I asked before, can anyone explain why Root Beer never tasted as good when drunk from a cardboard or plastic container as it did from a frosted mug?

```
┌─────────────────────────────────────┐
│                                       │
│                                       │
│       Snack at AL's SNACK SHOP        │
│        A really fine place to eat     │
│      945 Brooks Phone: Emerson 2-9748 │
│                                       │
│                                       │
└─────────────────────────────────────┘
```

* * *

WARNING

Should you see a "Closed" sign in the window, the Health Department has been there. Wait a couple of weeks after the shop opens so that the grill will have a chance to build that lip-smacking flavor we have all come to love. The mud and chocolate cake are good anytime!

LITTLE BUNGALOW
"People who know
Eat at
THE BUNGALOW"
545 West Grand Avenue
Phone: Emerson 2-9777

---

* * *

The Little Bungalow, the best restaurant in town to get a heaping stack of flapjacks, melted butter, pure wild clover honey, thick slices of crisp bacon and a cup or two of hot chocolate. Their home made apple pie with a chunk of cheddar cheese and a scoop of vanilla ice cream was good, too.

The original Little Bungalow was a favorite after the movie haunt and especially for a hearty breakfast. For lots of people, including me, The Original Little Bungalow appealed to me much more than did the new and improved diner that was erected. It seemed to me some how the hominess of Grandma's kitchen. The aromas, the creaking of the old wooden floor, the friendly old waitresses, the initials carved into the tabletops and the ambiance were lost forever when the wrecking ball swung. I remember the white clapboards with their peeling paint, the double green screen door and main door that were so badly warped that they let all sorts of winter cold in. (If you were smart, you sat in the back near the warmth of the kitchen. Beside, it smelled the best the closer you were to the kitchen.) The smell of bacon sizzling on the grill and Hills Bros. coffee brewing in the urn made your stomach growl and your mouth water. The new one with all of its chrome and vinyl somehow just wasn't the same.

Now the Little Bungalow is gone as is the City Bakery that was on the corner. Of course, in addition to the Spudnut Shop, Shower's A&W Root Beer Stand and The Little Bungalow, we cannot forget the Toot and Tell, Florieo's Pizza in South Beloit, the Corral were we took our special girl when we were flush with money. Lucas' Steak house was another one of those elegant eateries frequently attended when we wanted to impress our date, but, unfortunately, the last I knew they had all closed their doors. Ain't progress great?

The Dance Band played every Friday night after football and basketball games and most non-game Friday nights. Each of the members of the band was paid $3 per night. That stipend was usually spent that very same night when we would rendezvous at Florieo's for a pizza and a Coke.

Sometimes we had double pickle and catsup burgers at Al's or a late night breakfast at the Little Bungalow.

Perhaps playing for all of those dances is why I forgot all those dance steps that Jack Wolfram tried to teach me. I had a lot more fun playing in the dance band than I ever had dancing, although I missed out on a lot of close dancing, cheek-to-cheek time with my girlfriend.

CHAPTER FIFTEEN
Stormy Weather

Each region of the country has its own special weather problems. In Wisconsin, we did not have to contend with earthquakes, mud slides, hurricanes or even massive forest fires and floods like other areas of the country. Where I grew up, tornadoes and blizzards were the two most feared weather anomalies, with an occasional sever thunder and lightening storm thrown in for good measure. If you have never experienced being caught in the path of a Tornado, or have never seen close up the devastation that they leave in their wake, I hope that you continue to have that void in your memory bank.

I experienced my first tornado when I was about five years old. All I remember is that it was Good Friday afternoon. We had just returned home from the Good Friday services at church when all of a sudden I was whisked into my father's arms and carried to the root cellar in the basement while Mother followed closely behind with my little sister.

At first there was no sound. Sis and I wondered why we were hiding in the fruit cellar with its damp, moldy smell from the potatoes that were left over from last year that were sprouting as they were decaying. Orange mesh sacks filled with onions hung from nails that had been driven into the rafters. Some remaining winter squash hung in another mesh bag, as did a bag or two of parsnips. Our fall scavenging efforts for nuts, both Hickory and Black Walnuts, were hung in the very same orange mesh bags to dry. The nuts hung there, waiting to be cracked that next winter and their nutmeats mixed into one of Dad's Danish or French pastries. Dad always had a few tubers of horseradish hanging in a mesh bag as well. My sister and I made sure we were a long ways away from the horseradish.

There must have been at least a dozen or more large cans of V-8 Vegetable juice remaining from the last case purchase that father had made. One good thing I guess, our root cellar was well provisioned. It stunk, but at least if we had to stay there for any amount of time, at least we would have Mason jars filled with whole kernel corn, beans, preserved beef and jars of canned chicken to nibble on and scads of strawberry, peach and grape jelly and preserves to keep body and soul together for the duration. Strange thing, I do not remember any water being stored in the root cellar or any provisions for necessary bodily activities, not even a first aid kit. Guess Dad hadn't thought that far ahead.

The absence of sound was my father's first clue that everything was not going to be all right that Good Friday afternoon in Kansas (or in this case, Wisconsin).

After Dad made certain that we were settled safely in the fruit cellar, he ran to the garage and grabbed boards that he had pre cut and drilled so that they could easily be affixed to the windows to protect the glass from breaking. He only had time to hastily put the slats over the basement windows when the wind picked up force and sent Dad running back to the safety of the fruit cellar. We could see through the cracks between the boards covering the basement window that the sky was turning an eerie hue of chartreuse, a yellow-greenish color. When the wind started to blow, gently at first, then with a constantly increasing crescendo of sound and intensity, the hail pelted the roof and even put a dent or two into the hood of my father's car that had not yet been parked in the safe confines of the garage. Harder and harder the wind blew until it sounded like one of the freight trains that came steaming into town each day had jumped the tracks and was headed straight down Moore Street to 843 where we lived. "Dad, do you think the train is going to crash into our house? Do you, huh, do you?"

Luckily, our home was spared any damage, although many of the large trees, especially the Elm trees, had leaves, and twigs ripped from their branches. There definitely was a mess in our back yard. You see, Dad kept our garbage can and the barrel where we deposited used cans and bottles in the garage. Mr. Cox, our neighbor, on the other hand, kept his garbage and trash in open barrels behind his garage along the alleyway. When the wind gained enough strength, it must have hoisted Mr. Cox's trashcans, gave them a mighty ride before inverting them over our backyard and Dad's garden. It looked as though some ill-tempered kid had purposely tried to make our backyard look like the garbage dump in South Beloit. What a stinking mess! Did Mr. Cox clean up the mess? Hell no, Dad and I had to pick it all up and put it in his dented garbage barrels that had come to rest next to four of Dad broken tomato plants.

After the storm had passed, the sky had returned to its original light blue color and after the "All's Clear" high pitched wailing of the City's fire sirens were clearly heard, we exited the moldy confines of the fruit cellar and went outside to survey the damage. Of course, my mother insisted upon taking a drive to our relatives' houses to see if they were O.K. She took Sis and me to the car and waited for Dad to come out of the house with a first aid kit and lots of old sheets that had been torn into strips to be used as bandages, God forbid they be needed.

Along the way, especially when we were driving along country back roads on the west side of town, we noticed stand after stand of hardwood trees, pines and River Birch that appeared to have been twisted off as if Paul Bunyan and Babe the Blue Ox had trampled through the woods and snapped each treetop off as if it were snapped in two as a man would break a wooden matchstick.

What a sight it was to see straw sticking out of telephone poles, dead cattle in the fields. On one farm on the Afton Road about half way between Beloit and Janesville we saw a milk cow that had been hoisted by the wind and set down, legs draped over two rather large branches of a Chestnut tree. Boy could that cow bellow. I always wondered how the farmer would get his Holstein out of that tree. Do you suppose that he built a food trough high in the tree and just climbed a ladder to milk "Old Bossy?"

We saw overturned cars, trucks, tractors and other smashed and mangled farm implements that had come to rest in the fields and even on the roadways and the railroad tracks. What a mess! The landscape was strewn with shingles and wood debris from God knows where. Telephone and electric poles lay twisted and shattered with their downed wires emanating bright blue-white glow of the sparking wires. We even witnessed the muddy remains of a pond bed that had all of the water, fish and vegetation sucked out of it and dispersed God knows where by the storm. A small rowboat was smashed to smithereens against what remained of a less than mighty oak tree. Windmills, if they were standing, still spun with such ferocity that we could hear the sound of their spinning propellers from the road. The missing blades that had been ripped from the wheel of blades that propelled the windmill obviously made the wheel spin erratically. The empty spaces where blades once resided made a rather eerie high and then low-pitched sound that sounded not unlike a siren. Talk about a spooky day, a day to record in your memory bank!

As we passed one farm, we noticed the privy (the out house for you city slickers or you rich kids that had indoor plumbing) was resting high atop the barn's roof where the weather vane and cupola once stood. It was a tragic sight, but Mom, Dad. Sis and I got a real belly laugh out of seeing it. "I wonder how the hell the farmer and his family are going to get all the way up there to go to the John?" Dad laughed.

I forgot to tell you another memory about the storm. After the storm had passed, if you recall such an experience, how many of you remember running outside to pick up the golf ball size or larger pieces of hail to preserve in your iceboxes. Did you ever eat one? Mother saved a few of them in the freezer. Some times she would slip one into our glass of Kool-Aid or lemon aide.

I didn't mind the blizzards too much because they were an excellent opportunity for the school administration to close the schools. No school, and lots and lots of drifted snow meant that my sister and I could build a big igloo; go sledding at Horace White park or on the hills on the golf course. Blizzards and the inevitable school closings were one of the great pleasures of Wisconsin winters. The teachers may have never gone on strike when we were in school, but we could count on a least one or two snow days each winter. I wasn't smart enough at the time to realize that there would be such a costly tradeoff to be made. Every day the school was closed due to inclement weather, we would be required to attend school one day more in June at the end of the term. That realization was a real downer. There would be one less day to swim or to play baseball for each day that we frolicked in the snow. Did I enjoy baseball and swimming more than playing in the snow? Let me see. I think I will opt for the snow!

There was another positive that resulted from those blizzards. The opportunities to earn money by shoveling sidewalks and driveways were endless. Unfortunately, not being very muscular when I was young meant that backaches, sore muscles and frost bitten fingers, noses and toes usually limited the amount of money I could earn in a day. Come to think of it, I don't ever remember Dad paying me so much as a plug nickel for shoveling our sidewalk or our driveway so he could get his car in the garage when he came home from work. Everyone knew that my father was cheap, or as he called it, frugal. In Dad's defense, he probably thought that all of that backbreaking manual labor was good training for me. But, training for WHAT? Even at the tender age of eight, I knew there was no way in Hades that I was going to grow up to become a ditch digger.

Wisconsin's stormy weather had a lighter, a more fun filled side to it. When ever we were the recipients of one of those Midwestern thunder and lightning storms or just an old fashioned cloud bursting gulley washer, all of the children in the neighborhood would scamper to their bathtubs, retrieve their boats and floating ducks and congregate at the curb to race what ever toy we had down the gutter. Of course, we had to be fleet of foot so that we reached the sewer opening long before our toy did. More than once we watched as our floating toy beat us to the storm drain. I can still remember the sweet, clean smell in the air after a good rain. Have you ever smelled anything quite so clean? No, I will not accept Pinesol as a valid answer to that rhetorical question.

I will never forget the hundreds of night crawlers that came to the surface of our lawn on a night following a good rain. On such a night, I would take an old National Tea coffee can, put a little bit of dirt from father's garden along with some shredded newspaper and some crushed leaves in the bottom and collect night crawlers by the filtered light of a flash light. If the lawn had received a particularly good soaking that day, sometimes the night crawlers would be lying out in the open on the sidewalks and driveway. Weather permitting and with mother's approval, the next day I rode my bicycle with cane pole in hand to the old' Fishin hole in Turtle Creek at Shopiere.

Sometimes I collected so many night crawlers that I had enough to sell some to other boys and men who were also fishing at the old' Fishin hole that hadn't had the foresight to collect their own night crawlers.

I usually got a penny per worm, but occasionally, a nice old gentleman would give me two bits for a dozen. In retrospect, perhaps I should have become a worm farmer!

You know, now that I ponder those trips to the old fishing hole, all I can remember catching were a few small sunfish, one large Bullhead which I was afraid to take hold of and subsequently cut my line to free it and of course a case or two of poison ivy and scads of chigger and mosquito bites. Kind of makes one wonder who was the catcher and who was the catchee, doesn't it?

CHAPTER SIXTEEN
For What It Is Worth

Finally after nearly sixty-six years of life, this old man, unlike our philandering President Bill Clinton, really does knows what the meaning of IS is. Trekking through life and watching others climb the corporate ladder, amass vast sums of wealth, purchase every gadget that man can produce and hob-knob with the upper crust at the country club, I have learned that in the grand scheme of things, all of those things do not add up to a bucket of spit or have any more impact on what is important that a grain of sand on the beach or a piss in the ocean.

Once you have come to the realization that it is people, not things that are most important, you have taken your first step toward something significant. Caring, concern and compassion are not a Democrat, Independent or Republican character trait. Those characteristics are not the sole province of Protestants, Catholics, Jews or even Muslims. They are virtues that anyone can aspire to and attain if they really want to. You may very well have your very own life changing epiphany. Let me warn you, when an Epiphany hits you, it comes with like a charging elephant. I know, it happened to me! But to understand and be able to react to that Epiphany, any vestiges of pig-headedness, prejudice, and self-absorption need to have been wiped from your slate. I'm sorry folks; there is no easy way to say this. As far as Epiphanies goes, there is no room for "Do as I say not as I do."

I do not envy nor do I condemn country club membership; I am not proselytizing for a political candidate or any political movement. I could care less about blogging or marching in protest parades. What I do care about and what I am referring to when I say, something significant, is the God's honest rolling up of your sleeves and getting your hands dirty doing something to make the life of someone less fortunate than you more comfortable, more secure, or yes, even more loved. Search your heart for what really is most important to you, decide to make the first step and then do it with gusto. Sure, you will make mistakes along the way just as thousands of people before you have, bit if a man such as Ex-President Jimmy Carter, as inept a president as there ever was, could show his compassion by becoming involved with Habitat For Humanity, surely you, too, are capable of passing on the God given talents and blessings that you have received. Are you with me?

Over the last several years I have come to know several small children who have been dealt the hand of Autism or Cerebral Palsy. Getting to know and love them has been the impetus of my dedicating the rest of my life to working for the aid, comfort and benefit of special needs children through the vehicle of Santa Claus. What little money is generated from Santa visits is donated to benefit my little angels. The greatest assets in life cannot be bought or sold. They cannot be put into a savings or checking account or even in a long-term certificate of deposit. The blessings of hugs, smiles, giggles and kisses that are stored in you heart are much more precious than mere gold.

Try it some time. Give of yourself. Who knows, you may be able to lower the setting of your thermostat at home. I promise you, you will feel warm and fuzzy inside and you will wear a smile on both the outside, as well as the inside, knowing that you have made a difference in someone's life.

At the time that I wrote "Childhood Dreams Really Do Come True," I did not know the name of the originator of the sentence, "No man ever stands so tall, as when he stoops to help a child." I had tried to discover the authorship of that poignant phrase to no avail. Then out of the blue, a friend of one of my sons told me, "It was a great man who first said that, it was none other than Abraham Lincoln." Boy did I feel stupid. I am an avid reader of history and I didn't know that. I guess you are never too old to learn. See, at least I learned that from a friend of my kid. So I composed a photograph of

Abe seated with a book in his hands and his kittle boy Todd standing at his side to along with his words to remind me of his poignant statement. That photograph hangs proudly on the wall of my office, just to the right of my computer screen.

I believe in that poignant sentence with every fiber of my being both as a man and as Santa Claus. That brief sentence embodies how I have tried to live and how I will strive to spend the rest of my days. That brief thought, those fourteen words strung together, has become my credo, my mantra, if you will. We all have stresses in our lives. When the stress of everyday life seems to be getting the better of me, I usually go to my office with a steaming hot cup of Joe, read the sentence and then put fingers to the keyboard and write. I hope, for my sake and for the sake of my little angels that the Lord sees fit to grant me many more years to share with them as well as keeping the dreaded writer's block from invading my office.

Come on friends, you can do it. In Chapter eighteen, "T'is better to give than to receive," you will read about many of the charitable passions of some of our classmates. You, too, can stand tall, even when stooping! Pick your own passion. It does not have to be young special needs children. For example, there are hundreds of thousands of elder citizens being warehoused in nursing homes and extended care facilities that are lonelier than you can imagine. I make routine visits as Santa Claus to extend care facilities, nursing homes and hospitals to visit with the elderly. You would be shocked to learn how many of them haven't heard from or seen their children in years. Even more disturbing is that fact that many of them don't even receive so much as a greeting card from their children on their birthdays or at Christmas time. That makes me so angry that I could just spit! Why not visit one or more of them occasionally? Why not read to those whose eyesight no longer gives them the pleasure of reading for themselves? Listen up to an old man who has finally learned what IS is. Those senior citizens are a vast source of information, information that each and every one of us could do well to learn. If you are compassionate enough and want to do your part, you will find the energy, the verve and the wherewithal to get the job done. As Nike's ads say, "Just Do It!"

The following poem is a recount of a visit I had with a ninety-two year old lady in a senior citizens center and a promise that I made to her. I promised Emma to share her message with, as she called them, the younguns. So, I penned the following poem to honor her. Emma's message may only contain twenty-four or twenty-five words, but in my minds eye, it packs one heck of a wallop. I ask that you read Emma's message (Seems to Me) to your grandchildren often. Emma's message is one of those pearls of wisdom to be found in our senior citizens, a gift that just keeps on giving.

SEEMS TO ME

You may recall Christmases from a long time ago.
Rosy cheeked children playing in drifts of new fallen snow.
Some look forward to smelling pine boughs hung in the hall,
While others have fond memories of the caroler's call.

New pajamas and slippers we'd wear Christmas Eve
Christmas Day pictures, Mom would tell us, "Smile, say cheese."
But before going to sleep we would kneel by our beds,
Saying the prayers our parents taught us ought to be said.

"Now off to sleep children, pleasant dreams," Mama would say.
"Tomorrow is going to be a most glorious day."
No visions of sugarplums when I was a boy.
I dreamed of a bike, my sister a doll and some toys.

Next morning we'd rush to where Dad put the tree,
"Mom, has Santa Clause been here? Let us see. Let us see!"
Oak logs on the fire crackled, red-hot embers aglow,
While outside the window we could see fresh falling snow.

"Now times are a changing." Great-Grandfather once said.
But doesn't Santa still wear nothing but white, black and red?
Santa's goal never changes; it's the same year after year.
To bring good boys and girls blessed Holiday cheer.

Today's gifts may be pricier, but none can compete
With Grandma's hand knitted wool socks to warm our cold feet.
What ever we ate, turkey, ham or a standing rib roast,
T'was Grandma's homemade pumpkin pie that I liked the most.

We still trim our trees with cicles of ice.
Children still wonder, "Have I been naughty or nice?"
"What if I've sometimes been naughty or even real bad?"
"A stocking filled with coal would make me real sad."

Guess one could say, "Not much has changed since I was a kid."
We still celebrate Christmas as our ancestors did.
As Emma says, "The best presents tain't found under the tree.
"It's family and friends gathered around that means the most,
seems to me!"

So cherish you family and friends while they're still around
Tell them you love them; don't be afraid of the sound.
Enjoy friends and family as long as you can, don't you see.
You may outlive them all and be alone like Miss E.

CHAPTER SEVENTEEN
My Classmates and Friends Tell All

Now is when the book will get interesting. Now is the time to share with you the memories and pithy comments and suggestions from my fellow classmates.

That which follows will be the most significant part of the book. On the rest of the pages, you will have the good fortune of reading about the meaningful memories of fellow classmates. Enjoy their trips down their own special branch of Memory Lane and learn from their years of wisdom. Follow their example and either reconnect with old friends or don't loose track of them in the first place. Gold may be lustrous, but a good friend shines brighter than the most brilliant star. O.K. friends, it is now your turn to ponder your youth and let us in on your childhood memories and secrets.

I guess the saying, "You can take the teacher out of the classroom, but you will never be able to take the classroom out of the teacher," really is true.

Marilyn Ahrens Martingilio and her husband Jim are retired and currently split their time between their home in Brookfield, Wisconsin and their summer home in, as Marilyn calls it, amongst the critters in the beautiful north woods near Boulder Junction, Wisconsin. Marilyn is retired from her career as a schoolteacher. She now enjoys playing golf and is into stamping and scrap booking. Marilyn's interest in stamping and scrap booking has been influenced by the many years she spent in the classroom with her students. As I understand, she even teaches classes in the art of creative stamping and scrap booking.

Marilyn Ahrens Martingilio wants to share these, her memories, with you: I was born in Prairie du Chine, Wisconsin on April 11, 1942. My father worked on the family farm and my mother worked at home. My parents moved to Beloit in 1943 to work at Fairbanks, Morse. Fairbanks made diesel engines that were used in the war. After the war, my father started an excavating business that he had the rest of his life. I graduated from Beloit Memorial High School in June of 1960. I never lived in Beloit after college, but have been in Wisconsin all of my life.

It may sound strange at first when you read that my first and probably fondest memory is of "playing in the alley." Our block had a small road, an alley, running from east to west dividing the block in a northern and a southern half. There were no driveways leading up to the homes, but the alley was used to enter garages at the back of the lots. Our block had an incline at the west end, which made for a challenge when you biked through the alley. The alley was not paved, but was covered with loose rock. When new rock was applied in the spring, biking was difficult. I remember splitting my knee open when I took a spill. The bike tires went too deep into the stones and the bike became unstable.

When winter arrived the incline was the best sledding hill in the immediate area. We didn't have waterproof or windproof snow pants or jackets, but we would spend our weekend hours sledding down the hill and walking back up the hill to slide down again. I do remember having lots of hot chocolate breaks and then returning to the sledding hill. We would also sled after school, but it got dark early and so we would have to go inside. We did this for many years without the need for parental supervision.

Let's call the next memory the "Illinois—Wisconsin state line." As you know, Beloit is located on the southern border of Wisconsin, adjacent to Illinois. The street that ran along the border was called Shirland Avenue and that is where I lived. There was no visible sign to indicate that you were at the juncture of two states. The north side of the street was in Wisconsin and the southern side of the street was in Illinois. My best girlfriend from the age of two lived directly across the street from me. Every time we would go to each other's house, we would pause in the middle of the street. We always said we were in two states at the same time. Just today I talked with my friend of sixty-four years, Ginger Reindl.

What kid didn't enjoy "playing Hide and go Seek?" There were other children on our block in addition to Ginger. There was one vacant lot that seemed to be a magnet for we kids. We played ball in the lot and after dinner kids of various ages would play Hide and go Seek.

There was a large Box Elder tree at the side of the lot that was the "goal" or safe spot. The person that was "it" would close his or her eyes, lean against the tree and count to a predetermined number. All of the kids would run to find a hiding spot. The front of the lot had a hill that was always a good place to hide. When the person who was "it" had finished counting, he or she would try to find and touch us. You could try to get back to the tree without being tagged. That brought you "home free" and you would not have to be "it" for the next game. I can remember playing this game when I was a teenager! How times have changed.

Who could forget the "neighborhood television"? When I was little, we had no television. There were no television sets. We played outdoors or did crafts, read and played games inside. When I was nine or ten years old, in the early 1950s, my father surprised us with our first television set. It was housed in a large wooden box and of course the picture was black and white.

None of my neighborhood friends had TV, so everyone would come to our house to watch TV. The piano bench held several kids while others sat around the room. There were no cartoons or programs for children.

I remember watching "Arthur Godfrey's Talent Scouts." Remember, this was a black and white television set with such poor reception that it was like looking through a blizzard. A young talent on the program was a singer named Julius La Rosa. I just loved to listen to him sing! As I recall, he was also very handsome.

Oh yes, the "good Old days" really were good.

Eugene Bohrnstedt, as you will read in his memories, was the band director at Lincoln Junior High School for forty-four years. You have already read of the reverence and respect that I personally have for this most talented and kind man.

Mr. Eugene Bohrnstedt relayed the following to be included in our trip down memory lane: **I** was graduated from Northwestern University in 1940. After teaching in a couple of schools in Illinois, I became the Musical

Director for the Beloit School District. At that time I was responsible for all fourteen elementary schools and two junior high schools for both band and orchestra. Eventually another musical director was hired and the sixteen schools were evenly divided. Then, Orchestra directors were added to the staff and I was able to concentrate my efforts on my first love, teaching students the wonders of playing in the band. During that time thousands of kids took their first steps on a journey that for many lasted until the present day. Sometimes, depending on band need or physical characteristics of a student, I found it necessary to convince a student the he or she really wanted to play a tuba instead of a saxophone.

For the most part, the children that I came into contact with were polite, enthusiastic and well mannered. That is not to say that while my back was turned that a student or two didn't take the opportunity to toss a piece of wadded up notebook paper into the deep recesses of the sousaphone.

I have been known to show up at class reunions with my grade books from as far back as 1944. Perhaps we will have an opportunity at your 50th reunion of your graduation to review your grades.

Brian Brown was one of the many who entered a career of public service. If I remember correctly, Brian served on the Beloit Fire Department team for twenty-five years. Thanks, Brian, you and your colleagues did yeomen service for the people of Beloit. Brian writes: **A**s best as I can remember, my parents brought me home to an apartment above John O'Bryan on Euclid Avenue. One of my first memories was of the iceman and his horse drawn wagon.

As time went on we moved to the 1700 block of West Grand Avenue where we lived in a basement apartment for about three years. I went to elementary school at Gaston on McKinley. I remember friends and I would walk from West Grand Avenue to Shirland Avenue, the Wisconsin, Illinois state line and back just for something to do and to visit one of the basement apartments where they showed free movies.

I don't know if you will remember, but at that time Town Line Avenue was still a dirt road that ran through an apple orchard. I don't remember any homes on Town Line Avenue, just apple trees.

Some years later we moved to the 2000 block of Kenwood, but I still maintained my circle of friends from Gaston. Friends like Bob Gilmore, David Faust, Jim Burden, Marvin Paulson, Sam Bennett and of course Harry

Satness. During the summer we all walked to the swimming pool every day. Sometimes we made three trips in a day. When fall came we got some exercise by walking around town. We never got into trouble, but we had a lot of fun.

When I turned sixteen and was able to drive, we spent a lot of time going to Janesville to go roller-skating. When it got cold enough for the ice rink at Lincoln Junior High to be flooded, we'd spend hours skating and sitting in the little warming hut with the potbelly stove.

I retired from the Beloit Fire Department in 1997 where I worked with Art Palmer and Ken Sands. I will have been married to Susan for forty-eight years by the time I see you at our fiftieth reunion.

Not all of our classmates were born or even started school in the Beloit School District. One such classmate is **Avis Buchanan**. Avis Buchanan Rosser, better known as, Annie Oakley, lives in our hometown with her husband and is a staunch supporter of BMHS, especially the Class of 1960. We all owe Avis big time for the work she does on the reunion committee. You know, it's not easy to keep track of all of us chickens as we scatter from Florida to Alaska, New England to the border between California and Mexico. We even have a classmate living in Japan, so you can see the Herculean job she has trying to keep tabs on everyone. Avis, you will recall, Avis was the little Annie Oakley of our class. As you have read, she proves the song lyric, "You can't get a man with a gun," to be WRONG! Avis writes: **I** was born in Richland Center, Wisconsin and then moved to Milwaukee. For a brief period of time I stayed with my aunt. When she took me back home to my Mom, we discovered that Mom had gone to California to see my father before he was sent on sea duty. It was during WWII and Dad was about to be sent to sea to protect our country.

I remember Mom, her sisters and my grandmother and I all lived in one tiny house. As I look back at those difficult days of the war, it is hard to imagine how they could do what so many war brides and mothers did. My, what they did to keep body, soul and family together. They know what it means to do without and have to work for everything that they had. In other words, they had a great work ethic and a love of God that transcended all other things in their lives.

I don't remember much about life in California. I moved to Beloit when I was in the eighth grade. I do remember hearing my father telling of his experiences of taking the first occupation US forces into Tokyo. He also was at Iwo Jima at the time of the famous flag raising. While I don't remember the day that Dad came home from war, I do remember that mother and I were quarantined with Scarlet Fever. When the quarantine was lifted, we returned to Milwaukee. The day after our return, we were once again quarantined, this time with the chicken pox. Some homecoming, don't' you think?

As far as pets go, I had a toy Cocker Spaniel named Taffy, the color of her coat. She not only was a smart dog, but she was an excellent guard dog, too. For example, Daddy had trained Taffy to close the door behind us when we entered the house. One night Taffy bit my mother on the right leg as Mother was on a sleepwalking trip and wandered into my bedroom. Good ol' Taffy, she knew it was her job to protect me.

The Christmas that I remember the most was the year when my Uncle dressed up like Santa Claus and brought me an air rifle. I was always a bit of a tomboy and loved guns and cowboy stuff. You would most likely find me playing with anything except dolls. The irony of my youth and young adult life is that I had to hang up my six-guns and put my air rifle in the gun case to help raise my two younger brothers. One was ten and the other was fifteen years younger than I. No time for guns and fantasies of the old west when you have to play the role of Mother.

Please permit me to tell you of an E-mail message that Avis sent to me in reply to a message I had sent calling her Annie Oakley. Avis' response follows: "My father started teaching me how to shoot at bottles and cans when I was five years old. At that age, my father would hold the rifle and I would aim and shoot. I was actually quite good. When I was older, my boyfriend decided that I should learn how to handle a 22 Ruger. I missed the first shot at the can because the pistol was heavier than I expected it to be. So, I decided to hold it with both hands. After that, I did not miss the can in the next seven shots. He figured that I was good enough and didn't need any more lessons. Incidentally he ended up marrying me even though I did out shoot him that day."

I couldn't let that response go unanswered, now could I? I wrote back, "I seem to remember a line from a song, I believe it was I the Broadway musical, Oklahoma, that stated 'You can't get a man with a gun.' Avis, my dear, you have just shot that theory full of holes, haven't you?"

Ed Calkins is another of our classmates who enjoyed the movie serials at the Rex Theater and the activities at the various playground summer events. Those shoot-em-up westerns and the Three Stooges movies seemed to be so much better as we lay on our stomachs, head propped up by our hands, didn't they? Today, Ed is a dependable source for E-mail quips and quotations. Ed submits the following thoughts and memories for your edification: **O**ne thing I remember as a kid growing up in Beloit was our integrated school District. It seemed to me that no one ever made any "to do" about it. We were all Beloiters. However, to keep from offending one another, we all referred to each other as "Boots and Patties."

The blacks were boots and the whites were Patties. That's all there was to it. I know that doesn't seem like a big thing now and I didn't then, but it sure kept from hard feelings.

O.K., remember The National Clothing Store? Blue leather jackets were $25. Red Ball Jet and PF Fliers were two pair for just $5. Of course, if you wore them you were really poor.

How about the PTA shows at the Rex Theater every Saturday morning? A PTA ticket for all of the shows was $1.50. Whatever show happened to play, whether it was a cowboy show, a pirate show or a movie about the knights of the round table, we always took hours to reach home from the theater because we played and reenacted what ever we had just seen.

How about gym class in high school when we'd lock Harry Pohlman outside the small gym and he'd stand out in the parking lot blowing his whistle.

In the summer I lived at the swimming pool. As I remember, a season pass cost just $1.50 for the entire summer. I was also very active at the Vernon Playground on Hackett Street. I loved the outdoor movies they would show once a week after the sun went down. We played softball and competed with other playgrounds, i.e. Parker School and Burge School.

All through high school I was a cross between the "Hoods" and the "Pop House" crowds. I wore my leather jacket and did my share of beer drinking; I also hung with other classmates as well.

(Author's comments: Ed was, and I believe from the scores of e-mail messages that we have shared, still is a Renaissance man.)

Michael J. Cuthbert is the son of our beloved band director, Donald B. Cuthbert. Mike was a very talented trumpeter and as the photograph in the photogravure section shows, he was the drum major of the high school marching band.

Mike was two years ahead of us, but he was most cordial to the younger band members. Several years ago I was driving through Washington D. C. listening to the radio. The radio program I became engrossed in was a talk-radio show. It seemed to me like I knew tht voice, but for the life of me I could not place it. Then a caller to the radio program said,"Thanks for taking my call, Mr. Cuthbert." Instantly I knew it was the voice of my fellow band member and friend that I had not seen or heard from for over thirty-five years. As luck would have it, I used my cell phone and got right on the air with Mike. What a feeling to talk with an old friend. Mike has most cordially written the following for you to take with you as you stroll down memory lane:

One of my earliest memories of my father, D. B. Cuthbert, who was the band director at Beloit Memorial for thirty-two years, happened shortly after WWII was over. He had taken the band to Madison for an away game and afterward he and Henry DeBruney, the assistant director at the time and I walked around Capitol Square. Dad at the time wore a uniform hat with "scrambled eggs" on the brim. Three sailors came from State Street, distinctly under the influence. They saw the hat, the scrambled eggs on the brim and staggered to a halt and an anemic "attention" and all three saluted my father. Dad didn't stop walking. He snapped back a salute and barked, "Carry on, men."

Another memory is a Christmas Day ride to Clinton and most of the way back with Clark Swannack, who later died flying his own plane, and Rollie Barnett. We were all about ten years old and didn't tell our folks. It was ten above zero and windy. Clark and I had new Raleigh English bikes but it was Rollie and his hand warmer that saved the day. We'd get down in a ditch out of the wind and warm our hands before getting back on the route. It being Christmas Day, all the stores in Clinton were closed-something we had not anticipated. We struggled halfway back before remembering that Loretta Bradford lived on a farm and they saved us. Bikes in the back if a truck, we came home to amazingly calm parents and hot baths.

Yet another memory was sitting and talking with Barbara Griinke outside her house on a fall evening in October of 1957. We were talking about college the next year and what the future might hold for us. Music on the radio stopped and the announcer told us about the launch of Sputnik. I didn't realize the full significance of that launch until five years later when I got my Master's degree funded, in part, by an NDEA grant to my wife at the time, a grant program forced by Sputnik.

There are, of course, thousands of memories: Dad enforcing a "two Squares only" policy for toilet paper during the War (often violated); the "approval sign" at Strong Stadium for good performances; the morning sessions before school started in the band room with the stereo blasting away; playing for dances with other members of the band and getting paid for it; and the moment in every Commencement when the senior members of the band, having played their last piece with the band, got up in their caps and gowns and fresh-cheeked freshmen moved into their places. It was one of many signs that the force of time was inexorable and that life evolves, but it remains one of the most poignant.

The BMHS class of 1960 was fortunate to have a young lady that looked just exactly like "Gidget." "You look just like Sandra Dee." I am sure Peggy has heard that a million times. She told me the other day that she does relate to Gidget inasmuch as they both liked to act wild and crazy.

I wonder, do you think she has ever been to Paris? Do you think she knows Maurice Chevalier? Do you remember what a sweet, fun loving young lady Peggy was? From telephone conversations and scads of e-mail conversations, I can tell you she hasn't changed one bit. She may have been christened Peggy Fisher, but to her friends and classmates, she will always be known as Gidget. **Peggy Fisher,** from her home in Deltona, Florida, writes: Youth is such a wondrous time of life. It's a time that surpasses all other experiences in life. It is not limited to just a day, like the day you marry, the day your first born arrives or the day your family celebrates your life at your funeral. It is a life-long experience that shapes your life in so many ways. For me, it is filled with happy memories and laughter as I share them with my children. How often I have found myself saying, "I can remember when…" or "When I was growing up we…"

Growing up in Wisconsin during the 40's and 50's probably was not much different than growing up in any other small town during that time period. Like who doesn't know about collecting lightening bugs in a jar? If you grew up in the deep south where there seems to be no lightening bugs, you might not have had this experience. That truly is too bad. We took lightening bug collections a step further. We learned from the bigger kids in the neighborhood that if you squeezed off the end of the bug and rubbed it onto your skin, you too could glow in the dark. Now that I think of it, this was really a gross accomplishment, but it was fun.

Our neighborhood was the ultimate neighborhood. Our Moms and Dads would send us out to play after dinner and say, "Be home by dark." The older kids played with and supervised the younger ones. Well, most of the time. We were all "family." Some times we younger ones had minds of our own and would find our own trouble before the older ones were available to guide us in a safer path of adventure. I'll never forget the time Peter and I set the field on fire. We must have been around five years old. We were only trying to roast marshmallows in a small homemade brick grill our baby sitter had built behind her house. She wasn't home to supervise and as you might guess, we were sure we knew how to handle matches. We were still trying to roast our marshmallows as the fire trucks came screaming in. Boy did we get into some trouble. I think our rear ends were as hot as the fire.

The winters in Wisconsin were cold and my dad, for many years, would take us out of school in March for a month. Off to Florida we would go. There was a catch to that though. He would bring all our schoolwork from Wisconsin with us and then put us in school in Bradenton as well. We had double the work—some vacation for us. He was an avid Red Sox fan and that was the winter headquarters of the Red Sox. We stayed in the same complex as the team and got to know many of the ball players. One evening my brother and I sat around the table with Joe and Dom DiMaggio. I wasn't the baseball fan that my dad and brother were so I was not into the autograph stuff but they sure were. One day I was walking to school past Mickey Mantle's apartment and watched him peek out the shades to see if anyone was around and then tear out to his car and take off. He may have been famous but surely not friendly.

Baraboo, Wisconsin was the summer home of Ringling Bros. and Barnum & Bailey Circus. When they came to town it was the highlight of the summer. The railroad track was down the hill behind our house and we could watch the Circus train come around the corner. When the caboose left our sight we would rush to the Packard and drive to town to watch the train unload and the Circus parade that followed. Speaking of Parades, my father had been in the Calvary when the officers were assigned horses. Tony was his horse and when he left the Army before we moved to Beloit Tony came with him. I can remember as a little girl sitting on the curb of the street waiting patiently for parades to come into view. Soon I could see my Dad and Tony leading the parade. How proud of him I was and how magnificent Tony was. His head was held erect with his tail arched and steady. His parade gait was flawless. The two of them commanded the attention of all.

Our family has recycled as long as I can remember. My grandfather started the Beloit Box Board Company in 1907 and it has remained in the family for 100 years. Paper was recycled to make building board and boxboard and even wax paper. I hated having to take sandwiches to school wrapped in that yucky looking yellowish wax paper. But there was one good thing about the paper mill, that's where we got our comic books free. My mother wouldn't let us waste money, as she would say, on comic books. My dad felt sorry for us and would make up some excuse to go to the mill on a weekend so my brother and I could climb the bails of paper and pull out comic books to read.

Kite Day in Beloit was remarkable. It was a "boy thing" mostly, but it was so much fun watching the beautifully colored handmade kites of all sizes and shapes fly up into the blue sky, bobbing from left to right with the wind. Their multi-colored kite tails were equally as magnificent as they gently fluttered in the wind. The boys, with the help of their dads, (I don't know if this was allowed or not but you know guys) built the box kites themselves and competed for honors in numerous categories.

The Soap Box Derby was another great day. We would all gather to cheer our brothers and neighborhood boys on as they raced down a hill in their brightly colored homemade cars of different shapes. This was another one of those "boy things." Speaking of the Derby and hills, I can remember learning to ride a bike. I do believe my father put me on my bike at the top of a small hill and gently nudged the bicycle telling me to be careful on the way down. Could that be true? Probably not, but then it could have been. Maybe I learned to swim in much the same way. Who knows?

At the age of seven my father moved us to his dream house. He had spent at least a year drawing up plans for the "ultimate house on the river." This was his dream house, but the move was devastating to me. I lost not only my secure neighborhood but also the school I had become accustomed to along with all my school friends. It took several years in a new environment before some sort of comfort zone was reached and then my father died. I have to say that in those last two years I really learned a lot from him. Dad had already taught me how to swim and dive when I was about five years old. I learned to navigate Rock River and learned to hunt, fish and surf board behind our boat. Only Tommy Bartlett at Cypress Gardens had water skis. The next few years were hard and I took solace in the river, my dad's favorite pastime.

Ah, the radio! We had no TV so the radio was the ultimate entertainment. I can remember listening to the Lone Range, The Shadow Knows, The Green Hornet, Roy Rogers and Dale Evans, Hopalong Cassidy, Gunsmoke, Amos & Andy and our mothers listened to Stella Dallas and Perry Mason. And what about listening to Fibber Magee & Molly? Remember Fibber Magee's closet?

Ever play marbles? Well this was a great game during grade school recess. Now these are two words today's kids don't know much about. That is, grade school, which is now called elementary school, and recess which in some schools is nonexistent so there is no other word to describe it except maybe P.E. Anyway, back to marbles. If we didn't have string for a circle we would draw one in the dirt. Our marbles went into the middle of the circle in a plus sign shape and we would shoot them out of the circle with another marble from outside the circle. Each person had his or her favorite beautifully colored "shooter" marble. The one who shot the most out would be the winner. This fun friendly game lead to tournaments in every class up to 6th grade and the top shooters would compete in a citywide tournament. Parents came out by the hundreds to watch the final competition at the college football field. One year I was even a "Marble Queen."

Hopscotch, Jump rope and Jacks (remember the "onsies," twosies, etc.?) were definitely for the gals. While we would be concentrating on our sport the boys would run around acting stupid to try to get our attention. We all roller-skated though. Our skates clipped onto our shoes and heaven help us if we lost our skate key. We could either not get them on or not get them off without a key.

As time went by and we all grew a little older and entered Junior High School it seemed as though our lives still stayed simple and carefree. Our male teachers wore ties and our female teachers wore high heels. We had to wear skirts and slacks and jeans were only a Friday option. There were no "child-proof" caps as no child ever thought of touching their parents or sibling's medicine, let alone ingest it.

The radio was still our contact with the outside world. WGN out of Chicago was the favored station but we all had record players too and the old 78 RPM's had given way to the 45's and Elvis, Johnny Mathis, Nat King Cole, Jerry Lee Lewis and so on. I still have some of these old records but no record player. Now why in the world did I trash the record player and keep the records?

Watching Summer Stock in Lake Geneva was really a thrill. A bunch of us would go whenever we had enough money to buy gas and a ticket. Of course some of us were not old enough to drive so getting permission to ride in a car with an older non-adult presented somewhat of an obstacle at times. Maybe we snuck off without our parents' knowledge, who knows? Can't remember. I do remember seeing Paul Newman in a play however. Who ever would have thought that he would become such an accomplished actor? I look back now and wonder if there were others who went on to become famous.

Hayrides became a real craze during the 50's. We all looked forward to the sweet smell of hay or was it the stolen kiss under a blanket on a cold Wisconsin fall night? Probably a little of both as whether we went with a date or not we all still had a great time. Of course when we got home we were covered head to toe in hay as someone always started a hay fight. I am sure our moms loved trying to get it out of our clothes. We had to dump our shoes out before we were allowed into the house and probably had to pick the hay off our socks too.

Winter brought ice-skating and skiing. We had a huge ski jump in Beloit and it was great fun to watch the competition for many years but as time went on northern Wisconsin opened up many resort areas and we lost our spot in the competition and the ski jump started to decay. Skating would never disappear though as there were many places including the river where we could skate. The Lagoon was my favorite place as we could skate to music and had an area where we could warm up a little on the cold winter nights. We would even bring hot chocolate in a glass thermos to warm our souls.

High School days were exciting for most of us. It meant that we were old enough to drive, date, go to Proms and almost old enough to go off on our own into the wide world. What would high school have been without football and basketball and for some even wrestling? Homecoming and the Military Ball were also among the highlights of the year. Every town needs a Pop House like we had. It was the place to be with its dim lights, sodas, hotdogs, hamburgers and fries. There were rules and if they were not abided by, then you couldn't come back. We had a Wurlitzer jukebox filled with our favorite songs that we fed on a continuous basis. On special occasions we had live entertainment from teens in the town that had formed bands.

Our Marching Band in high school was the best in the State including Colleges and our formations during half time were something to behold. Our band director was ruthless and demanded absolutely straight lines in our marching whether we were on the field or in a parade. We practiced constantly to please him. I often wondered if we ever did.

Have you been to Cracker Barrel lately and seen the Beeman's Pepsin, Blackjack and Clove gum? Sure beats that awful pink slab of gum on the baseball cards doesn't it? Talk about a trip down memory lane. How about candy cigarettes, bubblegum cigars, milk in glass bottles with cardboard lids and the A&W Root Beer barrel in South Beloit, IL? I could fill pages with thoughts and memories of the past. The youth today are in so much of a hurry that I doubt many of them can remember much more than cell phones, the Wii and computers. Who said life was wasted on the young? Not so in our days but definitely in today's world.

Mr. Francis Fruzen: one of our Social Studies and History teachers whom later became Principal of BMHS remembers us from an educator's perspective. He writes: You might be interested to know that your class of 1960 was at Memorial High School when the Knight logo was instituted as a mascot. I believe that would have been either your sophomore or junior year. That grew out of a discussion in one of my history classes in the spring of 1957, and in 1958 the Knight logo became the official mascot of Beloit Memorial High School. So you and your classmates would have been there for that important event.

Regarding your question about the logo, we never had an official logo at Beloit Memorial High up until the time of 1958 when the Purple Knight became our official logo. We were called many different things in the newspaper, including the Stateliners and the Purple. The kids and/or the athletic team members sometimes used the name, "Saints," but that never was an official logo for Beloit Memorial High School.

As I have indicated previously, during a class discussion in one of my history classes we suggested the Purple Knights. That suggestion was put to a vote, and in the fall of 1958 the Purple Knight was used for the first time as a logo and on the athletic uniforms as well as on the cover of the yearbook.

You asked about the whereabouts of Mr. Barkin, Mrs. Reinholtz, Mr. Cuthbert, Mr. Oberg, Mr. Aubrey Wood and Coach Currier. I am sorry to say I believe all of those staff members have passed away.

Next is "Slugger," **Peggy Goetzke.** I am not certain how she got that nickname, but I do remember she was one heck of a softball player. I remember making it to second base on a series of errors in the outfield. That is the only way I would get to second base when a girl was involved. Peggy will always be remembered for her laugh and her beautiful smile. I am sure that some of the boys in the sixth grade will remember her powerful kicks, as Millie Rogers's memories of fifth and sixth grades at Wright Elementary School can tell you. I personally hope that she hasn't changed a bit even though she left me stranded on the dance floor after refusing my request of her hand in a dance at a junior high dance. She may have been the first to refuse my offer to trip the light fantastic, and she certainly was not the last, but Peggy has always been a special friend. I even got to second base with her! Yes, you read correctly. I got to second base. I stole second on a wild pitch in a softball game. (Come on folks, clean up your minds. This is I, the geek who was afraid of his own shadow. Why did you automatically think of something nefarious?) After many phone calls and pleading E-mail requests, Peggy relented and submitted the following to stimulate your memories of the 40s and 50s: There were five children in my family so we played a lot with each other when we were young. Sunday nights we would go down the basement where we had a large console with a radio and record player. We listened to The Shadow (with the lights out) and some other detective stories. It was really cool. When my grandson visits he likes listening to the old time tapes with me and having the lights out too. I think you pay more attention to the story and use your imagination more.

In the fall we would rake up the leaves in big piles and jump into them. We also raked out lines of leaves like they were floor plans for houses. Each of us had our own "house" and we put piles of leave for beds, etc. That kept us busy for hours. We had an empty lot on the corner and the neighborhood children would get together and perform plays. Some of the children would be the audience and other would put on the play. We did our share of playing statue and red rover (if those are the names).

I liked to climb trees and on the roof of the garage next to us and the barn behind us. We lived in a small town but there was an actual barn behind our house. I doubt my mom knew how much I climbed. Maybe that's where my son got his climbing genes.

During the summers there were city programs at the school programs. We played Zel ball there, got paper sheets with some games on them. We played softball too. I remember being hit in the face once. It really hurt. I don't remember getting a black eye.

Another thing, I used to take my younger sisters and brother down to the "Lagoon" and we would fish. The lagoon was a large body of water that connected to the Rock River. I thought it was large, but it was more like a big pond. There were several areas to it, including a cool bridge of the part where it connected to the river. Since we were poor, we had one cane fishing pole that broke down into at least five pieces. Each one of us got a piece and I divided up the worms. I also caught them. For several years I had a night crawler business. I loved catching them at night until my father told me what they were doing when two were stuck together. After that I quit!

In the wintertime we would skate on the frozen lagoon. There was a large building the city opened for us to change into our skates and to warm ourselves. The floor had wood on it for skating and someone played music over loud speakers.

The lagoon was across the street from what was the Fairbanks Morse plant. My father was a machinist there until he died. Among other things, they made engines there.

During the summers I slept on our front porch a lot. It was a large screened in porch. My bed was an army cot. I never had any fears sleeping there. Sometimes I would get early requests for my night crawlers. Occasionally I had frogs too. When we would visit my uncle's farm I scoured the creek edges and captured all the frogs I could. I would hit them on the head with a big stick. One time a herd of cows actually chased us back towards the farm. Since I was the oldest I had to protect the little ones. I helped them get under the barbed wire fence first. I don't know if we spooked them or if it was feeding time, but it was scary. We were right next to them except for the barbed wire. Their feet were much larger when you were lying on the ground and got a really close look.

On the farm we did something else kind of sneaky. There was a four-seated outhouse. I don't remember quite how it was situated now but we used to sit on one side and listen to people using the other side. It was certainly cheap entertainment.

We played for hours in the barn climbing on the square hay bales on the second floor. Just climbing to the second floor was cool. We could spy down on the animals below through the cracks. My uncle Dwight had a bull in the stall by the back door. We never messed with that stall. We put saddles on hay bales in the stall on the ground floor and pretended we had horses. We also watch the fish in the huge horse trough next to the barn. It's a wonder we never fell in. Of course, we climbed on all the tractors and chased the chicken and tried to catch the wild cats.

Best of all were the big family reunions there in the summer. Relatives came from as far away as Texas. I have two girl cousins who are six feet tall! The food was awesome. We could have all the watermelon we could eat. I had a cousin John. I remember he stopped my older brother from throwing corncobs at the horses when we girls were riding them. He was the only person who ever protected me from my older brother after my father died. My brother was a terrible bully. Now I know why, but at the time, he terrorized one of my sisters and me. I finally left home because of him.

In the winter I ice skated at the lagoon, sometimes at Cathy Christensen's house on the river (it was like skating on glass), at Scott Whiteford's house on Turtle Creek, but mostly at Cathy Kitto's house or on the rink at Roosevelt Jr. High. Cathy's dad was a wonderful skater and he taught Cathy. Every year he built his own rink in the back yard. One year I built one too. He was lucky because his yard was flat. Ours looked flat but it went down hill a little first before it was really flat. I would drag the hose out through the cellar door and hook it up the faucet in the laundry sink. I built one layer at a time just like Cathy's father said. It never looked like his did and after a week or so I abandoned the project. It was hard work.

One summer I went to day camp at Big Hills Park. It was boring except when I could catch baby toads in a paper cup when we were supposed to be doing something else. I would put a tiny bit of moss in the cup and then a toad. I thought it was wonderful.

I forgot about the times Cathy Kitto and I spent making candles form paraffin wax and whipping the stuff up with an egg beater and then patting it allover the candle to make it fluffy white. We were quite the pair!

As I reflect on growing up, the thing that stands out most is that we played pretty much without adult supervision. We created our own fun. We don't see much of that anymore.

I've been working on this for a week or so. This better wrap it up. Thanks for prodding me to remember years gone by Don.

Wilma Greenwood Dotter and her husband Bill live in Beloit. Thanks to Wilma's and Avis Buchanan's for their hard work on the Reunion Committee to keep track of the where abouts of the scattered flock of sheep. The next time you see Wilma, give her a big thank you. And to think we guys thought we did the cruising! You'll see.

Wilma sends this on to help you walk down her branch memory of lane: Here are just a few things that come to mind from my high school days: Fayellen Wedige (she goes by Ellen now) had a 1940 Ford Coupe in high school. Several of us girls used to pile in her car and just ride around (probably looking for guys, can you imagine that?) We would each chip in a quarter or so and fill the car with gas and just ride around. We never went out of town, as I think we would have been in trouble if we did. The girls that rode around with Fayellen were: Darcy Holmes, Joyce Markgraf, Linda Jensen, Nancy Bue, Carol Noss, Carole Kelsey and me. Needless to say we had a lot of fun and good conversation on our little jaunts around town.

I can also remember, towards the end of my senior year, I started working in the office at Beloit Foundry a few afternoons a week. When I did stop at the Pop House with friends, the guys of course were all lied up outside, watching us go in. I can remember a couple of those guys saying, "Here comes foundry dust," and they also asked me where my lunch bucket was. It was always good for a few laughs. I can also remember Miss Huffman, my homeroom teacher in high school. She was such a lovely lady and we corresponded with each other after I graduated from High School.

Harry E. Hamilton—I have a soft spot in my heart for Harry. You see, after knowing each other for over fifteen years, Harry and my sister, Diane were married. As related earlier in this book, unfortunately my sister died at age fifty of a series of ruptured aneurisms in her brain. A finer husband and a more loving and attentive father you would be hard pressed to find. Following, you will find some random memories of Harry's life during the 40s and 50s. I'd be willing to bet that many of us have similar memories. Harry writes: **I** remember ice-skating at Lincoln Field. We would put our skates on at home and walk the one block to the ice rink in our skates. I was just a kid, how was I to know that if my skates did have a sharp edge on the blade that the walks to and from the rink would dull their sharpness?

I remember the animated scenes at Brill's Jewelry Store.

I remember dragging my sled to the hills just west of the Beloit Memorial Hospital at the edge of the Municipal Golf Course and how steep the hill was just below the ski jump.

Being a little height challenged, guess who was always stuffed into the trunk of the car to be sneaked into the outdoor movie theater?

In the summer of 1957, two of my brothers and I worked on one of our relatives' farm. Our pay for the summer's long work we did was a used television set. It was our first TV and it was great. (That is if you could pick out the image through all of the snow.)

All of my brothers and I got hand-me-down clothing. One Christmases morning found one "Ace" truck under the tree for the three youngest boys to share.

As you can see, growing up in Beloit in the 40s and 50s had its share of challenges, but we had a large, loving family and that meant everything was just fine. Growing up the six boys in our family shared one dresser and the six of us slept in two double beds. Later on Dad purchased three sets of bunk beds from the Army Surplus store. Finally we each had our very own bed.

I remember when the whole family would pile into Dad's 1934 Chevy, all nine of us, and the drive from Beloit to Hancock or Coloma. Sometimes we even picked up a hitchhiker. Dad would always say, "If you don't mind holding a kid, we are going as far as Hancock."

Kathryn Hallock Hudson presents the following: This may appear to be brief, but this is my most significant memory, a memory that will last a lifetime. Way back when I was in the fourth grade at Powers Elementary school I met Ivan Hudson. We became friends and as time went on we decided to be boyfriend and girlfriend. After the school year ended, Ivan found another girlfriend. We didn't live close to each other, so I was quickly forgotten. As far as I was concerned, after that summer, Ivan Hudson was SCUM! In fact, Ivan was scum until our junior year when we once again became friends again.

On March 18, 1961, Ivan and I were married. From that union Ivan and I brought three children into this world whom have blessed us with four grandchildren. We celebrated our forty-fifth wedding anniversary in 2006. Ivan died from the ravages of a stroke that he had suffered four years earlier. I am proud to say that I married my high school sweetheart.

(Authors note) Kathy was married to Ivan "Butch" Hudson. You may remember Ivan's mother who worked at Al's snack shop as a waitress. She was always so nice and cheerful. For years Butch and Kathryn lived across the street from my cousin Shirley.

Cuz told me that on a warm summers evening that Kathy and Butch accompanied her and her husband Dave on a ride throughout the countryside around Beloit in my cousin's red convertible. Top down and the wind whistling through their hair the next thing they knew Kathy had pulled her tee shirt up over her head. I guess Kathy wanted to give the girls an opportunity to enjoy the warm summer breezes. When Butch saw that in the rearview mirror he said, "Kathy." At which time Kathy turned to Shirley and said, "I always wanted to do that."

Ann Marie Kernland Lamber—Ann Marie was a real heartthrob for the boys at Gaston Elementary School. One young lad in particular, Louis Warren, had a mega-sized crush on Ann when we were in the fifth grade. One afternoon after School, Louis and I walked Ann to her home on St. Lawrence Avenue home. We stood in her backyard when Louis decided to show Ann Marie his athletic prowess. He took one of Mrs. Kernland's aluminum clothes poles and threw it with all his might as you would throw a javelin. Poor Louie, his attempt to impress young Ann went sailing right through one of the screens on their screened in back porch. I wonder if Louie ever became an Olympic athlete?

Ann Marie has been coaxed into sharing with us these, some of her memories: Mr. Lafky used to pace the floor while lecturing our English class, going up and down the rows of desks and back and forth across the room. Since our class met near the lunch hour, some of our classmates brought their lunch bags into the classroom so they could go on to the cafeteria immediately following class. Well, Tom Pilgrim used to bring his huge lunch in a large grocery bag, and as I recall, Mr. Lafky would stop by his desk and snoop inside to see what he might like to be able to eat, himself. As a practicing Catholic, he wasn't supposed to eat between meals.

Then we come to poor Mr. Haglund. He had such a monotone voice. Some days it was extremely difficult to focus on what he was lecturing about and to keep from dozing off in class. My lab partner, Charles "Shorty" Krull and I used to keep track of the number of times Mr. Haglund would say, "Uh."

I am remembering Mr. Don Cuthbert and the band. I think being in the band was pretty much the high point of my days during high school. Mr. Cuthbert always told us that, "If you are going to make a mistake, make it a big one." I recall a time when the marching band was lined up on West Grand avenue for a parade when Helen Larson lost a contact lens and we were all on the pavement on our hands and knees trying to find it.

Then there was senior skip day. Marilyn Ahrens was allowed to drive her family's 1957 Chevy to Chicago for the day. I can't believe her parents let her do that. On the shopping trip, Sandy Jones stopped in front of Marshall Fields Department Store, set her purse down to tie her shoes, and walked on down the street. By the time we got back to Beloit, Sandy's mother met her at the front door saying something like, "You forgot something, didn't you?" A lady had found the purse and called Sandy's house to let them know she would send it to her; proving there are honest people in the big city.

Ice skating on the flooded and frozen field at Lincoln Junior High School was always fun, especially Tuesday night when music was provided over the PA system. Some of the nuns from Brother Dutton School directly across the street from the ice rink, used to come and skate there as well.

I remember ballroom dance lessons at Jack Wolfram's studio.

Our junior high school band used to play for the freshman football games. Eugene Bohrnstedt was our band director. He was a very mild mannered, soft-spoken man.

I remember junior high student council when we were in the eighth grade. My campaign manager was Carol McCarville. What a job she did for me since I wasn't even in school for the elections.

I recall attending a Governor's Conference on Youth where several of us went to Superior, Wisconsin for a 3-4 day event, staying in the homes of the students of the Superior schools. Other classmates attending were Sharon Wheat, Ed McBriar and John Johnson.

Now for the really way back memories: In the fifth grade at Gaston Elementary when Sandy Lindgren (a transfer student from Cunningham Elementary) and I used to discuss politics (I can hardly believe it) and how much we liked Adele Stevenson for President.

In sixth grade I was transferred to Cunningham where I met lots of new kids. One was Gary Fawcett who had the neatest party, boy-girl, in the basement of his house. He had the basement completely decorated.

Even earlier I met Sharon Putterman as we took dance lessons from Jack Wolfram and were in the same class.

Cathy Kitto is a very dear friend. Cathy and Rick and Penny and I spent a lot of time together. Like when we went to Picnic Point in Madison. Cathy sent me a photograph of Rick and me carrying a large watermelon in a blanket. It looked as though we were carrying a body bag. Cathy was a dedicated teacher and principal before she retired and moved back to Mineral Point. It is interesting to learn almost five decades after we last saw each other or even talked, that both of us are extremely interested in children with special needs, gardening and old stone farm houses.

Cathy is fortunate to live in a beautiful stone farmhouse while Judy and I are still aspiring to that treat.

Cathy has spent her entire working career in the field of elementary education from the classroom to the Principal's chair in the front office. Cathy and I share a common passion, the nurturing of Special Needs children. Following Cathy's memories and comments, you will have the opportunity to read an essay that Cathy sent to me that was written by her younger brother, Fred, which he wrote for a high school English assignment. I think that you may see yourself in the mental picture that his writing conjures up and that you will enjoy reading it as much as did I. But let's hear from his big sister first. To make my point that we all share similar memories, you have read of my experience at a YMCA dance. Wait until you read Fred's story. You will see what I mean. But for now, Fred's older sister, Cathy, writes:

My memories of growing up in Beloit in the 40s and 50s are just about perfect in every way. The first thoughts that come to mind are of the great neighborhoods, first when I lived near Summit Playground and then across from Wright Elementary School on Prairie Avenue. As kids we spent most of our non-school, non-sleeping hors outdoors playing softball, hide-and-seek (Ollie, Ollie Olson, All In Free, If you don't come now, you'll be I-T), riding bikes and hanging out at the playground in the summer.

The playground was home to everyone and where we'd spend hours on end playing Swiss Navy, checkers, box hockey, zellball and softball, or making lanyards and sniffing the banana oil that held it together when we were finished. And then there was the talent show—one at each playground—and then the all-city show at Horace White Park. I loved it so much that I became a playground director during my college summers. That provided a different perspective, but one that was just as much fun as when I was a little girl. Maybe it helped me stay in my childhood just a bit longer.

Summers were so safe, or certainly seemed to be, in "the good ole days." We were out from dawn to dusk, returning home for a lunch of egg salad sandwiches and Kool-aide. We were home for dinner at 5:30 on the dot. We didn't even think about being late for dinner, a time when family debriefed the day's activities and usually learned something from Dad. Dad liked to use dinnertime to introduce new vocabulary or challenge us with a number or word puzzle. However, during the day we rode bikes, often seeing how many kids we could pile on and still have someone pedal. Of course no one wore a helmet. I even remember riding around with my baby sister in my bike basket as if she were a doll. Can you imagine that happening today? My mother would be committed!

During the winter we spent every waking hour on the ice rink, usually the one in our backyard. The neighborhood kids showed u- at our house after school, after dinner, and on weekends with their skates over their shoulders. They let themselves in our side door to sit on the basement steps and change into their skates. Knocking wasn't necessary, or even allowed. Then it was out to play "Capture the Flag" or "I've Got It" until Mom or Dad flicked the lights off and on to alert everyone it was time to go home.

Twice, that I remember, a small group of us skated all the way to Shopiere on Turtle Creek. We'd go down to the Milwaukee Road ridge to start our journey and spend the day on our adventure. I don't think I've ever been more exhausted than after a round trip to Shopiere, but it took me two times to learn that I didn't want to do it again.

Ice-skating was such a big part of our family's life that my dad and I used to go to Roosevelt to flood the rink there. We'd go late at night, after flooding our back yard, and I'd climb down into a deep hole where the hose was stored and turn on the water while dad dragged the huge fire hose out to the rink. Dad had ice making down to an art. Occasionally we would put a new surface on the rinks at the lagoon and Lincoln before the Daily News Silver Skates Derby. What a wonderful childhood!

Another highlight of growing up was family night at the Y.M.C.A. My dad would allow each of us to invite a friend to come along on those Friday nights to play in the gym on the trampoline and use the pool. The guys had to wear suits on family night. I never really knew if they actually swan naked when girls weren't around, or if that was just a legend. But we girls always tried to catch a glimpse of some unsuspecting guy who didn't know it was family night. It never worked. But the "Y" was a memorable part of growing up in Beloit.

Life was pretty simple then. We didn't have more clothes than we could wear in a week—usually two or three pairs of shoes at a time—black patents for Sundays, saddle shoes or penny loafers for school and Keds for play. Remember collecting Levi tags from the backs of jeans?

Many of the staples of today were special treats during the 50s. On Saturday nights after we finally got a TV, a bowl of popcorn and a small bottle of coke were shared by the entire family. And on really special occasions, Mom would make a batch of fudge. We loved that. Credit cards didn't exist. My parents didn't buy things they didn't have cash for. We saved up for things we wanted, or sometimes put them on lay-away. So, while we didn't have a lot of "stuff," neither did we have a lot of debt.

Oh for the good ole days! But thank goodness for the great memories.

Just a couple brief authors' comment, (First, if the Kitto family wasn't the closest thing to a real life Ozzie and Harriet Nelson family or the Ward and June Cleaver family, I don't believe one exists. Second. Yes Cathy, speaking as a veteran of a boy's membership to the Y.M.C.A. and a victim survivor of the swimming pool, I can shine the light of truth on that particular legend you spoke of. It was not a legend. Embarrassingly, it was the truth. Not only were we forced to go sans bathing trunks; we were not to wear an athletic supporter either. Another oft spoken phenomena to which I can attest and confirm are the shrinkage properties of non-heated swimming pool water. Did you father know about your spying attempts?)

Fred Kitto's (Cathy's younger brother's) English assignment: My family belonged to the YMCA for as long as I can remember. I would walk down there and back every Saturday, rain or shine, to swim and play in the gym. It was about twelve blocks from home if I cut through the Beloit College Campus. I always took that route because I loved to look at the buildings. They emitted an aura of grandeur and majesty. I always wanted to go to school there, the halls looked so intelligent I just knew that anyone lucky enough to be taught in these hallowed halls couldn't help but learn everything.

When I was in eighth grade I went to my first dance at the Y. The two junior high schools; Roosevelt, where I went, and Lincoln sponsored it. I walked down to the dance and though I hadn't given it any thought, I would walk home, even though it was Friday night. This was 1960, it should be noted, and things were very different than they are today.

The dance was much more fun than I had anticipated. I danced with girls I knew from my school, and even a few from Lincoln, enduring the glare from some of the guys from there. Most of the guys I knew, either from Saturdays at the Y, or from playing ice hockey at "The Lagoon." I knew most of the girls from Roosevelt, some I had known since kindergarten; I knew them too well to think of them as anything but friends. At least that's how I saw them at the beginning of the dance. But most of the others I knew just well enough to say "Hi" in the halls. I didn't know any of the girls from Lincoln.

I found myself moving to the music with ease and a comfortable feeling that wasn't present when my sister, Cathy, tried to teach me the steps to the newest dance crazes over the past week. I think she just wanted someone to practice the "Stroll: or the "Twist" with. I was a reluctant partner for her, not realizing that dancing could be something that I would ever enjoy. If it didn't include cars, it didn't interest me!

Towards the end of the night a slow song started. I thought that was my cue to get a soda and take a break. As I made my way to the lobby and the refreshments, a hand touched my elbow. I turned to see what was the matter. It was Linda Nichols, whom I had known since we were five years old and had played together with for years. She said, "Will you dance with me?"

I had never noticed how pretty she was until then. Unsure of myself, I nodded and we moved onto the dance floor. Cathy hadn't taught me to "slow dance," so I placed my hand on her hip and held her hand up and away so that we were about ten inches apart. I was so tight. It didn't take long for her to start pulling me towards her and soon we were touching! The song ended and I hadn't an inkling of what to do next. Lucky for me, or so I thought at the time, the lights came on, signaling the end of the night's festivities.

I found my coat and made for the door. Outside, the cool September night air rushed over my sweating body and sent a shiver up my back. I hadn't realized how hot it was in there. Cars were lined up at the curb waiting like carriages at a ball. When I realized that I was going to walk home, I was suddenly embarrassed. I'm not sure why, even today. I guess it must have been pride, I don't know. One of my friends asked if I wanted a ride home and for some goofy reason that I have yet to figure out, I said, "No thanks, my mom is coming to get me!" I went back inside to find a phone. There was a line of kids waiting to call their parents for rides.

As I stood waiting for my turn, I wondered how my request would be taken at home. I had never called home to ask for a ride. There seemed to be an unspoken rule at our house that stated, "If you got there on your own, get home on your own." I say "unspoken" because being the third child; I don't ever remember being given a copy of "The Unspoken Rules." I suppose they were things I would have learned had I been paying attention.

When my turn at the phone came, I dialed and Mom answered, much to my relief. She agreed to drive down to get me. I knew I could count on her. I went out front to wait with the other kids. One by one their rides came and they departed until I was left alone on the steps of the YMCA.

Twenty minutes went by and I started to wonder where Mom was. About that time my dad walked up to me and said, "Hi Fred, I've come to take you home."

"Hi Dad," I replied as I jumped down from the steps to join him on the sidewalk. I looked about for the car but didn't see it. That's when I realized that he had walked to the Y and that he was going to walk me home! I sure was glad all of the guys were long gone.

At first, I was very upset and angry, but as we walked, I slowly calmed down, having learned long ago that anger wasn't an emotion that made much of an impression on my dad, especially in his children. As we walked across the college campus, past the library with its imposing columns, past the science building, dark and foreboding, and towards the beautiful fraternities and sororities, I began to see that he was trying to teach me something. Dad liked to use examples to teach us "Life's Lessons," as he referred to them.

Now, all I had to do was figure out what I was supposed to learn from this lesson. It wasn't how valuable his time was, of that I was pretty sure. After all, he had just walked all the way down to the Y to walk me home instead of driving the car. I finally came to the conclusion that he must have wanted me to be more self-reliant, to depend on myself for the things I was able to do for myself. At least I hope that was it. I never asked about that night nor did I ever ask for another ride.

Norman Kopp and **Judy Reynolds Kopp** were two of the fortunate few in our class who knew their future spouses when they were in school together. They dated, fell in love and married. I wonder how Judy felt riding in Norm's street rod going, as Norm says, "faster than the chassis had ever gone?" I know that Norman loved Judy as much as his street rod, but I wonder, was he as fast with Judy as his car was on the track? Well, how about it Judy?

I first knew Norman when we became friends at Sunday school at St. John's Lutheran Church when we were just little tykes. Here is what Norm would like to share about his childhood: **T**his remembrance probably won't appeal to many of the girls of the class of 60. It is how, in those times, a kid in high school could build a pretty fast, pretty "cool" street rod on a meager budget. It was a learning experience that would sustain me for a lifetime, and could only happen when the right set of conditions came together.

In my case, I was born into a family where my father and brother had the tools and knowledge and were willing to share and teach. I had the ambition, naiveté and a small budget from a part time job at Walgreen's. This job had to earn money for college, but of course I also had to have some "wheels."

My dad said, "You can drive anything that you can afford to buy, insure, feed gas and repair." So, before I could drive, I started collecting the basics. First I bought a pair of non-running 1932 Chevy two door sedans for $100. One was in bad shape, but the seller said I had to take both of them. I stripped the good parts from the one in bad shape and sold the rest for junk.

Next I bought a 1952 Oldsmobile Rocket 88. That supplied the engine, transmission, rear end, and steering and hydraulic brake system. That resulted in more 32 Chevy parts taken to the scrap yard. The rest of the components came from frequent trips to the auto recycler, then known as the "junk yard."

If you knew the guys at the yard, you could wander around the yard till you found what you needed. There was a good measure of "cut and fit" with saw, hammer and welder. The steering and suspension had to be modified to keep it safely on the road at speeds the chassis had never seen before. But in the end I had a muscle car engine to make it go fast and hydraulic oversized brakes to make it stop fast as well.

It did OK at the drag strip. It was the second fastest street rod in Beloit from the stoplight, and even carried me to college for years to cone. Not to mention, it was the car I owned when I was dating my wonderful wife, Judy, nee, Reynolds. Part way through college I sold it. I have lost track of it, but if I could find the car today, I would trade my Beemer for it.

Mr. James Lafky: English teacher extraordinaire and faculty advisor for the Increscent, the school newspaper. James Lafky was and still is a mentor for those of us who love the written word, both prose and poetry. At the time of this writing, Mr. Lafky is ninety-one years old and living in La Crosse, Wisconsin with his wife. I spoke with Mr. Lafky in early August of 2008. He was as sharp witted and sounded just as I remembered him so many years ago. After our conversation I sent him excerpts of this book's manuscript as well as excerpts from "Childhood Dreams Really Do Come True." By return mail he sent me a brief hand written note and a copy of one of his books of Poetry. He also volunteered to proof read and edit the manuscript for me inasmuch as he still remembered my penchant for verbosity. Below you will find a copy of the book's cover, as well as a photograph of Mr. Lafky when he was in his mid-eighties and a copy of the author's bio, which appears, at the end of the book. Enjoy and remember.

Mr. James Lafky was one of those teachers that you either loved or you hated with every fiber of your being. For me, Mr. Lafky was an outstanding instructor. An objective critic and an honest to God mentor. When Mr. Lafky was asked his favorite color; his sarcastic response was, **"Black Crepe."**

As you have read, some of our classmate's editorial comments about some of the teaching staff, I am sure that you quickly came understand that Mr. Lafky was the most respected instructor that many of us had. His influence on our fertile minds was much more pronounced than we realized at the time. That is why he is so revered by many of us. I wish I could sit down with him now, share a cup of coffee or tea and just pick his brain clean. What a mind! What a man!

Mr. Lafky probably knew more about the Bard On Avon than the Bard himself. Do you remember the hand-constructed replica of the Globe Theater that Mr. Lafky was so proud of? Can you imagine what Gloria Steinem would have said about men playing the roles of women? She would have burned more than her bra. Maybe that is how the original Globe Theatre burned down.

Mr. Lafky had a way about him that made studying the Classics almost enjoyable. I don't know what he is pointing to in the photograph on page 32 of your 1960 yearbook. As he pointed out various features he would probably have told the girl students in attendance that there were no ladies rooms in the Globe Theater. Like many of our classmates, I even took an after hours class from him on the Iliad and the Odyssey. Was Homer a real person or the penname for "Anonymous" or a host of unknowns from the late of the 9th or early 8th century B.C.? How about it, Mr. Lafky, got an answer for that question?

Yes, James L. Lafky was an unrelenting critic of our written words. The way he went through red ink, he must have bought it wholesale or had a brother-in-law that could get him a sweet deal on case quantities. Richard, David and I, just to mention three, were Mr. Lafky's most frequent victims of his sarcasm and embarrassing scolding. That withstanding, Mr. Lafky was the best teacher I ever had! He is and was my respected mentor. If he remembers me, I know he would be shocked to hear that, but it is true. It is because of Mr. Lafky's prompting that this sixty-six-year old retiree has taken up writing. Thank you sir, I owe you one.

A Brief Biography of James Lafky

According to the Minnesota State Records, I was born July 27, 1921 in St. Paul, Minnesota and was delivered by the very first female pediatrician in the state. At age five I went to live with relatives in Saskatchewan. Canada. I completed my elementary education there and I mention this factoid because it was there where I learned to read and to develop a warm relationship with the concept BOOK. And for more than eighty years I've been addicted. I even collected a small library while serving in the U. S. Navy.

At the time I entered the Navy I was twenty-0ne, weighed one-hundred eighty-five pounds and stood Six foot one-and one half inches in height. Because of prior experience, I went into the service as a "rated" man and I was a medic for three years, four months and seventeen days. My last fourteen months provided me with an invasion experience, one typhoon in the China Seas and endless juvenile military ceremonies.

After four or five years and attendance at two different universities, I became credentialized, licensed, and considered educated. From thence I went forth across the limitless miles of the republic in search of a career. After teaching for thirty-six years, fathering six children, marrying twice, I've been retired for twenty years, most of which I've traveled. At this time I am still writing prose and verse. (At the time Ventrographics II was written, Mr. Lafky was ninety years old). As a little sidebar, I sent a copy of Childhood Dreams Really Do Come True and asked him to critique it for me. I received a hand written note from him in today's mail in which he once again informed me in no uncertain terms that I am still verbose and included too many different topics in the book. I wish I had sent him the manuscript prior to sending it to my publisher. Good ole Mr. Lafky; ninety-one years old and still teaching. God love him.

I have asked for and have received written authorization from Mr. Lafky to copy and sharing one of his poems with you, a classic example of his quick wit and rapier like mind, so, read and enjoy. Oh how I wish I could sit quietly in the corner and listen to him read his poetry. His mind is so sharp, much sharper than ever was mine or will it ever be.

I didn't realize it until I pasted Mr. Lafky's photograph at the top of the previous page that my favorite hat and coat are exactly like that which Mr. Lafky is wearing, A Greek fisherman's hat and a Khaki field jacket. I wonder if he has a fountain pen behind the flap of his left breast pocket? I sure hope I look as good as he when I am in my late eighties.

After you read the poem below which is representative of Mr. Lafky's quick wit and rapier like mind, sit back, close your eyes and see if you can picture Mr. Lafky standing at the front of the room in his well-worn Harris Tweed sport coat with the suede elbow patches. I'll bet that you can.

To the colon

Today we take up the colon,
children:
not the lower, descending one,
nor an upper ascending,
(if one there indeed be),
but rather the intransigent
vertical snake-eyes of the
punctuation gamble!

Genealogically speaking,
The colon is derived from
The classic rhetoric (and prosody)
Of the sacrosanct Greeks,
Indicating a section
Of a period and used, of course
To provide balance:
One colon, two cola.

Conventionally speaking,
The colon has a variety of
Useful functions not the least
Of which are the following:
To signal a series, an explanation
Or an example, to announce, perhaps,
An extended quotation:

After the salutation of even
An insignificant business letter,
The colon is appropriate.

In Biblical references,
And whether prayer or curse,
The colon separates
Chapter and verse.

In time designation
Done numerically (the Arabic):
A colon ought to separate
The minutes from the second's tick!

:

Mr. Lafky died on November 27, 2008.

Kurt Leininger, a close friend of Don Marske, has an interesting story to tell about growing up in Nebraska in the 1940s and 1950s: **I** have no memory of my first years on the planet in Washington DC since I was two or two and a half when my family moved back to Nebraska.

One of my first memories occurred sometime in later 1948 when I was four and a half years old. I remember Mom walking with me to the corner grocery store in Lincoln as Mom pushed my baby brother Joel in a carriage. We parked Joel outside in his baby carriage and went inside. Shortly, we were alarmed to be told that a baby buggy was rolling down the sidewalk, and we rushed out to retrieve it. I don't remember anything more than how panicked Mom was and that we saved Joel and the carriage from going into the street.

In the same timeframe, I remember one morning running to the front window to watch Dad leave for his law class. I ran right into the window breaking it and cutting my forehead. (I still have a small scar.) Mom and Dad sat in their car in the driveway, with me in the back, debating whether to take me in for stitches. They decided not to. Funny, isn't it that I remember more about the time setting in the back of Dad's car listening to him and Mom debate my fate than I do about the actual accident.

In 1949 Dad joined a progressive law firm in Columbus Nebraska. We moved into an old house with a basement. I remember getting a punching bag as a Christmas present and practicing with it down in the basement. I also remember jumping off the garage roof, just to prove to myself that I could do it. So, I remember the cellar and the roof and not very much inside the main house other than when I was sick with German Measles and also Whooping Cough, both of which were going around in the early 1950s, we had a dog named, "Lucky." After a couple of years, we moved into a larger house, which is where I grew up. It was a two-story house "four-square" with a hip roof. It was a Sears Kit house. Yes, back in the 1920s you could purchase what we would now call a "Do it yourself house kit" The house was located near the elementary school that I attended, but sadly to say, a few years ago, expansion of the school necessitated the demolishing of our one time home.

Like most boys all over the country, I was in Cub Scouts during my years in elementary school, but instead of Boy Scouts, I joined several good friends who had formed an Indian dancing club. We made our own costumes and danced for local organizations and parades. We had a mentor who knew official dances of the Ta Tanka Indian Tribe in Southern Colorado. It was on this tribe that the club was based. It was most certainly an interesting experience. It was fun, you might even say, unusual. I know it might even seem to be a strange thing for a boy to do, especially to you city slickers on the East coast and the Left coast.

Yes, living in the western planes, I was fortunate to be able to go on fishing trips with my father and brother, Joel. Those were my most memorable events, along with playing baseball. I credit my choice of an engineering (water pollution control plants) to those days spent fishing in a stream, even drinking from it when I was thirsty.

My first car of my very own was a 1951 Mercury four-door sedan, (a "James Dean Mobile") which I drove only in the summer of 1961 before going to college. I sold it to a good buddy for a couple hundred bucks and later heard that it died on him after a year or so. Cars weren't made to last more than ten years back then.

In high school I sang in operettas, the most memorable of which was the role of Sergeant Luther Bills in South Pacific. If you saw the play or watched the movie, you will remember that Sergeant Bills did a belly dance. Well, so did I. It was a site to behold.

But the event of which I am most proud was as a sprinter with our 880-yard relay team, which qualified for the Nebraska State meet in the spring of 1961. We went to the state meet where we saw two Omaha high school athletes working out for their events. They were Gales Sayers and his brother Roger who was a champion hurdler. I didn't compete against either of them, but they were there on that field, and so was I!

Jeff Maiken, a fellow classmate, splits his time between his home in Austin, Texas and his summer residence on Washington Island in Lake

Michigan. Jeff tells me that he was the owner and manager of two wineries California following his days in corporate management. Now that Jeff has retired, Jeff's passion is an organization that was once called "Camp Heartland," now known as "One Heartland." One Heartland is a global effort to make life a little bit better for kids afflicted with HIV/AIDS. In an E-Mail conversation we had a week or so ago, Jeff revealed that he had just stepped down as President to give someone else an opportunity at the office.

Jeff wants to share with you the following: To me the biggest change that has occurred in the last fifty years is the communications revolution. As children, we had to find things to do—make up games—work together with friends to expand the fun activities. We didn't even have a television until about 1952 so the radio was our medium of choice. Today from television to IPODs to text-messaging etc., children have the opportunity to move much more quickly in learning things, expanding the friendship radius and the like. And yet, it has at the same time taken away the joy of learning, something that you found out yourself through trial and error, initiative and the confidence to believe in oneself. The key today with young children is that with the tremendous advantages and speed of information, we should establish ways and boundaries so that they do not lose some of what we had. Young parents today will say that things are different. You can't let your child run free. There are child molesters, and bad people that will take advantage of the children. Guess what? I am sure there are not any more violators today than when we were kids. But we had developed an independence and self-confidence that helped to ameliorate those bad things.

It is like the tourist who comes to New York City for the first time and wanders aimlessly down the busy streets, stopping every so often to look up at the skyscrapers. Unfortunately this tourist is easy to spot and becomes a victim. The New Yorker walks briskly down the street knowing exactly where he or she wants to go. He or she doesn't look up or down, but straight ahead towards the destination. You know what? They rarely become a victim.

Now for some of my fond childhood memories:

Living in Madison, Wisconsin, on the shores of Lake Monona from my birth until I was nine years old, a large hill leading down to the water gave us the opportunity every winter to build a toboggan slide. There was absolutely no need for us to go anyplace else to have fun. Our hill and our toboggan run provided exciting fun for all the kids in the neighborhood all winter long.

Even though I am certain that the mothers would look out of the windows from time to time, we certainly had no feeling that an adult was even supervising us. In the summer, of course, the lake became a large swimming pool. I remember pleading with my father to allow me to use the canoe. He finally gave in with this proviso: Before I could take the canoe out by myself, I had to prove to him that I would swim across the lake. To prove my swimming ability, Dad paddled me in the canoe to the middle of the lake and dropped me in. Apparently I went down once, rose to the surface and went down under the water for a second time. Thank God Dad jumped in and pulled me to safety. As I dried off, shaking partly with fear and also with shame, Dad said, "I guess you're not ready to use the canoe alone yet, are you? Don't worry, you keep working on you swimming and you will learn. I'll bet that by the end of the summer you will be able to use he canoe." Sure enough, I did learn to swim and I did get to use the canoe all by myself later that year.

Growing up in Beloit, I cannot ever remember my parents driving me anywhere for an activity. I had a bike that allowed me to go everywhere. I found the YMCA. I rode on Clinton Road out in the country. I rode my bike to Roosevelt Junior High School, etc. My world was really pretty large for a nine or ten year old boy. When Saturday came, my Mother would ask what I was going to be doing. I would tell her of the planned adventure for the day and she would say, "Be careful, watch carefully for the traffic and come for lunch or dinner."

Freedom to roam, the opportunity to build self-confidence and the beginning of an inner self that said I could do anything if I worked at it hard enough.

I can remember one summer when Gary Richard, Chuck Everill and I created a baseball league in our back yard. We had a whiffle ball and bat and large reams of paper to keep tack of hits, batting averages, home runs, strikeouts and walks for each game. I suppose now, kids would probably buy a program for their game boy or computer.

Permit another reminiscence. A memory of a summer a long time ago that occurred while staying at our summer place on Washington Island. Door County, Wisconsin is a prominent sour cherry growing area. In the summertime picking cherries at the peak of their ripeness was critical. Many Mexican migrants came up to the island for about three weeks after having picked peas or beans the previous three weeks further down the peninsula. I was probably six years old and was playing around the house when Mother came roaring down the driveway, obviously upset about something. As soon as she had stormed through the screen door, she grabbed some poster paper in one hand and grabbed me with her other and said, "We are going up the road." All of the way she was mumbling to herself, I think she was saying a few choice words that she would have punished me for saying.

We pulled up in front of the Log Cabin, a hamburger joint run by a very large and tall Icelander, Karl Anderson. Mr. Anderson was missing two fingers from his right hand. On the way into the hamburger joint, my mother ripped a poster off of the front door. It was later that I was to learn that the poster said, "No dogs or Mexicans allowed."

Mother, who was about five foot four inches tall stood there almost belly to knee caps looking up at Mr. Anderson with fire in her eyes like I had never seen nor have ever seen since that time. Mother yelled at him as she wagged her finger at him, "Karl, I am ashamed of you. You are a disgrace to the Island for putting up such a sign and not allowing the Mexican workers to come into the restaurant." She went on and on about human rights and Karl just stood there like a deer caught in the headlight of an oncoming car. He just stood there and took it. He was speechless. He said not a word.

"What's more, Mr. Anderson, not only has your sign been taken down, you will gladly put up this sign to replace yours, understand?" Mother's sign read, "Mexicans welcome." At the bottom of her poster she added a postscript inviting the Mexican workers to come down to our beach to swim inasmuch as they were banned from the public beach.

She turned around and we started to walk out of the restaurant when she stopped and over her shoulder said. "And I expect you to do as I say or I will run you off this island." Finally, Mr. Anderson had the wisdom to speak, "Yes, Grace, you are right, I am sorry."

Do you think that experience made an impression on a three foot five inch tall boy? Unfortunately, with all of the social progress we have made in the last fifty some years, I am not so sure our thinking has really changed; we just don't put signs up any more.

Our southern California dude, **Don Marske,** has lived in the state of Oregon and most recently in Orange County, California for over four decades. He has been a huge help with this effort. Not only did he offer to be the proofreader, and I can tell you there was a lot of proofing to be done, he convinced me that there are an awful lot of us Baby Boomers who would appreciate a positive read about their youthful days and that I should consider opening up the opportunity to contribute childhood memories to not only classmates, but to friends of classmates reared in the 1940's and 1950's. What a great suggestion.

Don has stopped hanging ten long enough to write the following to share with you: **I** was born and raised in Beloit in a tiny house on the Westside not unlike many in our class. I was the oldest of four siblings. My father worked for the Milwaukee Railroad as the local ticket agent at the old depot on State Street that is now the site of the Beloit Daily News. My mother was a stay-at-home mom who took in laundry and some daycare to help with the expenses. At the time, I didn't sense we were lacking for anything; however, it was a clearly a very different life from what my children experienced and certainly what my grandchildren are currently experiencing.

My parents, like many in those early days, struggled to make ends meet. The growing family necessitated expansions to the house to which I remember helping my father. With scrap lumber he had access to from the railroad and the volunteer help of his friends from work, he was able to provide us with a comfortable if spartan home. I am still appreciating what he was able to do in a time when loans for homes were harder to qualify for and certainly encumbered more cautiously.

As a kid in Gaston Elementary, I remember being a bit of a rascal. A neighbor reportedly characterized it as an angel with a broken wing. My mother would get notes from the teacher about my mischief including putting the girls' pigtails in the proverbial inkwell. Every time this happened, my mother would march me in to the teacher and ensure her this would not happen again. I would eventually win the teacher over when I would bring her a fistful of fresh cut lilac blooms in the spring. I'm afraid many parents today would blame the teacher for sitting me behind such clear distractions.

In the latter years of elementary school, I recall that one of my mischiefs included lifting a comic book from Bach Drug Store without paying for it. When my mother asked where I got the book, I had to confess whereupon when she marched me down to the store with my ear firmly pinched between her fingers to return it and apologize to Mr. Merritt Bach. Wow! That sure cured me of that mischief.

At Lincoln Junior High I started to use some of the things I learned from my father about building things. Like many other boys, I built a couple of Soap Boxes (never won a race). I also built a small runabout boat from plans I prepared from a book from the Public Library. Since these projects required resources for materials, I took on Beloit Daily News and two Milwaukee Journal Sunday paper routes. When I asked about taking on the second Sunday paper route, my mother said it was OK as long as I was done in time to go to church. To ensure this, my father helped by taking me out after he got back from meeting his Sunday morning train. My father was never very generous with his praise, but I'm sure he felt good about his kid who would periodically get a pay-as-you-go delivery from this big Beloit Lumber Company truck with a couple sticks of wood as the boat evolved over the summer of 1958. It's weird the things you remember.

During the summers between junior and senior high school, I had the opportunity to work on Uncle Fred's farm Up North. I don't know how this happened, but I suspect it was something my father felt would be good for me. In retrospect, they were two of the best summers of my life. On the 160-acre dairy farm, I learned a lot about what work and community was all about. The farm experience taught me how to drive and operate farm equipment, gave me an incredible mechanical background, an understanding of basic animal husbandry J, and an understanding of what real physical work meant. It also included two milkings a day, seven days a week. No exceptions! To this day, that commitment still has an impact on me.

Beyond the work of the farm, the experience also exposed me to what *community* was all about. My uncle was a leader in the local Township. He also had skills as a welder and he owned a thresh machine—an amazing piece of equipment that separates the oats from the chaff (straw). Because of his position and skills, he was constantly called on during the year by friends and relatives for help with equipment repairs, redemptions for bounties on gophers (my job was to count the number of heads in the coffee can), or to just talk local and national politics. My favorite time was threshing season. During this time, Uncle Fred, Aunt Viola, Cousin Roger and I would travel from neighbor to neighbor in the spirit of the old threshing bee. For a small fee, Uncle Fred would fire up the thresh machine and all of us, neighbors included, would gather the bundles of oats from the fields and bring them to the thresh machine where they would be magically converted to sacks of oat grain and a huge pile of straw. In the meantime, the women would be preparing a huge lunch and dinner rendered from the freshest produce of the farm. I never worked so hard, ate so well, or laughed so hard in my life. It was especially sweet when we all gathered to do Uncle's farm.

As I entered Beloit Memorial, I still needed resources to finance the fun times. Being too old to peddle papers, my mother helped me get a job stocking shelves at Bach, yes, the same, Drug Store. She accompanied me and vouched for me in an interview with Penny Finger's father (of Finger Pharmacy after Merritt Bach retired). It was a job I held for several years. During that time I got to know Penny and also developed a fond friendship with Judi McCarthy and her family. I can't help observe the irony of going from unstocking the shelves of my younger days to stocking them during high school.

I wasn't all that active in high school. No sports—too small, no music—no talent, and limited free time—the job. However, I enjoyed attending all of the events including the dances, proms and formals. I'm sure there is more than one female classmate who will remember, with some distress, this geeky little guy who tried to get first dibs on the prettiest girl in the class for the prom by asking them for the date six weeks in advance. I Gotta plan ahead!

Going to college was a given for me. My mother was certain I was going to be a doctor or lawyer, but I opted for engineering. I had no idea how I was going to pay for it. I must have assumed *they* would somehow take care of it. Boy, I was so incredibly naïve. Knowing I needed a job for expenses, I used my resume from Finger Pharmacy to secure a similar job at a pharmacy on State Street. However, as I related to my father in a phone call after work, I couldn't get back to dorm in time for my dinner meal. He replied, "Well, you better find another job." Wow! That hit me like a brick. It was the first time I realized that they couldn't help me. So much for my naiveté. Cured! Fortunately, I quickly found a job as a food trucker at our dorm's Commons. The University was very accommodating with my financial straits. I owe so much to the University.

At the end of my sophomore year, I had an opportunity to go to Alaska for a summer job with the Alaska Highway Commission as a surveyor. How exciting! It had the potential of paying for all of my college expenses, but would my parents let me go? When I asked, my father said, "Can you take me with you?" That was about the coolest thing I ever heard my Dad say. On the day we were to leave, I was sitting in a thermodynamics final exam while three of my compatriots were in a car on the curb waiting to go to Seattle. Needless to say, ALL I could think of was getting in that car. That was confirmed on the 4th of July when I got a letter from my father that said, "You got a letter from the University—I'm not sure what it means but I don't think it is good." Well, it wasn't. I flunked the exam and it was the course that would require me to sit out a semester. That winter I pumped gas on the swing shift in South Beloit where I vowed that would not happen again. I went on to get my BS and MS in Civil Engineering. Again I owe so much to the University.

Joan and I were married in 1964 in Beloit at the Second Congregational Church on my return from a 2nd summer in Alaska. We went on to raise three beautiful children. Now after 44 years we are retired and grandparents to five with finally—time to reflect. Where was this time when we needed it earlier? Today I compare the struggles that Joan and I endured growing up and just getting through the 44 with what we are doing for and to our children and grandchildren. As parents we naturally strive to provide a better life for our children. In many respects, we have succeeded, but in other areas, I often wonder whether we did or are doing them any favors with all of our provisions. In our quest, we have wrapped them in helmets, kneepads, elbow pads, safety belts, Purell, and SPF 40 sunscreen. We give them choices—white or chocolate milk, eat now or later, and Dora or Star Wars? And, their bedrooms look like a Toys-R-Us outlet. With all of this instant gratification, how will they learn to deal with adversity? Whoa! This is a big philosophical question that has spawned many "discussions" with Grandma. The discussions continue but I remain certain that we cannot provide our children with their every whim and wish. At the risk of sounding like my father who told me he had to walk five miles to school in the dead of winter, uphill both ways, we need the wisdom and discipline to select the right times to say, "No," so our children can learn the value of what they have without short changing them their childhood

One of the first classmates to respond to my request for shared memories of his youth was **Jim May** one of my best friends both at school and at church. Even though his given name was James and most people called him Jim, his closest friends, including me, called him Howdy Doody because of his freckles and the way he wore his red hair swirled atop his forehead. He was even a little bit high-wasted and walked a bit like Howdy. I could always count on Jim. He was and is a true friend. My friend, Jim May, AKA, Howdy Doody, currently live in Galveston, TX with his wife Lorna. He is retired from a career in information technology and is enjoying that exasperating game of Ah (expletive deleted), better known as golf. He says that way he keeps from getting under Lorna's feet. I've heard all sorts of excuses for playing golf, Jim, but that takes the cake. The last time I saw Jim was at our 20th class reunion. Then he looked like William Shakespeare. I wonder whom Jim will look like at the next reunion. I sure hope he doesn't look like Clarabelle.

In 2008 Jim and Lorna stayed in their home in Galveston while hurricane Ike blew his way through their area. Luckily their home suffered very little damage, but the weather raised havoc with all aspects of living. Jim, you and Lorna need to find a safer place to live. At least the snow up here doesn't cause a lot of property damage.

Howdy writes: **I** was born on a farm in Mitchell, Iowa in late March and my mother said that it snowed the day I was born and the doctor couldn't get to the house for three days because of the drifts. I guess that is as close as you can get to being born in a barn! This was the home of my grandparents and I remember it very vividly. The farm was a small 40 acres but it seemed to do very well for grandma and grandpa. I don't remember them having a cow but know they did at one time. I do remember the horses and the chickens and the pigs that they raised. We had an old tire swing hanging from a very large oak tree in the front of the house. I loved the garden that always had something good to eat when I grew old enough to know what was what. I could be found out there picking and eating raspberries, strawberries, peas, beans, onions, and almost everything else that they grew. I climbed the apple trees, helped grind horseradish, feed the pigs and chickens, gathered eggs and got hen pecked a few times. There was also good sweet corn in the late summer. We always ground horseradish when we were there in the summer and took enough back home to last a whole year. For those that like it, they should help with the grinding and find out how much stronger it is and how it will make you cry a lot faster than any onion you cut.

The farm never had an indoor toilet or hot and cold running water. The water in the house was from a small pump at the sink. You had to keep some water on hand to prime the pump before it would draw. The kitchen stove was a coal and wood burner, so it took time to get ready to cook. Of course grandpa made sure it was properly stoked before bedtime so that there were still coals in the morning to get things going. Somehow that stove made some fantastic cookies and grandma always made a lot of them. There were two earthen basements in that house. One of them was really for storage of all of the foodstuffs harvested from the garden. There always seemed to be onions, beets, potatoes, and I can't remember what all else. Grandma also canned beans, peas, corn, all kinds of jellies and jams that were kept in the second basement, which was close to the kitchen. She made lots of bread.

We lived on the Wisconsin-Illinois line (Beloit and South Beloit) for almost all of my first 18 years, but went to Iowa every summer when dad had vacation. It seemed that it was always timed for us to be able to help harvest hay in July. When I was real young, this was an interesting thing, but as I got older, I found out it was a lot of work. All of the mowing, raking, bailing and loading into the hayloft was done with horses. There never was a tractor on the farm until grandpa couldn't do the work himself and he rented the land out to other farmers.

Although we weren't there very often for it, I can remember helping cut and shock oats and then grandpa had another farmer with a steam driven reaper come and we ran the oats through separating the oats from the straw. Of course the straw was also saved as bedding for the animals. I can remember only once of helping harvest corn and getting all of it into the corn crib. I do remember getting into a lot of trouble when I would get into the corncrib and shell corn when grandpa didn't want it done. There were times when he wanted it and I didn't seem to be helpful and then when I tried it was the wrong time.

Anyone that likes a rhubarb pie would appreciate being able to pick fresh rhubarb, help cut it and cook it so that you could really enjoy the fruits of your labor. Grandma and grandpa had lots of rhubarb and it was another food that I would go pick and eat raw when I got the chance. When I picked strawberries or raspberries, it took a long time to fill the bucket, because I generally ate more than I put into the containers that grandma sent me out with. There is nothing better than picking and eating something fresh from the vine.

One memory of attempting a trip to Iowa was during the winter. As always, we left very early in the morning only this time it started to snow as we left Beloit. By the time we got to Brodhead, a blizzard had developed and dad wasn't able to see the road. I think we were driving about 20 miles an hour. When we finally got to a stop sign in Brodhead to turn on to a more major road, dad had to open the door to try to see where the road was. He decided that it just wasn't going to work and turned the car around and we headed back to Beloit. When we got back home and the car was unpacked, mother was missing a boot. The only time the car doors were open was at that turn around and from that time on, whenever we drove that way, the stop was know as the place were mom lost her boot. Today, they have changed the roads and that stop is no longer there.

Although I have many other thoughts and memories, I'm not sure how much more is wanted. I could talk about the Boy Scouts and the fond memories I have of my many years in scouting. I still try to see my scoutmaster every time I am back home. I spent 45 years in data processing and worked on many types of machines that kids of today would have no idea what they were. They have more capabilities in an IPOD than we had in a whole computer room.

If there is one thing that I could hope for with all of the younger generation, is that they would look for some of the simple things around them and not just be wrapped up in all of the latest technologies? Get out and enjoy the outdoors, play in the grass, visit a farm and learn about the animals, go swimming in a creek, overturn some rocks and look for the things that live under them. We enjoyed the simple life and there was a lot to it.

An author's postscript to what Jim has shared. Jim was very active in the scouting movement, earning many prestigious honors for his dedication to scouting. In addition, Jim had a most interesting family. He had a sister a year or two younger than he and a brother a couple of years younger than his sister. In December of Jim's senior year in high school, his mother gave birth to another child, only to be followed eleven month with a set of twin siblings. Ouch!

Donald Edward Nelsen: Alas, I am not the svelte lad of 170 pounds that many of you may remember. Today I am the poster boy for the ravages of a sedentary lifestyle, fine dining, and genes from my mother's side of the family running rampant. The **fa**ct that my wife is an excellent cook and the fact that one of my hobbies is gourmet cooking, couldn't have anything to do with my Santaesque physique, now could it? I must admit that every ounce of the rotund body beneath the Calabash pipe and the snow-white beard is real. In the age of indebtedness, at least the belly is paid for!

Even though I have lived up to my forty-year-old nickname of "Lard Bucket," I am determined to get as close to my high school graduation weight as possible before our reunion. Time will tell. Yes, I was successful in making a sow's ear out of a silk purse.

Next to my lovely wife, or seven children and so far seventeen grandchildren, my passion for the past forty-one years has been growing from a self-absorbed, wanna-be Santa to the real Santa Claus that I am today. A great man, Abraham Lincoln, once said a simple sentence that is every bit as meaningful as his famous Gettysburg Address. The brief sentence you are about to read has become my mantra, my reason for living: "No man ever stands so tall as when he stoops to help a child."

Almost ten years ago, two boys, one age eight and the other age ten opened my eyes. Their request for a happy home-life without bickering, cursing, hitting and the like as well as their request that Santa bring food to the people who are starving, was a louder wake-up call than would have been made by a thousand buglers blowing Reveille. At that time I had over thirty years of Santa experience beneath my ever-enlarging belt. Those young boys delivered a Christmas Epiphany to me to end all epiphanies.

You know, Christmas isn't just for kids. Please permit me to share with you a synopsis of a visit I had with a charming ninety-two year old lady living in an extended care facility. A full account of my visit with Miss Emma can be found in ***Childhood Dreams Really Do Come True.*** As I left Emma's room that evening, I made her a promise that I would relay her message to, as she called them, the younguns.

Emma is a self-described "Oldest Orphan in the country." Her husband was killed on D-Day at Normandy and the twin boys they had were killed in Korea before they married. So, Emma has no grandkiddies, as she calls them, and was a very lonely old lady when I first talked with her. To honor

Emma's wish and Santa's promise to her that December evening, you have already read my homage to her. Her message contains only twenty-four or twenty-five words, just two short sentences that contain the wisest truth learned over the span of her ninety-two years. Please read Emma's gift to your family, and read it often. Teach your children the heartfelt warmness, the sincerity and the absolute truth of Emma's words.

My wife and several of our children live on the periphery of the Amish farming community near Lancaster County, Pennsylvania. We admire the Amish folk for their work ethic, their devotion to family, their love of God and especially their Shoofly pie, pork and sauerkraut and their home made Birch Beer. But most of all, Judy and I love listening to the Amish folk speak. Colloquiums such as: "Throw down the stairs my hat."

"Make outen der light."

"The hurrier I go, the behinder I get,"

"Why ist der more horses asses dan der ist horses?"

"Kissin' wears out, cookin' don't."

"A plump wife und a big barn never did no man no harm."

"He who has a secret dare not tell it to his wife." and the best one of all, "Why ist ve get too soon oldt und too late schmart?"

In 1995 Judy and I purchased a yellow Mustang convertible with a 5.0-liter V8 stick. The license plate read, "O2B18." One of our favorite spring, summer and fall rides was through the Amish farm country. The Amish riding in their horse drawn buggies were always a delight to see, even if they were a traffic hazard. More than once I was forced to drive over and through a deposit if "Horse Apples" which necessitated washing the car before I put it in the garage. I loved the fresh air, especially in the spring. The aroma of the organic fertilizer being spread on the fields prior to plowing took me back to my childhood. "Put the top up, roll up the windows and turn the air conditioner on for God's sake. I can't stand that foul stench." Judy commanded. I, on the other hand, really enjoyed the smell and insisted that she should just enjoy what I called "Natures Perfume." Who do you suppose won that battle? An ice-cold mug of Birch Beer says you know the answer.

Judy Kepner Nelsen, Folks, I'd like you to meet my wife Judy. In addition to being my best friend, my wife, and my soul mate, she is also the best thing that has ever happened to me. I must confess, I have had a pretty good life and she has made it even better.

Even though I have spent hours going through old scrapbooks, shoeboxes filled with photographs and even an old trunk, I could not find a high school graduation picture of my bride. Finally she confessed that many years ago she had conveniently destroyed her high school graduation picture because she says she was so skinny that she looked like Olive Oil.

Judy tolerates my, as she calls it, masquerading as Santa Claus, but she has made it perfectly clear that she is not old enough, thankfully is no where near plump enough and not the least bit inclined to dress up in a long ruffled apron and ware a ruffled bonnet on her head. "And besides, there is no way in hell I am going to let my hair go white!" Do you think she might be the daughter of the Grinch?

I must say, however, she supports me one hundred percent in the work that I do for special needs children afflicted with Autism and Cerebral Palsy. Thanks, Babe. Even though you wouldn't be caught dead dressed as Mrs. Claus, you are still the best!

The light of my life, my best friend, my spouse, and my soul mate and without a doubt the best thing that has ever happened to me is perfectly capable of talking for herself, at least that's what she tells me. Sometimes the off the wall things she says reminds me of the George Burns and Gracie Allen radio and television routines. When that happens I just say, "Say Goodnight, Gracie." Our children grew up hearing me utter those words often. They heard me say that so often, in fact, that when Lori, our eldest daughter had a daughter of her own, she named her Gracie.

I was absolutely sincere when I told you that Judy is the best thing that has ever happened to me (and she didn't tell me to write that). She still comes up with some of the classic Gracie Allen witticisms as well as some of her own, like "Jackassic, a blinger of a headache, or Denmarkish when she refers to my ancestral heritage. God only knows what secrets she is about to reveal. However, I am confident that they will be interesting and may very well strike a chord with you. One other thing you should know about Judy. She a cardiac and radiology trained nursing executive, so you can imagine the persuasive arguments she makes for my attempting to reduce my girth. The significant question is, however, "Do I listen?" You bet I do if I know what is good for me!

After skillful negotiation, coaxing and significant pleading, (Babe, as I call her) has finally agreed to share with us some of her memories: Even though

I did not grow up in the Midwest as did the members of the BMHS class of 1960, and even though I am (as Don says, "The old gray mare") only eight months and eleven days older than Don and have just a tiny bit a little more experience with the 40s than he does, he asked me to share my memories of growing up on the Pennsylvania New York State lines to add an eastern perspective to your midwestern memories.

I grew up in Sayre, Pennsylvania, a small railroad town on the Pennsylvania, New York state line on the western shores of the Susquehanna River. You may remember having read about the Susquehanna river when approximately 100 miles down river, the Three Mile Island Nuclear plant was in the news. Even though Don and I grew up over a thousand miles from each other, Don's memories and my memories are very similar. I guess the common factor was the times we lived in and being raised by good, dedicated, God fearing parents and extended families of three and four generations.

I lived in a neighborhood made up of many families with children of similar ages. We made our own fun. I was the oldest of six children and our closest neighbor had only one child. She was my favorite playmate. Looking back, she was very much like the Aimee Godesy character on the TV series, The Walton's. When Patti came over to play she was always in a dress with matching shoes and socks with all the curls on her head in perfect placement. Patti may have dressed like Aimee Godsey, but she certainly had a much more pleasant personality than did the TV character. Believe you me; Patti never went home looking as pristine as when she came to our house to play. She sure did have fun at our house.

I remember one time Patti came over to our house to play before she was to go visit her grandma. She was decked out in the finest of matching clothes, including the nicest new coat that I had ever seen. We decided to put on a magic show for our parents and brother and sisters. Two of us held up a blanket. Patti bowed and curtsied politely in front of the blanket before walking behind the blanket and climbing into a large wooden box with a hinged lid. We said some magic mumbo-jumbo and dropped the blanket onto the closed lid of the box. Patti appeared to have vanished. Now, to complete the illusion, all we had to do was make her re-appear. Up went the blanket and more magic words were uttered. We dropped the blanket and Patti sprang up from the environs of the box, only to catch her new coat on a nail inside the box, creating a large three-corner tear in her coat. Her mother was just a little bit more than upset. Needless to say, Patti was not allowed to play with us for several days.

My brother Bill is six years younger than I. He was the only boy out of six children. (Don't you feel sorry for poor Bill having to wait for five sisters to finish in the bathroom?) Bill was a beautiful baby, too beautiful to be a boy. When he was a toddler, my sister, we called her Trigger, and I dressed Billy in girls clothing and took him to the corner soda fountain. We'd sit him on a stool and tell everyone that he was our baby sister. How we tormented the poor kid. No wonder he has grown to be somewhat of a recluse and a hermit.

I have often wished that our children could have grown up like we did. We could walk anywhere, any time of day or evening and be perfectly safe, not a worry in the world. We didn't worry about our safety and our parents didn't worry about our safety either. That's not to say that they didn't wonder what kind of mischief we would get into, especially Billy.

In junior high and senior high I was a "Rah-Rah," you know, a cheerleader. A highlight was the weekly sock hop after every home game. The entire school always attended.

Sayre was a football town and I mean the entire town. Friday nights, game night, the entire town would shut down and congregate at the Lockhart Street Bowl. We were always assured of a full house. In northern Pennsylvania, some of the later games were played in the frigid cold.

The night before a home game we would have a pep rally with a bonfire and with joined hands we would have a snake dance through town. At every intersection we would stop and lead a cheer or two for the residents who had gathered to see the snake dance. The local policemen would stop traffic, no matter how long it took us to move through the intersection and never complained that we were disrupting traffic. There was no traffic; everyone was standing at curbside to watch.

We were always trying to out do our rival school, the Athens' Bulldogs. Our school was known as the Sayre Redskins and we were proud to flaunt it. None of the local American Indians in the community objected to the name of our school's mascot and neither did any of the local veterinarians when it came to the Athens Bulldogs.

Two or three days prior to a pre-game bonfire, students would pile boxes, scrap lumber—anything that would burn- in anticipation of the night before the big game's bonfire. The night before our rival school's pep rally and bonfire, the night before our annual rivalry game, a group of our friends and I snuck into their stadium and ignited the fodder intended to be the fuel for their bonfire the next night. I don't remember ever seeing a bonfire quite as large as was that one. Even the smoke from that bonfire smelled sweet. It was awesome. (I cannot imagine this innocent thing being one of the pyromaniacs who destroyed their rival's bonfire material then complained because they beat them 17 to 12.)

We were so proud to have gotten over on them until game night. The Bulldogs took a big bite out of our Redskin's gluteous maximus, beating us by a score of seventeen to twelve. To make matters even worse and even more humiliating, they stole our beloved sign of our mascot, the Indian chief, from the wall of the press box, painted a line through it and painted the final score on the sign. Then they had the audacity to attach the sign to the grill of a car and drive all over Sayre blowing their horn and jeering at us. Too bad I was due to graduate the following spring. I would love to have been part of the payback the following fall.

My mother and father were very strict. Each of the older siblings had chores to do and we were expected to do them no matter what school or other activities we had on our plate. When I was on the varsity cheerleading squad, my sister was on the junior varsity squad. Before we could leave the house to cheer at a basketball game, we had to wash and dry the supper dishes. I washed and my sister was to dry. That is the way it was supposed to be. However, after wiping only one or two dishes dry she suddenly developed what I called "dishpan diarrhea," threw down the dish towel and left me to both wash and dry if we didn't want to be late for the game.

My family was not rich by any stretch of the imagination. That is we were not financially well off, but in many other ways, we were the richest people that I knew. How my parents could afford to purchase two cheerleading sweaters at $50 each and two cheerleading jackets at $75 each year is beyond my ability to comprehend. In the 50s, for a family of modest means, let alone a family of eight, $250 each football season was a lot of money to be taken from the family budget. Thanks, Mom and Dad.

I have already given you a clue as to how important clothing was to my sister and me. (Don will tell you that clothing still ranks high amongst my priorities inasmuch as I spend a lot of time and money in Talbot's. In addition to Talbot's I am a weekly or sometimes twice a week frequenter of Borders and Barnes and Nobles book stores.)

My sister and I were the same size so we could share our wardrobes. We didn't have a lot of clothes, but what we did have was of the very best quality. Mother taught us "If you buy cheap, you get cheap." That's why I shop at Talbot's. Mother told me to do it. So Don, if you have a problem with my Talbot's fetish, talk to my Mother.

One of my favorite memories is of my father coming home on Valentines Day with presents for my sister and me. He had purchased them on his own while on a layover he had in Syracuse or Buffalo on one of his routine train trips. He had purchased a skirt for my sister and the most hideous jumper I had ever seen for me. My jumper was gray with a flowerpot filled with flowers appliquéd on it.

I hated that jumper with a passion, but I wore it proudly because my daddy had thought enough to buy it for me. He was so proud when I would walk through the front door upon my return from school in the afternoon wearing that hideous jumper.

Don asked me if I remembered my first driving experience. I sure do. My father had inherited a 1942 Chevy. You know, one of those cars that were heavier than is a tank today. It had only 10,000 miles on the odometer and still had its original tires. The amazing thing is that Dad gave me the car in 1959 when he inherited it. It had a standard transmission with a stick shift on the floor, a hand operated choke that had to be adjusted as the engine warmed up, and a heater that was either off or blasted hot air from Hades out of the heater box.

I must have been a traffic hazard, or at least a sight to behold, as I tried to keep the car in a smooth, constant forward motion. I don't think that I ever did. (In fact, in 1995 Don and I bought a brand new yellow Mustang convertible with a 5.0-liter, V-8 engine and a five-speed stick shift. Don became frustrated with my jerking starts and turned over the responsibility of teaching me the finer points of shifting up and down shifting to one of our sons.) I know Don loves me but I also know that he will never volunteer to teach me anything about any mechanical device.

Let me take you back to my first car. I probably should not admit this, but each time I would back the car out or our driveway, I knew when I had gotten far enough into the street to turn and try to go forward when I would back into the telephone pole across the street. You know, they don't build cars like that any more. The hundreds of times that I smashed into the telephone pole with the rear bumper of the car, not once did the bumper dent. I even lost control of the car one winter's evening when I went around a corner, slid on some ice and banged the left rear quarter panel into a tree. I had scrapped a large section of bark from the tree, but there was nary a scratch or dent on the fender. Try doing that today and see how many hundreds of dollars damage will be done.

When I was graduated from high school I went immediately to nursing school at the Arnot Ogden School of Nursing in Elmira, New York. I have never been sorry for my choice of careers. Sometimes I wonder if I shouldn't have gone to medical school, especially when I had to teach some of the younger physicians the facts of patient care, cardiopulmonary resuscitation, electrocardiography and electrophysiology. (Time for another of my interrupting Author's notes. On more than one occasion Judy would come home after a particularly trying day of instructing, as she called the, "Sexual Intellectuals" to master the techniques of effective CPR. When I asked her to explain what she meant by "Sexual Intellectuals" shed said, "You know, blanking know it alls.")

Looking back on my youth there are some things that I did that would upset me if I knew any of our children had done the same thing. For example, when I was in my pediatric rotation at Buffalo Children's Hospital, we used to go to a local bar to dance and to drink beer. We always sneaked into the dorm by the always-unlocked back door until one night when it was locked. I wasn't about to go through the front door of the dorm and risk getting caught.

My dorm room window was directly across from the intern's quarters with about four or five feet of space between the buildings. To think, that four or five foot span was three stories above the ground and I was petrified of heights. I guess I had one or two too many Rolling Rocks that night.

As you might expect, I am a real white-knuckled flyer. That doesn't stop me from flying to some exotic or even some not so exotic location for vacations.

Raymond "Pete" Peterson was an exccellent musician in high school. I particularly liked to listen to him in dance band when he would play the

Glen Miller type trombone solos. I am pleased that Pete is still involved with music. Hold that tiger!

Pete adds a couple of twists to our trip down memory lane. He'd like you to know the following about his wonder years: While my dad was in the service (Army) during WWII, my mother and I stayed with her parents at their home in Brookfield, Wisconsin. One of my more vivid memories is a band rehearsal. Mother played the violin and bass in a dance orchestra. The band rehearsed at my grandparents' home and I got to listen and was treated royally by the rest of the musicians. The bandleader was a sax player named Don Murdow. I also remember being at some function the band was performing for at Pewaukee Lake.

There also was a fighter pilot that had come from the same Brookfield neighborhood. At least one time, he flew over the area in formation with several other planes and did the wing wave. I remember they flew extremely low and it was awfully loud, but thrilling.

After the war, we moved back to Beloit, across from Cunningham school. That was the edge of town then. There was an abandoned stone quarry west of Mary Street, between Merrill and Liberty. It had a small lake and an intriguing cave. We have a four-generation photo taken by a professional photographer in front of the cave. The place was strictly off limits because at least one kid drowned there, so we were there every chance we could sneak away. I don't remember getting caught, but I had a hard time explaining to Mom and Dad my soaked shoes and other telltale signs. The quarry later was converted into a landfill (a dump) and was a great place to hunt rats and shoot bottles with our bb guns.

I started in the music business in second grade with accordion lessons. My first teacher was Dallas Helms. Shortly after I started, he was drafted and my teacher was Shirley Clark. The studio was run by Clinton Voight and was on State Street I believe—2nd floor. Clint is still around and active in Star Zenith Boat Club. Eugene Bohrnstedt. The junior high band director talked me into taking trombone lessons during the summer between 5th and 6th grade. (I wanted to play drums until I saw that all you got to start with was a practice pad and sticks.) The first group to I played in to perform outside of a school function was with was "Tony and His Tigers." You are probably aware that Tony' Scodwell's latest gig was playing and managing the Doc Sevrenson Orchestra. Tony played a concert with the Rock Prairie Big Band last spring. I play trombone with that group so it was a nice reunion.

I am still active in several bands, including the Rock Prairie Concert Band. Eugene Bohrnstedt is a percussionist with the Band. I tell anybody that will listen that: If it wasn't for music, my wife would be dead and the dog would be in bad shape. That's enough of my yammering; I look forward to seeing all of you at the reunion

Daryl has been a life long resident of Beloit and has been an active participant in the Reunion Committee. As you have read, it is amazing, isn't it how similar Daryl's and my memories dovetail? At first Daryl was reluctant to send in his memories, saying that he wasn't a very good writer. Well, Daryl, I am glad tht you let me talk you into sharing your memories because they were heartfelt and right on the money. Thanks from all of your classmates.

"For the book, these are my humble memories of growing up in another century," says **Daryl Porter:** It may seem like a cliché but it WAS a simpler time, then. Growing up in Beloit in the 1940's & 50's was less hurried, certainly less electronic and much simpler. I was born in 1942 to parents who were older than many of my friend's parents. My mother was 38 and father was 43 when I was born. So if your math is good, you have figured that my Dad was born in 1899. Hard to believe, now.

Both of my parents worked at the Freeman Shoe Factory, in the "shop" as they called it. My mother stopped working when I was born to care for me and resumed working at Freemans later when I started school. Incomes earned by Freeman employees were not the best, but through good economic times as well as the not so good times, Freemans kept their employees working. If they couldn't provide enough work for a full five day work week, then they'd work four or even three days per week. Freemans was dedicted to their workers and would not hear of layoffs. My folks kept working and drawing some income to help keep the family afloat. I'm sure there were times when it was hard for my parents financially, but I wasn't made aware of it. And, I didn't know how other people lived.

The neighborhood we lived was on the far west side of Beloit in the last block of Roosevelt Avenue. We lived in a pretty modest home that I never liked because of the style. It was shaped like a traditional barn and had peeling yellow paint until covered with an ugly green shingle-type siding. My parents bought the house during the Depression for about $2,000 after the previous owners had lost it because of hard times. Mom and Dad paid off the mortgage many times only to borrow more for the next home improvement. It's my understanding that they didn't have running water or indoor plumbing when they bought our house. But, that was before my time.

I had my own bedroom which I liked because I knew many other kids who had to share with a sibling. The bathroom was located in what used to be a small bedroom on the second floor. Our water pump was in the basement. The basementat during my youth, seemed to me to be a small square cave that went out from under the house and under our driveway. We had a septic tank in the front yard until public utilities were available and there was a stoker type furnace tht I remember when I was very young. Frequently the hopper had to be filled with coal during the heating season. Of course, when coal burned it produced heat as well black smoke and "clinkers" which had to be removed from the furnace at least once or twice each day. Our small fruit cellar in the basement was always filled with jars of stuff my mom had canned.

Our neighbors were working class or retired people and the houses were mostly small frame homes. When I was real young there were large vacant lots between the houses and open fields beyond our block where we played, as children. As I grew, so did the neighborhood, filling in those open spaces with new but very modest homes. The only kid my age in our block was a pretty blond girl, but my interest in girls came much later.

Our closest neighbor to the west had a really decrepit single story house that needed paint badly. An old couple lived there, with their blind adult daughter and a son who brought home bottles in brown pager bags, every day. They must have been really poor but I don't think I knew that then. They had an outdoor toilet and no running water in the house. I understand that was not all that unusual just a few years earlier. They had a outside hand crank pump that we kids liked to use when old Bill wasn't looking. Even though they did have electricity, they had an ice box for food storage that required the delivery of a huge block of ice every few days. Delivery of ice may have been by horse drawn wagon earlier but I only remember an old faded red pickup truck. We neighborhood kids would follow the truck up the alley and beg for chips of ice to suck on like candy. That was quite a treat on hot summer days and the driver usually cooperated.

I had two brothers, Russ, whom my parents called by his middle name, Duane and Dean. I really didn't know them very well when I was a child because Russ was 18 and Dean was almost 15 when I was born. Yes, I know what I was. I've often said that if there had been birth control then, I wouldn't be here now.

My first recollection of Dean was of him in his Navy uniform just before going off to the south Pacific. Luckily he never saw any action because the Pacific War ended while his ship was half way across the Pacific.

My first memory of Russ, who saw a lot of action, was when he came home at the end of the war in Europe. At home, I had overheard much talk about the war. I remember Dad reading aloud comments found in the Beloit Daily News and broadcasts on WBEL radio. I had herd Mom and Dad talk about my brother Russ whom had been seriously injured several times. Each time he was hospitalized until his wounds had healed suffuciently that made him eligible to be sent right back into combat. In later years, he rarely talked about what he went through while in North Africa, Sicily, Italy and I believe on into southern France and/or Germany. I'm sure those weren't pleasant memories. I first remember Russ when he came home at the end of the war, charging onto our front porch in his army uniform. At 3 years old, I didn't know the difference between a US soldier and the enemy.Of course, I didn't recognize my own brother. So, he scared the hell out of me. It took a while to calm me down.

I remember fondly listening to the old radio as a child. There were no televisions around Beloit until I was around eleven years old and we didn't get a TV until I was about fourteen. We visited friends or relatives to watch there TV. Maybe that was when I began to realize there were have's and have not's."

For years, we just had a console model radio that had a record player inside. I believe it may have been a Philco brand but I'm not sure about that. To play records, you had to pull out the top of the lower front portion of the front which was where the speakers were concealed. Having done that, the speakers would then be facing diagonally toward the floor. I enjoyed many hours preschool and in later years, after school in front of that old radio.

I would lay on the floor much of the time looking at those speakers as if there was really something to see. I loved to listen to my favorite radio shows: The Lone Ranger, Hopalong Cassidy, Sky King, The Shadow and Tom Mix. I was devastated when Russ told me that Tom Mix was dead. And it was true, he had died years before I was born. Other radio programs that I heard were some of Mother and Dad's favorites, like: The Great Gildersleeve, Fibber McGee and Mollie, the Jack Benny Show, Red Skelton, Amos & Andy, Gang Busters and there were so many others.

Some of those old radio programs are replayed today on local radio stations and on satellite radio. They're fun to hear again, but I understand that some young people today don't understand the story lines and the sound effects used in those days. But, that was our "high tech."

I'm not sure how old I was at the time, but for a time I enjoyed listening to "Scholz Business" on WBEL with Bob Scholz. That radio show was on during the day so I must have listened to it during the summer or while home from school when sick. I don't know why I liked "Scholz Business" so much, but it must have been Bob's knack for finding unusual guests like a frequent cowboy band. Years later, Bob told me that that group was a wild, unpredictable bunch. That must have been what I liked.

When I was five I was reluctantly taken by hand to Cunnigham Elementary School where my older brothers had gone. Like some other children, I cried the first day when my mother started to leave. The Kindergarten was in a new section on the south side of the building and it was great. I don't recall my teacher's name but I really liked her. Many years later she was involved in educating elementary teachers like my wife, Mary at UW Platteville. Our Kindergarten room was very large, not just because I was little, but it really was huge. I believe it was as large a two or three regular sized school rooms. There were a lot of great things there to do like taking a nap on my little rug.

We stayed in school half the day, either going in the morning or in the afternoon. I don't recall whether I was AM or PM but that separation continued throughout our elementary years. What I mean to say is we continued with 2 first grades, 2 second grades, ect. until we finished the sixth grade. These separate classes of the same grade seemed a little competitive which may not have been the best way to educate.

I don't recall the names of my first few teachers but we will never forget our Principle, Miss Daisy Chapin who finished her career at the same time we finished the sixth grade. She and I didn't always see eye to eye but many years later I got to know her better while visiting her at the Caravilla facility where my parents would also come to live.

I only remember my teachers from the fourth grade on. Fourth was Miss O'Brien and she was beautiful. Fifth grade was Mr. Lee and it was his very first year teaching. We were quite found of Mr. Lee and at the end of the year we heard he was to teach sixth grade the next year and we wanted to continue with him but that was not allowed. The other class got him for the following year and we got Mrs. Pollman. She was nice but she kept saying, "People, People, People" to quiet us.

When I was about nine or ten I had my very own crystal radio set. It was very primitive, I guess somewhat like the very first radios. There were some electrical do dads on a flat board with a small metallic rock. I believe there was a single earphone. A needle was then moved to touch the rock and if I hit the right spot, I could hear music or talking from a radio station or what may have been a one sided conversation of people talking on short wave radio sets. I spent many hours in my room on that crystal radio.

The memories are flooding into my mind and I am afraid that I may bore you with a minutia of details, so permit me just a few more quick glimpses into my childhood, adolescense and teen age years. Who could forget the Saturday "Kid" movies at the Rex Theater.

Then, I headed off to Lincoln Jr. High, met other kids from all over the West side, walking all over town on my own, trips up north fishing with the family, hanging out at Al's Snack Shop, working in brother Russ' St. Lawrence Auto Body Shop, starting to drive, getting to know my brothers, off to High School and meeting the east siders, working at McDonald's Drive Inn, going off to business school, going to the Pop House and the Italian American Club, working at the First National Bank, Penneys, George Brothers, going to the DAL House and Frank & Mike's, getting married to Mary, joining Jaycees and later Lions, having daughters Amy & Beth, starting Gentlemen's Threads, Grandchildren, and much more. Well, I guess the rest of my life will have to wait for another book. We've run out of space in this one. Later….

Sharon Putterman Caplan: Thanks to Sharon's father, I was given dozens of orange and apple crates with which I made two Soapbox derby racers. Mr. Putterman encouraged me to build a fast car, but alas, I was eliminated in the first race my first year and in the third race during my second year. Thanks anyway, Mr. Putterman, we sure had fun trying. I hope you remember the aroma of fresh fruits and vegetables and fresh ground coffee that greeted your senses as you walked into the store. I'm getting hungry for a nice juicy plum as I think about it.

Sharon writes: I wanted to get right back to you; thanks for caring enough to do this. **A** few of my memories that I hope you enjoy reading about include: I felt special being part of the Beloit community with MANY outstanding memories.

—Bringing a menorah into elementary school each year to share the story of Chanukah with my fellow classmates.

—Being the only kid in junior high school to bike after school to work at her father's grocery store.

—Dancing rock and roll for the first time with Punch Wienke while our classmates formed a circle around us clapping

—Leading the high school's student council in "adopting" an orphan from Europe and chairing fundraisers in order to support this endeavor.

—Being "kicked" out of Jack Wolfram's dance class for talking too much!

—Spending many hours in the hallway during second grade for talking too much! (Does it appear that there seems to be a habit forming?)

It was a time of innocence and naivety that was so special. I loved every minute of it!

Ruthrae "Penny" Rowbottom Koth—"Penny" lived on the east side of town and I lived on the west side. In spite of growing up on opposite sides of Rock River, when we were ten years old we both appeared of a television talent show broadcast from WREX-TV, Rockford Illinois. Little did either of us know that when we got to high school that we would become sweethearts form the summer between our freshman and sophomore years all the way through our senior year.

Penny lives in Largo, Florida where she is an accomplished and award-winning elementary school teacher. I believe she also teaches Dance and Baton in her spare time. Penny's father was Comptroller of the Freeman Shoe Corporation. I think one of the reasons that her parents approved of me was that I wore nothing but Freeman shoes with the exception of my stinky PF Flyers in gym class.

Now for Penny's memories: **P**robably one of my fondest memories from childhood through high school was my father standing out in the middle of the night, cold as all dickens, with the garden hose in his trembling hand, spraying water on the packed snow so my brother and I could ice skate on it come Christmas morning.

My next memory is also of my father. He took on the responsibility of driving me to Janesville every week for baton lessons. We had such good talks and sang, terribly, a lot. He never seemed to mind being Penny's dad. (Author's note: How could he, Penny was a special, very talented little girl)

Many memories of skating on Rock River whether it was for an ice show or just for fun.

I remember having to deal with my mother being a teacher at the high school and how restricting it seemed.

The bonfires at the pep rallies were something our children would never see or take part in. It was such fun to cheer, talk with old friends and of course for us…check out the guys. (Author's note: I didn't realize that my steady girlfriend of three years was scoping out the guys. Man is that a shot to the ego!)

I really felt privileged to be the head baton twirler. I often think that that had a great deal to do with my getting my scholarship to college and many other opportunities I otherwise would not have been afforded.

Since I am a teacher, I thought as a child in elementary and middle school that it was great to be able to walk to a neighborhood school. Of course high school, being the only one, we were driven. Many a day I thought we wouldn't make it when my mother ended up going down the big hill that led down to the river, sometimes sideways, backwards and going in circles.

Mandy Teare submits the following to hopefully remind you of similar happenings in your life: **I** grew up outside of Chicago—a family of four living in a two-family house. My parents, my sister Madeleine and I lived on the first floor level and our neighbors, Blake and Faber O 'Hagan, another set of loving adults for my sister and me, lived on the second floor.

Blake was a home economics teacher in the Chicago School District. She taught me to sew, paint by numbers (remember them?) and much more. One time, we made a dress for me—purple with rows of rickrack in pastel shades of pink, green, yellow and white. It was a secret! When it was finished, I put it on and went downstairs to surprise my family. They were amazed that I had made it all by myself (or almost by myself!) How proud I was. Blake gave me lots of self-confidence and taught me skills that I still use today.

Her husband, Faber, owned a bookstore. I spent a lot of time in his bookstore where my life-long passion for books was kindled. He used to let me come in the store, sit on the floor and read away. No charge. He also gave me lots of books. I especially remember the Landmark books series. They are still available on eBay and elsewhere. I particularly liked reading books about Joan of Arc, Daniel Boone, Clara Barton, Abraham Lincoln, Benjamin Franklin—a few of the people that I read about. I loved biographies.

We had no TV back in those early days. We spent our days outside. I remember an annual carnival that my friends and I created. For a penny, kids could buy popcorn or lemonade; visit the Fun House (wet spaghetti dripped over their heads. We told them they were worms or snakes), get pushed on a swing, have their fortunes told and other fun activities. I don't recall that we ever needed any adult supervision.

Those years were a time of discovery. We planted tomatoes and flowers along the side of the house. I remember seeing rabbits eating away at our crops and being fascinated. Mom made tons of chili sauce. Does anyone make that anymore? (Author's request: Mandy, my mother and her sisters used to make homemade chili sauce, too. Unfortunately their receipt died with them. If you still have your mother's receipt, I would sure appreciate a copy of it.)

We had a funny routine we went through when we wanted to play with a neighborhood friend. I would stand outside his/her house and yell: Oh, oh Betsy…, Oh, oh Betsy in a singsong voice. We didn't ring the doorbell or call first on the telephone. This method of summoning a friend seemed to be the custom in our neighborhood.

When we finally got a TV it was an instant success in our home. Blake and Faber said that after we got the TV they never saw us outside again.

"I Love Lucy," Milton Berle, Sic Caesar, Imogene Coca, Howdy Doody, Kukla-Fran and Ollie, The Today Show with Dave Garroway, were classic early TV shows that I remember so clearly.

I went back to this suburban town a few years ago for the first time in forty-plus years. I certainly had never driven there as we moved to Beloit when I was about fourteen years old, but the car seemed to know the way I found my house and elementary school right away.

Later I had lunch in a small restaurant in the center of town. After I had finished eating, I mistakenly exited through the wrong door into the lobby of the building where the restaurant was located instead of exiting to the street. I was instantly aware of a long-forgotten smell, and I realized that my dentist's office was in this building, somewhere off the lobby. I can't imagine that there is still a dentist's office in that same location, but I smelled it. They say that odors provoke the strongest memories and I believe it.

I send my best to all of my classmates. Mandy.

Arthur "Punch" Wienke, one of Beloit High's infamous thespians shares the following with you all the way from his home in Sioux Falls, South Dakota: **M**y memories of high school revolve around Mrs. "R" (Mrs. Reinholz) and DB Cuthbert. This is of course after I was cut from the track team having been told that I was too slow even for the mile and half mile events. I recall one meet in my sophomore year at Rockford East I rounded a corner in the half mile and was so far behind, several of the Rockford East students were moved suggest to me…"they went that-a-way," pointing toward the rest of the pack! I think I quit track the next day!

After my sophomore year with Mr. Cuthbert and failing to measure up I joined choir. A side bar to my experience with "DB." During my last lesson in his office, (remember that frightening time?) he indicated that he wasn't going to flunk me and hoped that some day I may be the only person on some Army base somewhere that knew which end of a trumpet the music came out of. That in fact occurred. Dateline: Werl, Germany, November 1963. I was the only person on that small post familiar with a bugle and the only soldier that could play for the ceremony honoring our fallen President. I was able to relate the story to Mr. Cuthbert some years after the fact. He seemed to be very pleased!

"Would anyone care for some tea while the actors try to remember their lines?" That is the promise Mrs. "R" threatened every cast in every play I was in if they forgot their lines. I don't remember it happening but it encouraged all of us to memorize our lines. A theatrical memory that comes to me occurred during he production Pirates of Penzance. The Pirates were to sneak up on the police and do battle. There was a huge green ground cloth put down on the stage to simulate grass. It was secured with carpet tacks to the stage floor. The stagehands did great work until they forgot to pick up the extra carpet tacks left strewn all over the fabric. In came the Pirates, in bare feet, singing the sneak up song and stepping on carpet tacks, causing them to grimace in pain!

Another occurrence was when Marty Peebles was cued to brake thru a fake brick wall about a full script page before it was time. He just sat there and observed the play until it was his time to deliver his lines!

The final production in high school was, "Father Knows Best." All of the male parts called for red hair, so Mrs." R" had arranged for all of us to have our hair dyed red except Rich L. who already had red hair. We all met at the beauty salon and had our dye jobs and came out with flaming red hair. There was an older gentlemen sitting out side the salon, on East Grand Ave I think. He was more than a little confused when we all came out with the same shade of flaming red hair.

Some of the dialogue in "Father" was a bit racy for 1960 so Mrs. "R" would sit down with "geometry" Thompson and read her the lines she wanted to test. Some lines made it through while other didn't. For instance the word "damn," became "damnation," more suitable for our young ears. Seems egregiously tame by today's standards!

What a great time and place in which to grow up, Beloit Memorial High School, class of 1960!

Sharon Wheat Grieves' grandmother lived just a few houses from my home. Sharon and her husband James live in Beloit. Sharon is an AKC licensed dog show judge.

Sharon has three children and two grandchildren. If you have watched the dog shows on television, you have probably seen this pretty lady on TV. If I remember correctly Sharon always was an animal lover, especially horses. Someone told me that she was an excellent breeder of Black Labradores, my frvorite breed of dog.

Sharon writes: **M**y favorite classroom memory is of my first day in Mr. Barkin's chemistry class my senior year. I had Mr. Barkin for biology as a junior, so he knew me. The summer between our junior year and our senior year he married Miss Hanson. His opening statement was that he would have given us homework for the first day, but he was really busy that summer.

I remember an announcement on the Public Address system that the theater wanted to hire a student. I applied right away thinking that would be such a fun job. The girl's counselor (I can't remember her name) told me my typing grades were too good for that job and sent me to the Commercial Credit Company where I worked part time during the school year and full time for two summers. That job was O.K. but I was really disappointed that

I didn't get the theater job. As a side note, I did get into trouble in typing class because I would get my work done quickly and then help out those around me. I have no idea how she could tell, but I finally got a note on my paper saying, "Please do only your own work." I also made a few extra bucks typing papers for classmates.

I can still remember just trying to get to and from school. We had to walk as the school bus didn't come past the Municipal swimming pool (I lived several blocks past it) and it didn't matter what the weather, we had to walk. I can remember walking backwards against the wind when the temperature was well below freezing. I would arrive at school/home practically frozen. When I tell this to my kids, they say, "Sure, Mom, and it was up hill both ways." They have had it waaaaaaaay too easy.

After almost fifty years of living all over the country, **Janice Witte Prinzi** and her husband, Phil, have just moved from the Denver area to the little Pennsylvania town that my wife and I have lived in since 1978. It is going to be great having a fellow classmate live so close by. Janice and her husband Phil are presently staging their home in Denver for sale so they can move to eastern Pennsylvania to be closer to their children. Janice and Penny were the closest of friends all through school. My wife and I are anxious to show Janice and Phil around town. It will be nice to have a fellow classmate living near by. Howdy, neighbor.

As you will read, one of Janice's fondest memories is the aroma emanating from her Grandma's kitchen. Recently Judy and I were guests at Janice's home for a pasta dinner. We were treated to Janice's grandmother's sauce. It was magnificent! Janice writes: **T**here are many events, which spring to mind when reflecting on life in Beloit in the 40s and 50s. I grew up on Keeler Avenue across from Roosevelt Junior High School. In the winter, the "Hollow" was an ice rink maintained by the city of Beloit. I spent many afternoons and evenings ice skating there and sitting in the little warming house talking to my friends. When school started in the fall, the football, track and baseball teams from Roosevelt Junior High would practice there and also have school competitions at the "Hollow." In the summer, baseball games were played there and would continue long after I was sent to bed. We did not have air conditioning, so our windows were open and the noise from those games would drift through the window screens. It took a while to fall asleep.

My Italian grandparents also lived on Keeler Avenue, about four blocks away. I was allowed to ride my bicycle to their house and I visited them almost daily. My grandma's kitchen was scented with daily baked bread, meats fried in olive oil with garlic, and sauces simmered to perfection. Garlic, basil, parsley and onions were kitchen essentials as were vegetables from the garden, fruit from their trees and tomato paste from jars stored in the cellar. I can still remember those wonderful smells. My grandpa had a grape press in the basement and I would help at Christmas time delivering wine to all of our relatives and friends.

My childhood memories include many picnics at Leeson's Park, located off Milwaukee Road. It wasn't too far from our house. My mom didn't work until I was in High School so she would take my brother and me to Leeson's Park in the summer for afternoon picnics and wading in the creek. We would go swimming at the Municipal Pool on the west side of town. When I was in junior high at Roosevelt, I started playing golf with Cathy Kitto. Cathy's mom got me interested in golf and I played frequently at the public courses. I still enjoy the game but never improved much. Girls never had varsity and junior varsity teams in any school sport back then, only intramurals.

One of my favorite memories from High School was a camping trip. I can't remember the name of the woods, but we got there by crossing the creek behind Judy Bogg's house and walking through the woods to a clearing and setting up camp there. (It may have been called Murphy's Woods). We cooked our dinner over the campfire and spent the night there. I doubt if anyone slept.

Maybe I didn't realize just how special Beloit was or how many good memories I had until Don Nelsen started e-mailing me about this book.... I look forward to reminiscing over many memories with my classmates at our 50th reunion.

Barbara Wood Whitlow and her husband of eight months live in Oldsmar, FL. Living with them are her mother, a graduate of Beloit High in 1937, and her 26 year old grandson. Barb is retired from US Airways where she was a Senior Maintenance Planner. It recently came as very sad news to learn that Barbara's husband died in his sleep in early August of 2008. Barb, be confident in knowing that we mourn your loss, too.

Barb would like to share these; some of her memories, with us: (Author's comment: Yesterday I telephoned Barb and her mother answered the phone. I told her who I was and she said, "You know, I graduated from the old Beloit High School in 1937." What a delightful lady. I wonder if she attended her seventieth reunion last year?)

Now let's go back to Barb's memories. **I** attended kindergarten at Strong Elementary School. Barb told me that she remembers her report card comments informing her parents that she seemed to have difficulty sleeping during naptime. She went on to say that now all she hears are complaints about her sleeping too much. Any way, Barb went on to say, "I remember walking to school through Mechanic's Green on East Grand Avenue, then up the hill to school. One day I heard that one of my classmates that I really liked was having a birthday party. I was sure that I would be invited, so I wore y handmade pink dotted-Swiss dress to school that day—she had one similar to it only hers' came from McNeany's—"THEEEEEE Department Store to shop at." Of course, I was not invited, so I decided I should just walk home at lunchtime and not come back. Oh-oh was I in trouble!

So, from Strong I was transferred to Cunningham, where I spent the next three grades where I became friends with Ruth Thorson Greenberg. We remain friends today and see each other a few times each year.

I also met Ronald Lee. I had a big crush on him, especially after he let me ride his Schwinn bike with its handlebar streamers! He is gone now, and I always regretted not seeing him again.

Times were great back then. I lived with my aunt and uncle and two cousins. We would put on puppet shows in Donald Alton's garage in the summer, have lemonade stands, collect Coke bottles in a red wagon for the deposit refund and make endless trips to Hart's grocery store on Satin Lawrence Avenue. The Fourth of July always included a picnic at Rock County Park or at the Lagoon and then we would lie on our blankets and watch the fireworks over Fairbanks Morse.

At Lincoln Junior High School I met two more girls that have been part of my life to this very day. They were Mary Alice Connors and Judy Yonts. We spent every Monday night walking around downtown. It was usually guys on one side of the street and the girls on the other. We'd window shop in McNeany's (where they had a tube system used to send your money upstairs), J. C. Penny's, Three Sisters, Ben Franklin (where you could buy opera creams and box turtles), and lastly to Walgreen's for their yummy hot fudge sundaes. Sometimes after movies at the Majestic, State or Rex theaters we would hit the Little Bungalow for a pickle-ketchup hamburger, fries and a Coke. Of course, I can't forget our regular stops Al's Snack Shop for a piece of chocolate cake with a side of "mud" for a whopping price of twenty-five cents.

During junior high, Saturdays were confirmation classes at Our Savior's Lutheran Church as well as church and Sunday school. We no sooner were released from public school only to be enrolled in Bible School during the first part of the summer. Choir practice always brought unlimited opportunities for Mary Alice to play pranks on us, which she continues to do to this day. I think her best prank was when she put up "Garage Sale" signs all over Brodhead with Judy's address on them. People cat at eight A.M. demanding she open the garage door.

High School was a blast! I had Miss Orpha Thompson for Geometry (never could understand those angles). She was my mother's homeroom teacher when she was in high school in the 1930s. Since she decreed we be seated alphabetically, I ended up behind Art Wienke. We cheated like crazy and passed jokes back and forth. I was trying new mascaras then. One of them was dark blue and **not waterproof!** Art was in rare form that day and since my eyes water when I laugh, I had blue running down my face. That was the consequence of vanity and the lure of beauty.

In my junior and senior years I became involved with The Increscent and worked many long hours after school to get it published on time. James Lafky was the greatest mentor ever when it came to newspaper work and always made his English and Journalism classes come alive. I treasured the special Journalism award I received from him the last week of high school.

Four years of French class with Darlene Nelson left me able to converse reasonably well during my one and only trip to Europe, but since I've lived in San Diego and now Tampa, Spanish would have been a better choice.

Since I was the first of "our gang" to turn eighteen, it was my duty to go to South Beloit to purchase 3.2 beer. One of the guys had a car, so we'd drive down to Sugar River Forest Preserve. We girls would drink one bottle between us, just to show we were way cool. It was all very platonic, and we had great times. On Saturdays we'd walk eight miles our St. Lawrence Road to ride old Dan Kelly's horses. He had a big house on a hill with no indoor plumbing or lights. He also had a big old rickety barn. We'd scare ourselves silly at slumber parties there. One of us always got locked out then we went to the outhouse. We spent many happy times out there.

Over the years I have had dreams in which I am going to be late to class because I had forgotten my locker combination. Another recurring dream was that I'd be walking into class with no shoes on my feet. I guess those high school days stay buried in your brain forever, and I am so happy that they are still there.

Frank Young and his wife, **Judy Patton Young** live in Ft. Myers. Florida. Frank and Judy are another couple who met in school and who tied the knot. Frank, Judy and Judy's sister put their heads together and came up with the following memories, memories that I am sure will remind you of times you had thought you had forgotten. Judy writes: **My** sister, Frank and I came up with the following snippets from our memories of growing up in Beloit in the 40s and 50s. We fondly remember going to the Rex Theater on Saturday mornings for an all-day movie watching fest that cost only twenty-five cents. Remember, you could stay as long as you wanted to. Boy, was that a bargain.

Lots of our memories centered on the radio and eventually television. Before television came along, we listened to The Shadow, The Lone Ranger, Fibber McGee and Molly, The Great Gildersleeve, Sky King, Buster Brown. Boy, those were the days. Then came along television. We watched programs like Howdy Doody, The Mickey Mouse Club, and American Bandstand with Dick Clark.

Being in the Brownies and Girl Scouts taught me many skills that have come in handy as an adult. I remember going on picnics at the Big Hills Park. Yes, we were some of those nuts who climbed the huuuuugh ski jump. We also went in the wintertime to watch the ski jumpers. We'd always go to the county fairs, especially the Walworth county fair at Elkhorn where my parents met. I thoroughly remember the class trips to The Cave of the Mounds, Little Norway, The Talmah House in Janesville and of course our trips to Chicago and Milwaukee. Do you remember those awful grade school class pictures and the grade school programs that our parents had to endure? What about the school district's marbles tournament, playing with paper dolls, (Frank, did you play with paper dolls?), playing dress-up, making tents on the clothesline with blankets, running through the sprinkler, sliding down the hill in the park on Grand

and Bluff on an old cardboard box, waiting for the Beloit Daily News to publish home room assignments, mud cake at Al's or roller skating with skates that clipped onto your shoes and were tightened with a skate key hung around your neck from an old shoestring. Those were the days; we remember them well.

CHAPTER EIGHTEEN
'Tis Better To Give Than To Receive

Something amazing has occurred to me as I read and enter the memories and comments of my friends and classmates into this compellation. I have come to learn that many of the people who have responded to my invitation to journey with me down memory lane have dedicated themselves to the service, aid and comfort of others less fortunate than we. It appears that my classmates and I have more in common than where we lived, were educated and lived through those wondrous years of the 40's and 50's. In retirement, many more than I expected have surrendered to their passion for helping the disadvantaged. I am so very proud of each and every one of them, almost as proud as their mothers and fathers would be.

Therefore, I have asked, and they have agreed to share with you the myriad of charitable and service oriented projects that they are working on. I hope their selfless dedication is not unique to just members of our class.

For example, **Jeff Maiken** writes the following: When I first got involved with Camp Heartland in the mid-90, it was somewhat self-serving. I wanted my winery to be able to join up with a non-profit organization for fundraisers so that I could find new consumers, and equally important, that I could attract young people who liked wine but had not really began to think about what they should give back to society.

At our first fund-raiser held in the city park in Wauwatosa, we had four chefs each preparing a different dish and our various wines at the tables to match with the foods. We had a good crowd. Just before going into the auction to raise the big bucks, one of our campers who was about to speak to the crowd, came running up to us after she had used the restroom facilities. She tugged on the sleeve of our Executive Director as he prepared to address the group. The young lady said to him, "You know Neil, in that restroom I just used; they had a can of something that said it would kill all bacteria. Do you think it could get rid of AIDs?"

I instantly knew that my heart would remain with Camp Heartland. Just hearing kids like this young lady speak of hope for the future as she did, made me realize that I needed to get seriously involved.

That afternoon I had to ask Neil, (our Executive Director) to make the pitch to the audience inasmuch as I knew that I could never keep it together as the young girls words rang in my ears.

In March of 2008 I stepped down as President of the Board of Camp Heartland, a global, non-profit organization, dedicated to helping children affected and infected with HIV/AIDs. My heart and my soul continue to beat to its tune. Now Camp Heartland is known as One Heartland. It is a global effort to make life better for children with HIV/AIDs. Wow, such a long way from Beloit, Wisconsin in 1960.

Don Marske has lived in the state of Oregon and in Orange County, California for many years. Now that he and his wife have retired, like most of us, he has a fair amount of time on his hands. Don shared the following with me through an E-mail conversation that we had the other day:

"I am involved in Paint Your Heart Out, a non-profit organization in Orange County, California. With the help of about a thousand volunteers, we paint and otherwise spruce up the homes of the low income elderly in cities of Aneheim, Orange, Santa Ana and Brea. On successive weekends we prep and paint upwards of fifty homes per year."

Like many of us, Don's wife probably had to nag him to wash the windows or paint their bathroom, but he found it in his heart to help others. Way to go, Don. Paying forwards really does paint your wagon, doesn't it?

Don Nelsen: As for me, I officially entered the realm of Santa's Service in 1969, almost forty years ago at the time of this writing.

Christmas parties for friends and relatives, parades, hospital and nursing home visits and several broadcasts on local radio programs were the extent of my service to Santa for the first thirty plus years of wearing the red suit with white fur trim. Then in 2001 I was asked to pose as Santa with children at a photography studio. Of course, each child had a list as long as your arm of the goodies that they hoped I would lay beneath their Christmas tree on Christmas Eve. One little boy climbed up on my knee and pulled out a lengthy letter that he had cut out and pasted pictures of just about every toy in the Sears Christmas Catalog. Accompanying each picture he had written reasons why he needed each item. I had to give him credit; he knew what he wanted and he was bound and determined that I know what and why, too.

Then there was a surprising exception, two boys who turned out to be two of the nicest, most caring boys to ever sit on Santa's knee. The boys were eight and ten years old at the time. When prompted to tell Santa what they wanted Santa to bring them, the eldest said, "I'd like you to bring happiness and peace to my family. I would like there to be no more fighting, no cursing or hitting. I would like you to make it possible for my brother and to see our dad. He don't live with us any more. I would like to be able to go to grandma and grandpa's house for Christmas dinner like we have ever since I can remember. I want my family to love each other, not fight all the time. That's all, thank you Santa."

It was now the younger brother's turn upon Santa's knee. "Santa, do you bring food as Christmas presents?" he asked in a very grown up sort of way. "I learned that there are lots and lots of people who don't have enough food to eat. At church last week I learned that some people are dying caus they don't got no food. Could you please bring them some food so they don't have to die?"

After Mom and the two boys left the studio, I asked the photographer for her name and telephone number so I could call the Mom and tell her how impressed I was with her two young men. During the conversation she told me that she had just learned that afternoon upon their arrival at home that the money they had been saving all year long for a Game-Boy was missing. She went on to say that she discovered that the boys had put their savings into the Mission Box at church to help feed the homeless.

Those young men opened my eyes to the obvious. As Santa Claus, I should be helping those less fortunate, too. To make a long story short, I started charging for the parties that I attended as well as the appearances at community and social events, the profits to be donated to organizations that supported children afflicted with Autism and Cerebral Palsy such as the Easter Seals, Summer Camps and Equestrian riding lessons.

After my retirement, I quickly became disillusioned with Jerry Springer and Oprah Winfrey. I went in search of a part time job to help me retain what little bit of sanity that I still retained. Driving a school bus part time got me out of the house as well as introduced me to some of the most interesting children. Some of the children were afflicted with Autism or Cerebral Palsy. Even though most of them were non-verbal, in their own special ways, they taught me the meaning of compassion, empathy and unconditional love. My life has been so enriched by meeting and getting to know my special little angels that my passion is to do what ever I can do to make their lives a little happier.

To that end, several years ago I began to take the Santa thing to an all-new level. I purchased a professionally made Santa suit from the costume designer whom made the Santa Claus suits for Tim Allen in the Santa Claus movies. My totally white beard seemed to grow longer and bushier each year. While at times my wife Judy laments that I let my beard grow too long, that I begin to look like a homeless person. After over three decades of marriage I know I had better go to the barbershop for a trim and a buffing of my baldhead. Somehow I have managed to keep my wife happy and I have I persevered and now sport a magnificent Santa beard, if I do say so myself.

With the white beard, the great Santa suit, the rotund belly and the nearly bald head, not to mention the well rehearsed Ho-Ho-Hos, I have become known as Santa 365 days a year. In fact, on July 19, 2008 I attended the birthday party of a seventy-year-old grandmother. I don't mind telling you, it was hotter than blazes in that suit. I am most thankful that Christmas comes in December.

Inasmuch as children are constantly looking at me and wondering if it could really be, I have resorted to carrying a black leather fanny pack on my belt that is filled with small candy canes. When I see that look of awe, I just reach into the fanny pack and pull out a candy cane for each of the children and just walk away Ho-Ho-Hoing. That gets them every time.

Even Santa Claus has to put up with the naughty side of life; once in a while I've had to deal with the dregs of humanity, if you will. Not all encounters that Santa faces are with little children. Sometimes an infamous adult raises his or her ugly head. I have explained every last disgusting point of the true incident in *"Childhood Dreams Really Do Come True"* but I will give you a brief synopsis here. What I am about to tell you turned this normally docile Santa Claus into a raging bull, a Santa that would have liked to throttle the man and give him nothing but coal for the next fifty years.

An editor of our local newspaper wrote an article about the work I do as Santa Claus. The day after it was published and hit the news stands, I received a telephone call from a young man who wanted to offer me an opportunity to be in an independently made Christmas movie that he was shooting locally, to be shown at the Sundance Film Festival the following fall. To read a blow-by-blow description of the movie plot and story line as he described it to me over the phone, you will have to read the afore mentioned book. Suffice it to say that this misguided filmmaker wanted me to star in a movie about the murder of Santa Claus. I blew my stack. I said to him, "You, Sir, need to get off whatever dope you are smoking and go see a psychiatrist immediately, if not sooner."

"Gee Mister, calm down," he said, "I don't understand why you are so upset; it's just a movie. If you won't do it, can you suggest where I might find an old man with a white beard like yours who would be willing to help me?" he had the audacity to ask.

"The type of sorry individual you are looking for will probably be found on Skid Row, drinking Thunderbird wine from a brown paper bag! I never!" I slammed the receiver down and called for Mama to join me in my office. I was PO'd and not a Depends in sight.

Fortunately, that is the only example of bad times that I have experienced as Santa other than a group of teenagers who shot beans through their bean shooters at me as I rode on a float in a Christmas parade in the early 70s. In "Childhood Dreams Really Do Come True," I tell of scores of funny and heart tugging experiences while wearing the red suit. I think you might enjoy the read, at least I hope that you will.

My uncle, Henry Case portrayed Santa for the Chamber of Commerce or the Kiwanis Club some time in the late 40s or the early 50s. Perhaps you or one of your siblings were in the audience gathered around Santa Claus Henry?

Now, Uncle Henry, who did you think you were fooling with that God awful fake beard and wig? Why didn't you grow a real beard like all of us real Santa's do? I know personally that you had a real substantial belly under that red coat. Would it have been too much to ask for you to grow a white beard? You were an old man at the time, maybe twenty-five or thirty years old.

All joking aside, my experiences have taught me two very valuable lessons, lessons that confirm the Amish saying, "Man ist too soon oldt und too late schmardt. First, I have recognized that even an old geezer like me can learn from young people, especially from young people who have the courage of their conviction like Billy and Thomas and those special needs children that I have met who exhibit the intestinal fortitude to play the hand that they were dealt and enjoy it with a positive attitude. Thanks kids.

Secondly, I have realized that it truly is more blessed to give than it is to receive. It truly is a shame that I had to get so old and worn out to realize that our Lord put us here on earth to truly be our brother's keeper. Better late than never, I guess.

The funny thing about giving of yourself is that you reap much more than you sew. The smiles, the giggles, the hugs and the kisses I have stored in my heart from those precious children are more valuable to me than silver and gold or a chest filled with the crown jewels.

Janice Witte Prinzi and her husband **Phil** have recently retired and have moved from their home in Denver to the little berg that Judy and I live in to be closer to their two daughters. Phil has had an avocation of videography for several years. In retirement, Phil and Janice have purchased a video franchise called "Home Video Studio of Downingtown." Last weekend, Judy and I hosted Janice and Phil at one of our favorite Italian restaurants. During dinner, we talked about memories, our children and all the usual polite dinner table topics of conversation. Phil described for us the new business that he and Janice are involved in. He told me the following that I think you will find interesting and will give you an insight to the charitable nature and character of so many of our classmates and people in our age group:

I am certain that many of our classmates, even though they have not contributed to the written words of this project, have been and are committed to one or more charitable causes. I thank each one of you for society as a whole for your efforts and selflessness.

EPILOGUE
Th-th-th That's All, Folks

Well, there you have it, as many different perspectives of growing up during the 1940s and 1950s as there were contributors. Was I right? Did our friends' memories take you back to a much simpler, calmer time and place? Did their stories remind you of people, places or events in your life? Did they remind you of you? I sure hope so. I said it before, but I believe it bears repeating, "We have many more memories and experiences in common than we have differences."

I suppose progress in most cases is a good thing. But when it comes to the effect that modern-day information-technology, television, MTV, video games, Gangster Rap and the like is having on the younger generations, I am made painfully aware of why, without our help, our grandchildren and great grandchildren are doomed to never have the kind of life we grew up with. Most of us were on the not so rich side of life. And yet, I believe we can honestly say that we led a well-rounded, abundant childhood filled with friends, neighbors and extended families. I wish that for all of our offspring, but honestly, I question whether they will ever be able to experience the simple life as we did. I don't think they stand a snowballs' chance in hell of ever experiencing anything like we were able to live.

Look at what our generation has accomplished. We followed our dreams of climbing the corporate ladder, no matter where it took us. By moving vast distances away from grandma and grandpa, we, in a way, robbed our children of what we were fortunate enough to have. It is hard to enjoy a hug from grandma if we have taken up residence a thousand miles away. How are our children going to learn of and from the vast stores of knowledge and common sense bottled up inside their grandparents if they see them once every two or three years.

Now my friends, I am fearful that we are about to reap the fruits of our country or worldwide relocations. Those of us who have children and grandchildren living hundreds and thousands of miles from us will someday pay the price when we are no longer able to travel to see them and we are wasting away in a nursing home or senior citizens center.

I can't help but notice that our grandchildren don't seem to have the passion for reading that we had as a child. They do not appear to have the desire for reading that would transport them to a fantasyland, times of yore or beyond. Oh brother, now I sound just like my Grandfather Case.

To continue, it appears that our grandchildren require that everything today seems to have to be graphic, bold and on the television, their computer screen, their MP3 player or their Blackberry. I concede that they have most vivid imaginations when it comes to killing space aliens, navigating Mario through the maze of obstacles or decoding the latest CD of Gangster Rap. But do you honestly think that being able to master the wizardry of electronic games such as Grand Theft Auto will ever become a salable skill? What a shame.

Has your grandchild ever written you a letter? Not the scribblings of a child with a Crayola crayon. You know, an honest pen or pencil to paper stuffed into an envelope type of letter? A birthday card or the like does not count. I'll bet that they have not. What's more, I'll bet that they think a text message; an instant message or E-mail is what writing is all about. Wouldn't you like to receive just one honest to goodness hand written letter from them before you die?

I made a wager with you at the outset of this book. Remember, I wagered that no matter where you were raised, if you were born in the early 1940's, didn't our memories mesh with your memories? Well, did I win or lose the bet?

Permit me to make yet another wager. I am willing to bet, if you are willing to take the time to share your memories and your very own dreams, in a conversational, non-instructional way, the sharing of your memories may be just the psychological tonic that the younguns need to excite their own imaginations in a positive way. Wouldn't that be fantastic? Wouldn't it be a wondrous thing to watch your grandchildren as they daydream themselves into what they may think of as a distant fantasyland, but really is the life that we were so fortunate to be able to live? Wouldn't it be great to see your grandchildren clustered on the floor around you as you reveal the secrets, mysteries and blissful times of our youth?

It has been said that those who do not remember the past are condemned to repeating it. Well, I'd like to think that if we tell our grandchildren about our youthful beginnings, and the blessings of growing up in the 40s and 50s, maybe they would be blessed with the opportunity of experiencing at least some of them for themselves. Maybe they will put down the video game and go outside, climb an apple tree and eat their fill of sour apples or go outside at night and catch fire flies, break off their luminescence and smear it on their foreheads like their grandparents used to do. If presented with the opportunity, they may even enjoy listening to the old time radio shows.

I'd be willing to bet that if you take the time to tell your grandchildren about your good ole days, you will be inundated with questions. What's more, I'm willing to bet that they will say something about or ask, "why did your parents let you do that, didn't they worry about you?" "Weren't you afraid some bad person would get you?" Answer them honestly. Help them to understand that times were different, people were much more friendly and concerned with the welfare of each other, that each of us in our generation had responsibilities and that with the acceptance and honoring of those responsibilities came the freedom to do the things that we did. If that doesn't work, my friend, you are on your own. I don't have even so much as an inkling of what to do. As the old saying goes, "You can lead a horse to water, but you can't make it drink."

On the other hand, if you keep leading the horse back to the water trough, eventually the horse will get so thirsty from all of that exercise walking back and forth to that blessed water trough. Just keep trying.

Remember, in the tradition of time honored family structure; we are still the leaders of our families. We are the tribal elders and chieftains, if you will. At least, I hope that we are for at least a little while longer. In the vernacular of Ebonics, that abomination of the King's English that we hear far too often these days, "we needs to conversate with the younguns!" We need to not only teach them by our example and hope that they will covet our glorious days of wine and roses and the years of splendor in the grass, so to speak, but that they will try to emulate the freedom and charmed lives as much as possible.

Thank you for sharing your memories of your good ole days and for reading the memories held so dear by those who shared their memories with you. May you have many more years of pleasant memories to pass down to the younguns. Perhaps if we introduce our grandchildren to some of the experiences we had, (like a trip to the local fishing hole, a hay ride, S'mores cooked over an open fire or catching fire flies) we may be able to relive the good old days vicariously through them.

Th-Th-Th That's all folks, at least until our sixtieth class reunion in 2020. Perhaps then we will collaborate on another book called "The Golden Years."

ACKNOWLEDGEMENT

I wish to thank each and every classmate whom contributed his or her childhood memories to this venture.

With deep gratitude, I acknowledge and appreciate the many photographs and yearbook scribblings included between the covers of this book.

The Alma Mater is courtesy of its composer and lyricist, Mr. Donald B. Cuthbert, Director of Bands.

Thanks to Mr. Paul K. Kerr, Director of the Beloit Historical Society, I have been able to include some of the photographs found in the Photogravure section, many of which that were taken by Stuart D. Klinger and published in Century of a City by the Beloit Historical Society as well as the "Winter Fun" photo-graphs and commentary which were also provided courtesy of the Beloit Historical Society.

Mr. James Lafky has authorized me to utilize his photograph, author's Biog and one of his poems as found in Ventrographics II for my fellow classmate's reading pleasure.

Thank you one and all for your contributions. Without your support, your photographs and pithy comments, this book would not be complete. Left to my own devices, I fear this would have been a very dull read.

Author's Bio

Born in mid November of 1942, the author is a descendent of a long line of storytellers, including Ralph Waldo Emerson on his maternal side of the family. Don was one of the youngest, if not the youngest member of the 1960 Graduating class from Beloit Memorial High School. Being one of the youngest members of the class was by no means a bed of roses.

Beloit at that time was an industrial city of approximately 30,000 residents. Even though large business like Fairbanks Morse and the Beloit Iron Works employed many of Beloit's residents, equally as important to the overall community were the hundreds of farms and the multi-generational or extended families who lived on and ran them. Kids had ample opportunities to experience milking cows, gathering eggs from the hen house, seeing a calf or a lamb being born, mucking out a stall and yes, even being paid ten cents an hour to de-tassel corn stalks in the summer time.

Back in the days of our youth and innocence, those glorious days that memory can in no way do justice to, being in the band was the cool thing to do. Learning at an early age that practice makes perfect, commitment to extended families, meals devoured at the dining room table, (attended by all), outdoor exercise that was actually fun and a strong dedication to God and country made our generation what it in fact became. Our class was born early enough in the decade of the 40s to position us a few years ahead of the baby boomers, the flower children, hippies and the peaceniks.

Growing up between the "Days that will live in Infamy to the Dawning of the Age of Aquarius," My friends, fellow classmates and I are some of the luckiest people to have ever walked the face of this earth. Just ask us. We'd love to tell you what it was like growing up during the 40s and 50s.

D. E. Nelsen has retired from a lifelong career in sales and marketing management of medical electronics and diagnostic pharmaceutical research services that facilitated FDA mandated successful compliance with the regulations for a New Drug Application approval of the release of a new pharmaceutical.

D. E. is the father of seven and the grandfather of seventeen so far, five granddaughters and twelve grandsons.

Other than his wife, children and grandchildren, for the past forty plus years Don has had two passions. The first of the passions has been being Santa Claus for children of all ages, especially children with special needs such as Autism and Cerebral Palsy. Don's second passion is much more self-indulgent. He enjoys standing knee deep in a cold trout stream, casting flies up stream in the attempt to entice a rainbow trout or a brown trout to gulp down his artificial presentation as it floats atop the rapids or tumbles along the rock strewn bottom. It matters not how many fish are caught inasmuch as Don is a firm believer in "Catch and Release." The experience of communing with God in his Nature's Cathedral and the oft chance of tricking a trout to suck in his fly is all the rewards needed for a most outstanding afternoon.

Don and his wife Judy live on the periphery of Lancaster County's Amish country in Pennsylvania. As stated before, Don loves the quaint, well-kept farms, the smell of nature's perfume, (Horse apples dot the country roads assuring an ever present source of nature's perfume.) and the Amish dedication to God, family, mother earth, not to mention their colloquial speech and tradition. Lest you forget; "A plump woman und a large barn never done no man no harm." Perhaps the most poignant Amish saying is, "Man is too soon oldt und too late schmart." Do you think at our advanced age means that we are finally smart?

As Don has oft times been quoted to say, **"You can't very well carry on family traditions if you have no memory of your past."**

CPSIA information can be obtained at www.ICGtesting.com
Printed in the USA
LVOW080659281011

252449LV00004B/6/P